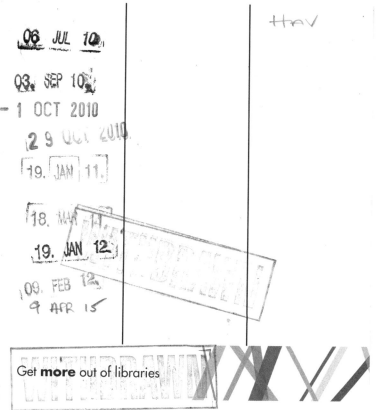

# THE
# SOUTH DOWNS

Little more than a tiny church, a large farm and house or two remain of the shrunken settlement of Tarring Neville in the Ouse valley south of Lewes, its 'straggling sparseness of tenements almost fatal to its title of village' as A.F. Cooke remarked in his *Off the Beaten Track in Sussex* (1911). A similar process of depopulation has prevailed in the Downs over many centuries.

# THE
# SOUTH DOWNS

## Peter Brandon

Phillimore

First published 1998
Corrected reprint 1999

Published by
PHILLIMORE & CO. LTD.
Shopwyke Manor Barn, Chichester, West Sussex

ISBN 1 86077 069 X

Printed and bound in Great Britain by
BUTLER AND TANNER LTD.
London and Frome

*To the loving Memory of Alexia (Sally) Jenkins*
*in Friendship and Gratitude*

It was still the unending summer of that marvellous year 1912 …
This was the first time I had seen the South Downs as it were from
the inside and felt the beauty of the gentle white curves of the fields
between the great green curves of their hollows; I have lived close to
them ever since; and have learnt that, in all seasons and circumstances,
their physical loveliness and serenity can make one's happiness exquisite and assuage one's misery.

Leonard Woolf, *Beginning Again* (1968)

# CONTENTS

Founded by 1803, Findon Sheep Fair (photographed in 1931) continues to be held on Nepcote Green.

# LIST OF ILLUSTRATIONS

*Frontispiece:* The shrunken settlement of Tarring Neville

# Colour Plates

# ACKNOWLEDGEMENTS

I owe thanks to the late Barbara Willard for suggesting that I should write about the South Downs and to Tim Hoof who helped me in the initial stages of the collation of material for this book. To Susan Rowland of the University of Sussex especial thanks are due for her exceptionally clear and accurate maps. Ann Winser supplied the index, clarified expression and has been very supportive throughout. Numerous other persons have given specific help including David Allen, Stanley Baker, Judith Brent, Nicola Frank of the Council for the Protection of Rural England, Charles Granshaw, John Goldsmith, Harry Goring, the late Eric Holden, George Holleyman, Mrs. Christine Isitt, Geoffrey Mead, Sylvia and John Jenkins, David Monnington, Janet Pennington, Brian Poole, Dr. Peter Reynolds, Dr. Francis Rose, Richard Williamson and Dr. Andrew Woodcock. I also greatly valued the help and encouragement of Mrs. Ann Money, Dr. Harry Montgomery and Christopher Passmore. I am also indebted to the staffs of the East and West Sussex Record Offices and of the Hampshire Record Office, to Joyce Crow and Richard Philcox of the Sussex Archaeological Society, to Esme Evans of Worthing Reference Library and to the staff of the London Library, without whose collections this book could not have been undertaken. Noel Osborne and Nicola Willmot of Phillimore have exercised great forbearance with an untidy manuscript and have been unfailingly supportive towards its improvement. As a personal tribute I have dedicated this book to Sally Jenkins' memory.

The author is grateful to the following individuals and institutions for photographs and other illustrative material and giving permission to reproduce them. Photographs not listed were taken by the author.

Professor Mick Aston, 41; Adrian Berg, R.A., XXIII; Dennis Rothwell-Bailey and the Sussex Collection of Sussex Stationers, XII; Trustees of the British Library, 106; Professor Barry Cunliffe, 36, 37; East Sussex County Council, 33, 136; East Sussex County Record Office, 72, 105 (upper), 117, 121-4, 132-4; Alan George, 3, IX; English Nature, 106; Findon Wattle House Trust, X; The Game Conservancy Trust, 147; The Lord Hampden, 8; George Holleyman, 27, 34; The Imperial War Museum, 1; The Landmark Trust, XI; Peter Mercer and Douglas Holland, XVII; Mrs. Margaret Malton, VII; Dr. Harry Montgomery, 6, 7, 11, 13, 16, 23, 24, 30, 55, 56, 59, 60, 62, 76, 81, 90, 93, 97, 138, 148, 152, 153, II, IV, V, XIV, XXII; News International Syndication, 127, 128; John O'Riley, 130; Andrew Nicholson, 114, XVIII; Dick Passmore, 53; Edward Reeves, Lewes, *frontispiece*, 83, 100, VII; Dr. Peter Reynolds, 26, 35; Susan Rowland, University of Sussex, 2, 19, 20, 22, 36-8, 42, 43, 45-9, 51, 69, 82, 92, 94, 95, 102-4, 106, 146; Royal Commission on Historical Monuments of England, 32; Ronald Smith, 44; David Streeter, 103, 104; Surrey Archaeological Society, 74; Sussex Archaeological Society, 17; Sussex Downs Conservation Board, 4, 111; A. Thorley, 102; Rodney Todd-White and Son, VI; J.A.M. Tomson, 22; The Towner Art Gallery, XIX, XX; The Weald and Downland Museum, III; West Sussex Record Office, p.viii, 70, 79, 96, 98, 99, 113; Miss Ann Winser, 5, 15, 25, 29, 39, 58, 61, 63, 64, 67, 68, 86, 91, 139, XXVIII, XXIX.

The opportunity has been taken to acknowledge corrections provided by a number of persons, including David Lloyd and John Pile.

# PREFACE

To know the South Downs we must get out of our cars, breathe in the salty tang in the air, tread the chalk rock, and experience something, at least, of the life of plant, tree and animal, and of the ways in which man has shaped the landscape in the past, is shaping it today, and may shape it in the future. This book is written in the belief that as people acquire familiarity with the countryside they will want to extend their active enjoyment and understanding of it and will seek opportunities of doing so.

Much of the history of the Downs relates to the history of the land itself and how it has been re-shaped repeatedly by the activities of its past farmers. This book's central theme is thus change, physical change and social change, and change from 1939 when the impossible was suddenly possible and this distinct and lovely landscape was altered out of all recognition. This was so irreparably destructive of the past that many people at the century's end who knew it earlier still feel unable to regain their former organic relationship with it. The new world of the Downs is incomprehensible without understanding the old. The hope is to enlist all who love the Downs and share my concern for their future, including all who have responsibility for them, whether landowners and farmers, countryside planners or conservationists. Knowledge of the historical, literary and artistic associations which the Downs have acquired may help to a better understanding of what happened, is happening and what may be about to happen in our own time. The past may be a foreign country but travel in it broadens the mind. For these reasons I have used few technical terms and surveyed a great sweep of time with a minimum of detail. The result will I trust be an appropriate background for an appreciation of the Downs from the various standpoints of interested groups.

The book is written from my own perspective, in part inherited, in part arising from my own experience and interests. Ancestry has largely determined that I should live only a mile from my birthplace below the Downs where a former signpost bore the directions '⇐ TO THE DOWNS  ⇒ TO THE SEA' that as a child I thrilled to read. As I glance up from my word processor and see my own familiar green ridge of the Downs overlooking the Holmbush superstores where the Brighton bypass emerges from a tunnel under Southwick Hill and cleaves through the Downs like an open wound, I realise that the Dorset, Berkshire or Wiltshire Downs are as beautiful, possibly more so (and certainly less spoiled) than the South Downs, but they do not move me so deeply, for the South Downs are my native hills, known to me since I could remember the smell of chalk dust, wild thyme and the tang of the sea. Many generations of the simple working people of my mother's country have made me what I am and they are responsible for my love of the South Downs—one of the strongest emotions I possess. These maternal forebears, rising to positions of shepherd and foreman before sinking back in old age as bent-backed hired labourers, have also really determined what kind of book this is.

**1** 'The South Downs', a Second World War poster designed by Frank Newbould (1887-1951) for the famous 'Your Britain: Fight for it now' series issued by the Army Bureau of Current Affairs. Depicted is Birling Farm and the former lighthouse of Belle Tout. It encapsulated the English heritage the nation was fighting for. Other subjects by Newbould for this series included 'Alfriston Fair'.

# INTRODUCTION

The South Downs are no ordinary hills. They are perhaps the most familiar hills in England and before the mid-1920s they were regarded as its most beautiful stretch of downland. Their exquisitely smooth yet deeply sculpted landscape imbued with the tang of the sea remained unspoiled, its loveliness only enhanced by man-made associations arising from its bountiful corn and Southdown sheep. Although prized as the jewel of the Sussex crown, eulogising by Rudyard Kipling, Hilaire Belloc and many others ensured that they were not merely of local but of national, even international importance. With 19th-century urbanisation the rhythmically-rolling Downs came to be regarded as peculiarly and beguilingly English, the landscape of dreams. Consequently, few landscapes have spoken so potently to each generation to transpose their inspirational and spiritual qualities into verse, landscape painting or orchestral sounds. To Arthur Mee, the far-travelled editor of the King's England series of inter-war county books, Sussex was 'the county of counties for sheer English beauty'[1] and the South Downs 'the natural glory of our island'. So many similar public declarations were made that Hilaire Belloc claimed the South Downs as a national institution which lifted people's experience of them to something approaching a religious creed. Drenched in verse, 'country writing', painting, photography and advertising, and promoted with no hyperbole too great, Kipling's 'blunt, bow-headed, whale backed downs'[2] were created into a national icon of a landscape regarded as quintessentially English, which men and women from all over the Empire thought about when they were most homesick and where they planned to end their lives.[1] In the English arts and crafts world the Downs had a special resonance and they became a major part of a national identity for an urban society with a taste for Old England, nostalgically harking back to a past rural idyll. For these various reasons the Downs became world-renowned as a focus of English culture.

The images that sustained this nostalgic idea of the South Downs so healingly to the heart were a kind of golden dream based on a half-imagined, half-recollected, notion of pastoral England. In this dream the real and the tangible merged with the imagined to such a degree that the Downs became as much a state of mind, like Atlantis, Utopia or Brigadoon, as a physical reality. The stereotyped South Downs were much easier to take on board than the complicated reality. Thus the history of the Downs is full of myths. A major scourge of these, so drawing a distinction between the mythic and the real Downs, is a major objective of this book.

Inevitably the Downs became a victim of this urban rediscovery of the countryside. As early as 1926 Kipling lamented in his verse *Very Many People* that the dawn of the motor vehicle was exposing the Downs to the day-tripper and weekender (though he himself had earlier created a new genre in literature with his joys of motoring across Sussex). People took the Downs at the valuation of Kipling, Belloc and other writers, saying in effect, 'If the Downs are such an ideal place, why not plan to end our lives there?' Many who came to the Downs destroyed what in fact they revered. Kipling's Sussex became besmirched with indiscriminate development. It was on the Downs, and particularly at Peacehaven, that inter-war suburbia in England reached its nadir, creating one of the ugliest townships in England and destroying some of our finest landscapes in the process. Almost wrecked between 1920 and 1934, the Downs became a place where despoliation awakened England to a sense of its wider self-destruction and ever since they have been part of the landscape conscience of the nation and have had a special role in the story of landscape protection in England.

Yet despite being in the forefront of pioneering new ways to protect and enhance them, more damage has been done to the Downs within living memory than at any time in their long history. Swathes of downland have been scythed away, or threatened by road improvement and out-of-town development despite their ostensible protection and some of their tranquillity has been shattered. Even the pleasure of what beauty remains is impaired by the uncertainty of how long it will last. This erosion of the fabric of the Downs has been accompanied by a transformation of the Downs' agricultural landscape from the early 1950s on a scale which would have been inconceivable a generation earlier. The process of putting much of the downland under cereal monoculture, has caused increased run-off of rain, loss of soil, as well as the depletion of wild plants and fauna. Much former priceless archaeological heritage has also been obliterated, wildlife species that were once a familiar part of the everyday farming scene have declined dramatically, and the very essence of the Downs has drained away. The Downs' rolling ridges and wide skies still have the power to raise the spirit and lift the heart but the monoculture of the modern cornfield affords less refreshment for the soul than the satisfying smooth turf and more diverse landscape of the past.

So dire were the threats to the Downs that the Sussex Downs Conservation Board came into being in 1992 as a unique experiment in the management of a threatened landscape. This was regarded as a flagship for similar Areas of Outstanding Natural Beauty and at the end of its six-year experimental period its functions have been extended to 2001 with reduced funding. At the time of writing it is not known what form the permanent new body administering the Downs in the new millennium will take or what area it will protect. It is because of doubts about the long-term future of the Downs that calls are being made by some for a nationally co-ordinated scheme of development and conservation which would have the status and funding equivalent to that of a national park.

*Chapter One*

# THE CHARACTER OF THE DOWNS

To take to the road with the aim of keeping Hilaire Belloc's 'great hills of the south country' in sight westwards from their spectacular white cliffs of Beachy Head until their majestic sweep comes to an end, means a journey of more than eighty miles well into Hampshire. An observant traveller may well feel in a kind of limbo when the formidable north-facing escarpment of the Downs, the most imposing sight in southern England, finally peters out. True, the same unvarying dry, flinty chalkland continues on towards the great chalk table land focused on Salisbury plain, but it becomes low, broken and indeterminate. It is round about Old Winchester Hill (12 miles east of Winchester), where the skylark sings above the most dramatic situation of the Iron-Age hillforts, that one becomes aware that the landscape has a different 'feel'. So it is about here that the South Downs may be reckoned to end (or have their beginning).

This is the definition of the South Downs adopted for the purpose of this book. It is broadly comparable with that of two government quangos, the Countryside Commission and English Nature (though both extend the Downs to Winchester itself). It is also approximately coincident with the bounds of the Ministry of Agriculture's South Downs Environmentally Sensitive Area Scheme which pays farmers for maintaining or adopting agricultural methods which promote the Downs' conservation and enhancement.

This modern definition fits our age of the motor car and the new sciences of landscape analysis. When travel was slower and more arduous, the local background to people's lives was

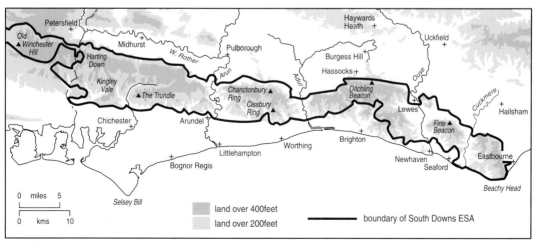

**2** The South Downs Environmentally Sensitive Area. Note its extreme vulnerability to urban encroachment in the Brighton area and in the hinterland of Portsmouth.

I

much more restricted, and many local differences, now blurred, were formerly more marked. A farmer's or parson's notion of the South Downs was then more limited. In 1800, and before, as for a considerable period afterwards, the South Downs were associated in people's minds with their most renowned product, the celebrated breed of Southdown sheep which, improved by John Ellman of Glynde and others, became the progenitor of all the other English down breeds and had a powerful influence on sheep farming worldwide. Originally, this native breed did not graze the whole extent of the range now called the South Downs but was confined to the eastern stretch of the Downs between Beachy Head and the Adur valley. In their minds' eye the old farmers identified the South Downs with stark, bare downs open to the sky and rolling down to sea cliffs. They knew them as endless miles of old chalk grassland, feeding immense flocks, bordered by cornland at lower levels, made productive by the sheep's dung. Farmers of more than two thousand years earlier would have recognised this same austere landscape with its plough-oxen and shepherds. The 18th- and 19th-century downland farmers in these Eastern Downs thought of the wooded Western Downs beyond the Adur river, as if it were another country (which in several respects it still is). This landscape of the Eastern Downs has almost totally vanished since the second World War, though people over the age of 60 years wistfully recall the life, sounds and scents of its immemorial past as familiarly as does the modern child the present great blocks of wheat, superstores and country parks.

This 18th-century idea of the South Downs is confirmed by the parson-naturalist Gilbert White who described his native village and the Downs with such charm and affection in his *Natural History of Selborne* (1798).[1] He recorded that the Sussex Downs 'is called the South Downs, properly speaking, only around Lewes'. He also observed the two distinctly different breeds of sheep divided by the river Adur, each adapted to its different terrain which had

3   The chalk cliffs at the Seven Sisters.

evidently been long lasting. The contemporary agricultural writers, Arthur Young and William Marshall, adopted the same customary use of the name 'South Downs'[2] but it was not only people with farming interests who accepted these limits. Dr. Gideon Mantell, the pioneer geologist of the South Downs, explained in his *The Fossils of the South Downs* (1822) that his book was originally intended to comprehend only the eastern part of the Sussex Downs as far as the Adur valley 'which constitutes the western boundary of the South Downs'. Later 19th-century writers adhered to the same usage, the famous archaeologist Lane Fox (who later adopted the name Pitt Rivers) noting the limited usage of the name South Downs as late as 1868 when he wrote his pioneer essay on the archaeology of the Downs.[3]

It was not until the late 19th century that the public began to think of the South Downs as extending right across Sussex to the county border with Hampshire. W.H. Hudson in his classic *Nature in Downland* (1900)[4] observed this change in the perception of the South Downs and noted that general use then had it that the name then comprehended the whole range of the chalk hills in Sussex. This recognition of the physical and cultural integrity of the larger area is presumably due to more general travel by railway which had the effect of blurring original differences in dialect, folklore and farming and made feeling for landscape less local. The new fashion for historical and descriptive writing on a county basis also contributed to the changed view.

It is only in recent years that writers have chafed at county boundaries and treated the South Downs from a geographical and ecological point of view, so extending the definition to cover the continuation of the Downs into Hampshire. Thus the South Downs may now be said to have three component parts, the Eastern Downs, the Western Downs and the East Hampshire Downs, together with the river valleys which cut across them and the land immediately below them (the scarpfoot). The scenic and cultural heritage of the blocks of downland varies one from another in several respects, and each has its admirers, but it is the primordial shapes and ancient presences of rounded hills such as Mount Caburn, Firle Beacon and Windover Hill and the toy villages and half-hidden little country churches of the Eastern Downs that came to be regarded as the epitome of the South Downs and the most beautiful of all the English chalk country. It is this section of the South Downs that acquired worldwide fame with Kipling's verses which seeped so deeply into the mind as to bring tears to the eyes of exiles who longed for home. It is significant that the most recently published book on the South Downs, Michael George's *The South Downs* (1992), celebrates in photography not the whole range of the chalk hills but the special feeling engendered by the 'White Cliff Country' where the Downs meet the sea and add 'their magnificent white cliffs to the outline of England'.

Few lines of hills have caught the public imagination for generations as has the steep northward-facing escarpment of the Downs, whether rising smooth-shaven abruptly from the flat Weald, 'so noble and so bare' in Belloc's felicitous phrase or mantled with hanging woods. This virtually unbroken steep wall forms the horizon for hundreds of thousands of inhabitants in southern England and has remained unchanged for centuries. Those who know the Dorset or the Berkshire Downs are unprepared for its formidableness and grandeur. For the people of the Surrey and Sussex Wealds this great wall is the familiar backdrop to their daily lives. They feel more comfortable having it there, unspoilt, a reassuring image of home which greets them on return. Persons who have loved that view, but are now too infirm to visit it, value it as profoundly for simply being there. It is reckoned that views including the distinct skyline of the South Downs increase the sale value of almost every country dwelling—even if binoculars are needed actually to identify them! With the knowledge that beyond the Downs is sea, the crest

4    An aerial view of the line of the escarpment, looking westward from Mount Harry near Lewes.

has also been a constant source of fascination and inspiration, a boundary between the seen and the unseen, which to William Anderson of Clayton near Ditchling signified a point of departure for imagination and invention.[5] It has been spared from building in past times by the depth of wells needed and more recently by the determination of landowners, planners and amenity societies to preserve it inviolate, so that hardly a building breaks the smoothness of the skyline. Only national authorities have outraged it. A 'supergrid' of electricity pylons from the now vanished power station at Shoreham Harbour strides over the Downs with the insensitivity of the mechanistic Martians in H.G. Wells's *War of the Worlds*, blundering over the skyline, as at Fulking north of Hove, and crashing through valleys and spurs instead of following the lines of the land more naturally as on the West Dean estate. The same sense of reverence due to the Downs is lacking in those now erecting a rash of telecommunication masts.

Alec Clifton-Taylor, in a memorable television broadcast on Lewes,[6] was asked where he would most like to live. He replied, without hesitation, 'two miles north of the Downs, looking at them'. It is evident that the affluent have had the same preference certainly for some two thousand years, witness a long line of Roman villas, including Bignor, and country houses, mostly of Elizabethan or earlier origin, which lie in the calm beauty under the northern edge of the Downs, neither too close nor too far away, which fulfilled all the requirements to enjoy the special character of downland country. Passing from west to east the great houses and estates included Lavington (now Seaford College), Burton Park (until recently a girls' school), Cowdray, now a ruin, but once the greatest of all, Pitshill, Parham, Wiston, Danny, Streat Place, Glynde Place, Firle Place, Wootton and Folkington Manors. It was much more convenient and much more amenable for grandees to farm the rich soil below the Downs and run great flocks of sheep on the downland itself rather than to live there, for the Downs can be bleak in the winter. This is probably the reason why the once numerous country houses in the Downs themselves have not lasted as long as those at the Downs' foot, e.g. Halnaker, a ruined medieval mansion, Michelgrove, Muntham Court at Findon and Hangleton Manor near Brighton.

It is to the way the Downs stand in marked contrast to the Weald and the sea, and not because of their height, that their impressiveness is due. As W.H. Hudson observed, the pleasure in looking over a wide prospect does not depend on the height above, because whether the height be 500 or 5,000 feet, we experience much the same sense of freedom, triumph and elation in an unobstructed view all around.[7] H.G. Wells, who spent part of his boyhood at Uppark, has expressed the effect of this matter of height differently but with the same meaning: 'It is after all not so great a country this Sussex, nor so hilly. From the deepest valley to highest crest is not 600 feet. Yet what greatness of effect it can achieve. There is something in these downland views, which like sea views, lifts a mind out to the skies.'[8]

As one explores the Downs, one also comes to the realisation that the downland can impinge on the senses on a scale that feels more vast than the actual extent, for this, too, is only relative, and has nothing to do with the actual size of the country. The range of the human eye is only about twenty miles and seeing that distance conveys the same exhilaration as would be experienced on the Russian Steppes. Thus seeing the horizon all around one, or at least in an arc or a semicircle, as is the arrangement of the hills in southern England, induces a notable feeling of expansiveness. The uneven lie of the land in the Weald sharpens this impression, for, standing on one of the many vantage points on the crest of the Downs, we see the horizon sinking below eye level. This seems to make the sky the inner side of a sphere enclosing the earth, and this increases immensely the sense of the apparent distance.

Thus with their considerable elevation, their abrupt rising and dipping, and with deep, ravine-like valleys cleaving into the escarpment, the Downs feel more nearly true mountainous country than other chalklands and, in views across the Weald towards Blackdown, Hindhead, Leith Hill and the rampart of the North Downs closing the horizon, one can savour something of the solemn grandeur and sublimity which was the 'sort of delectable mountain feeling' which tranquillised Bishop Wilberforce at East Lavington, near Duncton Hill.[9] In certain light, as when the Downs disappear mysteriously into cloud or mist, or silhouetted against the setting sun, this feeling is reinforced and it recalls Gilbert White's

5 This ruined terrace is almost all that remains of Muntham Court near Worthing.

description of the Downs as a 'majestic chain of mountains'.[10] Even in reality some of the downland slopes are steeper than those of some mountains. It is a stiffer climb, for example, up Kingston Hill, near Lewes, than over parts of the Mourne Mountains in Ireland—and the air is as keen.

## The Eastern Downs

The absence of trees or hedges bestows a striking individuality on the shape and form of the land because chalk, whether grazed or cultivated, retains an impressive and monumental simplicity wherever gently curving lines are not masked by woodland or engulfing scrub which makes the form of the hills scarcely discernible. The peculiar smoothness and bareness results from centuries of shaving by sheep and plough (villages and farmsteads being visible only in hollows). This has given rise to broad, bare, round and smooth sensuous outlines of hills which have long appealed as the shape of the human figure. W.H. Hudson likened them to 'the solemn slope of mighty limbs asleep',[11] F.W. Bourdillon saw them as 'softly rounded as a mother's arm about a cradle'. In the present sexually-liberated society Alan Ross has explicitly identified the chalk's contours to the beauty of the feminine body.[12]

**6**　A view towards Ashcombe, near Lewes, from Housedean Farm. In this 19th-century landscaping the beech trees are both functional and ornamental and there is a diversified land-use and refinement lacking in much of the present-day Downs.

The visitor's experience here is distinctively different from that of the Western Downs. The wide open stretches of the bare-sloped Downs are to be seen at a single glance. They hold fewer secrets. It also means that a developer cannot hide anything ugly from the public eye and, because any building breaks this smooth outline, there can be few English landscapes less suited to any form of development. The sense of space and height created by these broad, bare expanses can be overwhelming. The emptiness is very evident, and it engenders a sense of antiquity, a feeling for the age of earth and of the oldness of man's possession of the Downs. With tumuli outlined against the sky it feels like a vast sacred burial ground. Where trees exist, they are weather-beaten and stunted. Woodland has survived only fragmentarily, typically in small patches on steep slopes on the escarpment, as at Clayton Holt, Offham, above West Firle and Wilmington Holt. Possibly some such patches may never have been completely cleared by man, in which case they may contain relict ancient woodland species. In a few places elsewhere great landowners have left their mark on abandoned downland by creating plantations and shelter belts over the past two hundred years. Some of these are in the form of positions held by the armies at Waterloo or in the shape of the Duke of Wellington's hat or boots, as at Falmer.

Traditionally, these Eastern Downs were the principal sheep rearing area of the South Downs and the most arable. Its glory was the fine sweet turf singled out by botanist John Ray as early as 1691[13] as its most distinctive feature. This chalk country had been originally covered with forest. It was cleared by early man because it was easier to use rudimentary cultivation tools on chalk than on the heavy clay of the Weald. Ultimately, cultivation gave way to grazing animals on the higher ground and gradually the traditional old chalk grassland came into being on the sheepwalk. Thus chalk grassland is very much the creation of sheep, it being a 'sheep-adapted' community of plants which were capable of withstanding their constant cropping. Consequently it is a vegetation type that is entirely dependent on grazing by sheep both for its initiation and continued existence. Since the last war, almost all of this habitat of the old chalk grassland has been lost to ploughing, and although the billowing swells of the chalk are as distinctive under corn as they were once under turf, much of the special charm of the Eastern Downs has been lost. It is now like an efficiently-run factory, where most of the wildlife in the regimented wheat has been killed off by pesticides, herbicides and artificial fertilisers. The skies are emptier, too, and much of the archaeological heritage has been obliterated.

It was in the Eastern Downs that Kipling was stirred to write his verses entitled *Sussex* and numerous others by the magnificent white towering cliffs and the sea. He loved the solitary places below the cliffs, seeing and hearing the surf crashing against the rocks. He also captures skilfully the essence of the then intangible atmosphere of the Downs such as the voice of the shepherd, the barking of his dog, the cries of the sheep, the far-off clangour of sheep-bells, the jingling of harness and the calls of birds, all so simple and familiar to downsmen since the very beginning of man's farming on the Downs some five thousand years ago but now as irrecoverable as Atlantis. It was the almost unbroken turf to the edge of the cliffs that Kipling loved especially:

> Clean of officious fence or hedge,
> Half wild and wholly tame,
> The wise turf cloaks the white cliff edge,
> As when the Romans came …[14]

This 'Kipling' country is the insuperable stretch of downland that forms the 'blunt, bow-headed, whale-backed downs' in Kipling's own phrase, which lies between Beachy Head and round about Lewes. It is still possible to savour it, for example, along the Seven Sisters' cliffs, but were Kipling to re-appear he would find the landscape with which his poetry is expressive of his intense identification, utterly transformed by arable farming, despite its cultural importance and outstanding natural beauty. Although one does not have to be a farmer to appreciate a well-ploughed expanse of earth as trim as a garden plot, it may be that, in the future, past literature and landscape painting may play some part in the re-creation of landscapes recalling some of the enchantment Kipling knew before it was ploughed up wholesale.

Several viewpoints on the crest have entered the national consciousness, views which stand for many as the emblems of their Mother England, notably the beacon hills on which fires told of the most important events in English history, such as Ditchling Beacon, made famous by Richard Jefferies and by Charles Knight's arresting image of the inter-war years (Plate XIX).

From Black Cap or Ditchling Beacon, the highest point in the Eastern Downs, the vast view across the Weald towards Crowborough Beacon and the North Downs is matched by the splendid line of the steep escarpment of the Ouse valley running like a pier from Kingston Hill, or the deep vale between Mount Caburn and the distinctive profile of Firle Beacon, opposite one of the most 'mountain-like' views in the Downs. The most popular and accessible of these vantage points is the Devil's Dyke, first 'discovered' by Regency tourists from Brighton for the contemplation of the view which enthralled Constable. Ever since it has been trippers' paradise, collecting in the past a funicular railway, an overhead walkway, a railway station and a zoo, and now the resort of hundreds of car-borne tourists. A different type of landmark on the crestline in the transitional belt between the Eastern and Western Downs is the now severely windblown clump of trees on a Roman temple within an Iron-Age hillfort at Chanctonbury Ring, planted in his boyhood by Charles Goring of Wiston in 1760. This led to many imitative

**7**   Chanctonbury Ring, before the Great Storm of October 1987.

coronals on the Downs, each beautifully arched by nature in conformity with the smooth rounded hilltops, the outer trees being stunted by the wind and the inner ones rising above them in the shelter, seeking light. By its presence felt for miles around, Chanctonbury has acquired a mystical and symbolic force without equal in southern England. Its recent replanting will ensure that the magic of its ancientness and sanctity will inspire future generations.

Although such vantages are memorable, it is the secretive hollows and secluded places which provoke stronger emotions. Hospitable, sheltered refuges from the rather bleak, windswept chalk uplands are provided by two types of dry valley. These were familiar to the Saxons who contrasted -denu (dene) valleys from -cumb (coombe) valleys. The latter are bowl-shaped troughs with steep sides usually etched into the escarpment or on the side of a main valley, as at the Devil's Dyke or at Coombes in the Adur valley, which takes its name from this feature. When wide enough, a village or hamlet has snuggled into it, as at Coombes. The denes are generally winding valleys, sometimes several miles long. Although now dry, they are the watercourses of ancient streams. They have relatively wide, flat-floored bottoms and interlocking spurs, just like normal headwater valleys, such as the one in which Balsdean lies, north of Rottingdean, or that above Bishopstone or Telscombe. Whole tree-like branching systems of these old river beds exist. Their sides are so steep that they sometimes carry scrub or a smooth thin covering of grass that has defeated the plough, so creating welcome ribbons of biodiversity in blocks of cereals. They invariably contain derelict farm buildings used in the 'Golden Age' of downland farming before the 1870s. They penetrate so deeply into the heart of the Downs and form such an intricate maze, and so empty are they now of human life, that one can easily get lost, yet the thickly populated coast between Brighton and Worthing, with its noisy highways, is only a few miles away. Exuding peace and quiet, they are home to most of our native orchids, many of the other beautiful wildflowers of the chalk and have relatively large populations of butterflies. Hence most of the Sites of Special Scientific Interest are located on their valley sides, whereas intensified agricultural activities elsewhere have robbed the Downs of much of their former interest and character. It is also here, in the tiniest of hidden folds, that are found little squat downland churches, snugly crouching against a hillside, 'little better in appearance than dovecotes', as Gilbert White described them, together with mellow cottages, huge barns with steep sloping roofs encrusted with orange-coloured lichen, and renowned pubs. Many of the elms planted around the villages to provide shelter still survive the Dutch Elm disease on account of their isolation. These comfortable, cosy and home-like villages convey a sense of timelessness because such places as Bishopstone near Seaford, West Firle, Glynde, Alciston, Telscombe, Stanmer and Falmer were for long estate villages and still survive little altered, bearing the imprint of estate stewardship over many generations. Even modern buildings have not destroyed the sense of the past which seems to have taken hold of these places.

## The Western Downs

To even the most superficial observer, the South Downs change character as they begin to strike obliquely inland away from the white cliffs and rise higher and wider as they extend westwards towards Butser. There is no abrupt transition between the Western and Eastern Downs but west of the Arun one is acutely conscious of entering a different country, although a part of the single range of the South Downs, special and distinct, with a cryptic and compelling fascination of its own. Whilst undeniably chalk country, its more wooded nature contrasts

**8** Glynde Place is really the focus of two estate villages grafted into one; the older lies on the hillside below the great house and the church; the other arose from lime-quarrying and dairying in the 19th century and is focused on the railway station.

with the bare downland of Salisbury Plain, the Dorset, Marlborough and Berkshire Downs, as well as the Eastern Downs, which are more commonly thought of as archetypal chalk scenery. The glory of the Western Downs was never the turf that made the Eastern Downs famous and loved, though locally, at Harting and Levin Downs, for example, this exists as an important habitat. Their chief feature is the high beech forests with their spectacular autumn tints. Thus savouring the Western Downs is a distinct experience. There is a special 'language' to be learned. The eye is not set free along curves and hollows spread like an ocean without check. Much of the surface of the rolling hills is fenced off with a girdle of trees and one is forced into narrow ways between trees at every turn. The woods mask the forms of the chalk hills and the antiquities and wildlife are not instantly visible as on the Eastern Downs. They are kept 'secret' and have to be sought out. Those devoted to the austere bare Downs are inclined to regard the Western Downs as 'downless' Downs, and so hardly proper Downs at all.

Yet the Western Downs are invested with a particular charm and significance. They are less touristy, being more remote from seaside resorts than the Downs further east, and have so many ancient, unobtrusive places hidden away that extensive landscapes belong more to folklore and memory than to the present. There is an air of the North Downs and the Chilterns about these Downs with their large patches of acid soil above the chalk bedrock, their beechwoods, the long rural tradition of wood-using industries, and the smaller, often hedge-bound, fields.

Walking or riding over them brings the realisation that they have rather a different topography from that of the Eastern Downs. Missing, except at Amberley Mount and the dramatic Great Coombe of Butser with its mountain-like steep sides, and Rake's Bottom, also in Hampshire, are the curving forms of great promontories jutting out from the escarpment, and the deep, winding coombes etched through the escarpment itself. Rare, too, are Kipling's 'blunt, bow-headed, whale-backed downs', for gently rounded scenery is less prominent, being generally wide plateau surfaces. On these flatter surfaces, and also on the less elevated country seawards, the chalk is plastered with a cover of Clay-with-Flints which is more retentive of rainwater than the chalk itself. On the highest ground, as at Tegleaze Farm and the Mardens, rainfall is considerably greater than in the Eastern Downs, and it is cooler and less sunny, so the climate can be harsh for southern England.

This distinctive milieu is a land of magnates, Norfolks, Richmonds, Leconfields, Cowdrays and others with a locally sporting and farming tradition evolved over centuries. Although sheep and corn have always figured in the economy, neither has been as prominent as further east. A good deal of land has been preserved traditionally for sport, and much of this was not suitable for anything else, given the state of the farming art in the past. As early as the Saxon period extensive areas on the higher parts of the Downs were zoned for hunting which after the Conquest were owned by successive lords of Arundel Castle and other wealthy lay and ecclesiastical magnates. In the 17th century these famed hunting grounds attracted the 1st Duke of Richmond to the district. The vanished glories of the Charlton Hunt are still imprinted on the face of the Downs in the form of widely planted fox coverts. One cannot walk far when undergrowth has died down in winter without encountering clear evidence on the ground of an old deer park or Forest. This is normally a prominent bank with an inside ditch, in contrast to wood boundary banks where the ditch is outside. This was to keep the deer inside rather than out, as at East Dean Parkwood.

Some patches of woodland are survivals of uncleared ancient wildwood with 'indicator species' of flora, including lichens, Dog's Mercury, Anemone, Lily of the Valley and Bluebell. Other woods originated on poor sheep pasture in the 16th and 17th centuries. Yet the present

scene is largely Georgian, the result of conscious artistry in the late 18th and early 19th centuries. This involved the visual remodelling of the land surfaces of entire estates such as Arundel, Goodwood and West Dean so as to combine beauty and utility in a tradition created by John Evelyn in *Sylva* (1664), and according to the then prevailing Arcadian aesthetic of The Picturesque. The woodland and farmland that embellishes the present scene reflects the great landowner's desire to make his home good to live in and to look at and to provide his incidental sport and leisure. It lends a tranquil, serene, spacious air of grandeur and ease which is generally missing in the stark landscape of the Eastern Downs, the traditional preserve of the peasant and yeoman. The English landscape is seldom as *grande luxe* as on the 12,000-acre Goodwood estate with its grandiloquent views across downland, coastal plain and sea or in the Duke of Norfolk's estate where traditionally the opening cricket match against an overseas Test team takes place in May. H.G. Wells, recalling his upbringing at Uppark, noted of the Western downs: 'In no other country in the world has such a continuous effort been made to elevate leisure, or the appearance of

**9** The 3rd Duke of Richmond (1735-1806), essentially the creator of Goodwood House and its estate.

it, to a finely judged art'. The romance of the old deer park at Uppark in heavenly rolling downs captivated him:

> About that park, there were some elements of a liberal education; there was a great space of greensward not given over to manure and food grubbing; there was a mystery, there was matter for the imagination. It was still a park of deer. I saw something of the life of these dappled creatures, heard the bellowing of the stags, came upon the young fawns in the bracken, found bones, skulls and antlers in lonely places. There were corners that gave a gleam of meaning to the word forest, glimpses of unsullied natural splendour. There was a slope of bluebells in the broken sunlight under the newly green beeches in the West Wood, that is now precious in my memory. It is the first time I knowingly met beauty.                                                     (*Tono-Bungay*, 1909)[15]

Similar experiences are to be had in the present high woods as at Monkton on the West Dean estate, now the haunt of the Buzzard and other occasional raptors such as the Red Kite and the Marsh Harrier. Overall, the woodland on big estates has a striking individuality which somehow seems to retain its new-mindedness despite some recent planting mistakes, such as the over-enthusiastic planting with conifers. Such landscapes, although maintained largely at private expense, are national assets which give a much needed quality and style to our rapidly degenerating countryside. Year after year the edges of these woods are adorned with a lavish succession of snowdrops, celandines, wild daffodils, primroses, bluebells and campion, rounded off by a display later in the year of foxgloves and hemp agrimony. Part of the enjoyment of this chalkland is the pleasure of plunging into the cool freedom of mysterious woods on a summer's day, or watching the fox with his rabbit in the evening. Then fallow and roe deer, in herds of a dozen or more, come out of the woods to feed on growing corn, their eyes shining like the rays of miniature torches in a car's headlights. One of the loveliest scenes that man and nature have jointly created are the hanging woods on the escarpment of the Western Downs and on the East Hampshire Hangers, so called because the trees literally hang from the steep hillsides, as above Heyshott, Graffham, Duncton, Barlavington, Sutton, Bignor, Harting and Buriton. These woods contain patches of scrub interspersed with groves of yew, beech and ash, through which there are glimpses of soaring views across the Weald.

The most remarkable of the woods are the yew groves of Kingley Vale National Nature Reserve which has become famed as the finest yew forest in Europe through the ecological research of Sir Arthur Tansley, who became the foremost authority on British vegetation.[16] Although yew has growing habits which make it difficult to date, several gnarled old yews in the core of the Reserve stand on the edge of former dew ponds, suggesting that they began to grow when the downland was abandoned for sheep grazing with the fall in population towards the end of the 14th century, making them about 600 years old, no more, though they look and 'feel' much older. Higher up the steep slopes of the northern edge of the great coombe are masses of bird-sown yew up to 100 years old, marking another time when sheep grazing was on the wane. In the midst of the Reserve is a commemorative sarsen stone (from Wiltshire!), marking Sir Arthur's favourite view in Britain across the Sussex coastal plain and the creeks of Chichester Harbour to the Isle of Wight, of which the spire of Chichester Cathedral is the focal point. It also acknowledges Tansley's 40-year-old ambition to protect the yew forest for all time, at last achieved with the first tranche of British nature reserves created in 1952, when he was the first chairman of the Nature Conservancy. Richard Williamson, warden here for more than 30 years, managed the downland scrub, chalk grassland and trees for wildlife: some 228

**10** Sir Arthur Tansley's memorial in the unforgettable setting of the Kingley Vale National Nature Reserve.

species of downland flowers, including 12 species of orchid, 39 species of breeding butterflies and 57 species of breeding birds have been recorded, including many rarities.[17]

The crest of Bow Hill, the dramatic backdrop to the Reserve, commands a most beautiful view, encompassing nearly every place described in this book, eastwards to Beachy Head, southwards to the sea, westwards towards the Hampshire, Dorset and Wiltshire Downs, and northwards over the wooded Downs near the Mardens as far as the Surrey hills. Breaking the skyline are four enormous Bronze-Age barrows, visible for miles, consisting of two ditch bowl-barrows and two bell-barrows, the latter being about 500 years later. Nearly a mile to the west is a very fine twin bell-barrow, a great rarity. A long barrow lies just to the north of the four barrows. A prehistoric field system with prominent lynchets lies on a spur running down into the Reserve, and on a spur of Bow Hill is a slightly hollowed trackway interrupted by a group of flint mines, possibly *c.*3000 B.C., or earlier, which indicates that the trackway was in use in or before the Neolithic period, making it one of the oldest humanly-made features on the Downs.

This quintessential downland landscape of Kingley Vale retains that rare and almost inexpressible charm that springs from an ancient human landscape in the possession of natural beauty and which has been made and re-made countless times by successive generations. Here its richness and verisimilitude can be savoured at leisure in the kind of countryside that has more or less vanished elsewhere in the Downs. The past seems to pervade everywhere, for every considerable earthwork created by prehistoric and later peoples has survived the bulldozer. The four barrows are known locally as the Devil's Humps or the Kings' Graves and the tradition was that if one ran round them seven times without stopping the Devil would appear. The Kings were legendary figures thought by local people to have fallen in battle with the Vikings *c.*A.D. 900.

The thickly wooded downland west of the river Arun was 'the hills of the South Country' which so profoundly moved Hilaire Belloc as to become his spiritual home. He always wrote of Sussex as if it were the crown of England and the downland bordering the river Arun as the jewel of that crown. Spiritually, the Sussex of his verse and other writings is Slindon and the surrounding downland where he spent his Sussex boyhood. He wrote with great gusto of the high woods, 'noisy in the loud October', through which he rode on horseback, tramped on foot,

11  View along the escarpment towards Ditchling Beacon from Barlavington Down.

12  Hilaire Belloc wrote with a depth of feeling unequalled of the 'lonely, tall and silent woods' of the Western Downs.

or viewed from the deck of his sailing boat in the English Channel. We catch glimpses in his verse of that most special West Sussex view, the long curving line of the wooded escarpment of the Downs against the pines on sterile sands at its foot. Belloc evoked the Western Downs, not as a dream but as a number of specific real places, so that he can be placed in his setting of sea, grassy glades, high woods and waving corn. Halnaker Mill, still standing on the skyline near Boxgrove, is the subject of one of the favourite modern poems in the English language, expressive of the heart-rending signs of agricultural decay which he took as a sign of national decline. The chapter including the poem *The Boy that sings on Duncton Hill*, which closes his book *The Four Men* (1912), is an evocation of mysterious Barlavington Down at nightfall on All Souls' Day (2 November) when the invisible dead emerge from their graves as a cloud of human ghosts to re-people briefly their ancient landscape of boundary dykes, lynchetted fields and rough woods.

Walkers who have traversed the South Downs Way through the high Western Downs beyond Butser may find the low chalkland of the East Hampshire Downs an anti-climax. Yet it has an individuality of its own. The best way to become acquainted with it is to walk or ride along its unfrequented footways and bridle ways, for example, the old trackway between West Meon and Warnford which offers views across serene country. Another good introduction is along the Wayfarers' Way long-distance footpath between Emsworth and Inkpen Beacon in Berkshire which takes to the higher country between Hinton Ampner and Droxford, and yet another beautiful and instructive route follows the South Downs Way to Old Winchester Hill, which commands the best views. Standing on the ramparts of the great Iron-Age fortress is a green mantle which once clothed the high chalkland but is now only an oasis amongst regimented rows of winter wheat where similar rich habitats have been ploughed and sprayed out of existence. The magnificent views are in a full circle of the horizon towards Salisbury Plain, the Berkshire Downs, Hindhead, the Vale of Fernhurst, the Western Downs, the Isle of Wight, the Solent, the New Forest and the Dorset Downs. So remote, still and empty is the landscape that it is impossible to believe that it is the immediate hinterland of the large towns of Portsmouth, Eastleigh, Fareham and Southampton.

Another major element of the Downs is that of the river valleys by which they are divided.[18] Although these wetlands so contrast with chalkland as to have been omitted from the Sussex Downs Area of Outstanding Natural Beauty when its boundaries were initially drawn up, their water meadows (brookland) have traditionally been integrated into the sheep-and-corn farms on

**13**   The Adur valley from Topfield near Henfield, looking across to Chanctonbury Ring. New Inn Farm in the foreground supplied bargemen with refreshment when the river was improved for navigation from 1806.

the low, smooth hills on their flanks because they offered rich summer pasture. The waters of the Cuckmere, Ouse, Adur and Arun are gathered in the muddy Weald and are strongly tidal when they find their way through magnificent gaps in the chalk range, so they lack the pellucid quality of the Hampshire chalk streams Meon, Test and Itchen, whose clearness and trout fishery is proverbial. Nevertheless there are few more beautiful places in England than all these valleys, visually connected in the mind with peacefulness and an extraordinary sense of time. Several of the villages were little ports engaged in sea fishing and salt-making before farmers began embanking the rivers to reclaim farmland in the early middle ages. The rivers sweep hard in places against almost precipitous cliffs, relics of former river cliffs of great age, and the white scars on these hillsides marking an abandoned quarry add greatly to the attractiveness and historical interest of the scene. The quiet reaches of brookland are cut by formerly interconnecting but now choked channels and remnants of abandoned control hatches, signs of traditional skills of drowning and draining the meadows, now lost, but for centuries matter-of-fact and seasonal. Since the last war the rivers have been confined into massive embankments which has permitted an extension of arable and improved pasture into the floor but which has greatly reduced the flora and wildlife. The least changed of the river valleys is that of the Arun. The stream itself is lined in places with overhanging willow, elm, poplar, sycamore and alder and the river banks are still clothed with waterside plants, seen at the best in late summer, such as the bright flowers of Balsam, Tansy commemorated in the novel of that name by a local name by a local naturalist-parson, Tickner Edwardes of Burpham, and the Great Hairy Willowherb.

The Amberley Wild Brooks in the Arun valley are a classic example of a wetland. They extend over 900 acres in a depression in the natural flood plain where the river crosses the Gault Clay vale. They consist of wide, peaceful dyke-drained grazing pastures with an endless variety of grasses and aquatic and marsh plants, with an occasional stretch of reedbed or swampy woodland. In the north the woodland grows on the only natural peat bog in south-east England outside the New Forest. The Brooks are thick with dragonflies, grasshoppers, butterflies and snails as well as wild flowers and they are one of the main wildfowl haunts of bird-watchers in southern England. The Wild Brooks have a numinous quality for some people. C.E.M. Joad wrote of them in the 1950s: 'Here, if anywhere, one felt, the nature gods still stayed; this was one of their last lurking places …'.[19] It has also been a constant source of inspiration to artists of all kinds, and has notably been immortalised in music by John Ireland's piano piece 'Amberley Wild Brooks'.[20]

## The Scarpfoot

Immediately below the chalk escarpment of the Downs is a chain of villages, hamlets and isolated farms standing normally on a bench of land where the Chalk and the Upper Greensand, which are permeable and soaked with rainwater like a sponge, comes sharply up upon the impermeable rock of the Gault Clay marking the southern edge of the Weald. Along this line burst out hundreds of deliciously-clear running springs filtered through hundreds of feet of chalk. These emerge more or less exactly at the same geological boundary, the 'spring-line', which has more than anything else created this line of settlements. The springs ran mills for corn-milling, fulling cloth, watered meadows and orchards, spread into teeming fishponds and provided pure water for drinking and farm use at no cost. In places the spring-line is so close to the escarpment that villages like Edburton near Henfield and Didling and Treyford on the Hampshire border are cast into shadow in low winter light when the countryside immediately to the north may be free of frost and mist and enjoying sunshine.

**I** The majestic profile of Firle Beacon and the dipslope of the Downs decline to the sea cliffs near Seaford Head, a fine example of Kipling's 'blunt, bow-headed, whale-backed downs'. The distinctive stepped profile of the Beacon is due to successive stages in the erosion of the Weald by rivers. The fertile cornlands at the scarp-foot are notable as is also the tree belt marking the boundary with traditional sheepwalk on the escarpment, maintained as a source of fuel, fencing, wattles and hurdles.

**II** For skyline and situation none will dispute the grandeur of Kingston Hill, near Lewes, made famous by W.H. Hudson's opening chapter in *Nature in Downland* (1900) when thistledown showered upon him from the then extensive sheepwalk. The deep scallops on the face were caused by freeze-thaw erosion during the last Ice Age.

100 BC

300 AD

1000 AD

**III** The changing landscape over time at Singleton, in the Lavant valley, adjacent to the present site of the Weald and Downland Museum. An explanation of the changes is given at appropriate places in the text. The stability of the hill pasture in the context of the continuously changing middle slopes and the valley is notable. The depicted changes, in general, were gradual. The earliest scenario shown followed clearance of woodland. (Based on research by Ruth Tittensor and created by Pat Donovan.)

**1600 AD**

**1880 AD**

**PRESENT LANDSCAPE**

**IV**  Wiston House, seen from across the gardens to the Downs in the background, *c*.1668, unidentified artist. The house was built by Sir Thomas Shirley in 1578-85, who embezzled public funds to pay for it. When this picture was painted, the estate was in the possession of Sir John Fagg, MP in the Long Parliament. He leans on the fence as part of the sporting frieze.

**V**  Lewes High Street from the Castle ramparts. The gracious Georgian fronts indicate 18th-century prosperity before the rise of Brighton as a watering-place. The absence of urban sprawl and the small scale of the town adds much to its attractiveness and individuality. Almost every building in Lewes, except the post-war County Hall, blends quite artlessly and accidentally into an agreeable total effect.

**14** Duncton Mill, now a commercial trout fishery, was for long milling corn and cloth.

These spring-line villages are linked by trackways to the crest of the Downs deeply worn into the chalk. The oblique inclination enabled oxen and horses to draw heavy loads up and down them. They are called locally 'bostals', a name probably derived from the Saxon beorg, hill and stig, a path. Some of these tracks are very ancient, doubtless prehistoric in many cases, and lie on former long-distance droving routes leading from coastal and downland settlements out into the once heavily forested Weald (p.17). The villages were probably for centuries virtually self-contained, communicating mainly with the Downs and the Weald by north-south routes, rather than between themselves. The narrow lanes which twist and wind along the northern edge of the Downs were presumably added later to the network in order to communicate with the external world and were so local in importance that they have remained byways which one enjoys at their best drawn by a horse or by beetling along in an open Morris Minor. These include the unhurried underhill road now a track between Berwick and West Firle, which is known as the old Coach Road because 18th-century stage-coaches used it as a highway to Eastbourne before the present A27 road was constructed. The east-west road is also very distinctive below Ditchling Beacon and between Poynings and Upper Beeding, where it is one of the most delightful roads linking a group of Saxon 'ings' and 'tons'. Near Wiston House, Mouse Lane at Steyning leads into a greenway and further west, as at West Burton, Bignor, Sutton, Barlavington, Bepton, Treyford and Didling, the road has a special magic of its own, being invariably a hollow-way up to twelve feet below the surrounding fields as a result of age-long traffic and periodic heavy rain. In this district the motorist must be prepared to be held up by the regular passage of dairy cows or to be distracted by extravagantly beautiful downland.

The scarp-foot country in West Sussex is very special terrain made up of very different types of scenery in a shorter distance than probably anywhere in Britain. Patrick Heron, explaining the sources of the inspiration of the distinguished landscape painter Ivon Hitchens, of

Lavington Common, near Petworth, remarked: '… The lush force of nature regulates itself into a disordered order, a fertile wildness'. Heron noted the variegated, overgrown beauty where miniature hills and valleys running through wooded heaths, flat meadows, marshes and fields, conceal small lakes, hammer ponds, waterfalls and streams amidst rhododendron tunnels, massive oaks and chestnuts lapping up against the smooth chalk-grass-woodland rampart of the Downs.[21] It is a landscape of such remarkable diversity (as seen from Tillington Church or the nearby Manor of Dean) because of the rapid sequence of narrow geological outcrops, similar to those so famously described by Gilbert White in his natural history. Eleanor Farjeon in *Martin Pippin in the Apple Orchard* (1921) evokes this 'secret' country at Greatham, near Pulborough, 'where everything was so intricate that it might be Eden grown tiny', and D.H. Lawrence, who lived there in 1915, uses the fields, heaths and woods in a short story in the collection *England, My England* (1922). The novelist Ford Madox Ford rented Ford Cottage (now Redford House) in 1919, describing its setting as 'a nook, a little sweet corner, the tiniest of hidden valleys'.[22]

Although this countryside is so brimful of unregarded historic landscape features that one thinks of an over-packed suitcase bursting open at the seams, it has only lately come to be appreciated by home-seekers. It is alarming that the part of this delectable scarpfoot district near Storrington has lured so many people to south-facing slopes looking towards the Downs that their houses have destroyed, or are threatening to destroy, its special character and also damaged the view from the Downs themselves. The little wooded valley of the Stor is in many ways a microcosm of the whole. Its little brook rises in a powerful spring at the foot of Chantry Hill and flows vigorously through a series of wooded dells of still great, but fast fading, beauty in the wake of repeated house-building which now threatens to destroy it irretrievably.

## The Old Market Towns

The site of the beautiful cathedral city of Chichester is greatly enhanced by the backdrop of the Downs and so is that of Arundel of which Robinson has remarked that 'The Downs roll back to reveal the careful 18th-century planting and model farms of a great estate, a red-roofed hillside town climbing to a ridge crowned by a huge French Gothic cathedral and a still more huge castle backed by a dramatically wooded park. As an overall landscape composition is generally considered to be among the grandest and most wonderful creations of the Romantic imagination.'[23] Petersfield, too, has a special relationship to the Downs as a flourishing market town and home of one of the earliest of the naturalists who established the reputation of the South Downs. He was John Goodyer (1592-1664) who lived at the Spain and was the first to identify the Small Woodruff, or Squinancywort as it is more usually known, one of the most typical plants of the Downs.[24]

A fascinating form of rural settlement is the decayed small market town. Alfriston (p.125) is an example as is Hambledon. If the special place of the South Downs in our culture lies in its recognition as a 'quintessentially English landscape', then Lewes is a quintessential English town with its castle, former markets, coaching inns and merchants' houses in their superb setting. It is the only town to lie in the heart of the Downs. As Graham Greene remarked, it is both a hill town and a valley town which for long was a seaport. Not the least of its attractions are glimpses caught from its steeply-plunging lanes or from upper floors of houses in the long thoroughfare of High Street. It is every bit as much a hill town as any place that can be found in Tuscany and it is exactly the right size for comfort. Its combination of medieval and Georgian domestic architecture makes it a gem. Its population in 1700 appears to have been no more

**15** Hambledon was well-known to Cobbett as a decayed market town. It is now a large, compact, downland village but with its greatly enlarged 13th-century church above an agreeable mixture of half-timbered, flint and Georgian brick houses and former shops it still retains the air of a small-scale town, as does Alfriston in Sussex.

than at Domesday Book in 1086 and even with its modern growth it is really only a town in miniature. At the end of the 19th century William Morris viewed it 'lying like a box of toys under a great amphitheatre of chalk hills'.[25] This remains an apt description. He also thought Lewes set fairer than any town he knew. Both he and his stalwart in the Arts and Crafts movement, architect Philip Webb, were distressed at the decay of the old trades and traditions. There was also an apparent unwillingness of people to step in and save dilapidated buildings, so making the town, in Webb's view *c.*1900 a 'slipshod-looking, 19th-century slatternly object of scorn'.[26] Lewes has spruced itself up since, notably in the inter-war years, by examples set by such as architect Walter Godfrey and Mrs. Alice Dudeney, the novelist.[27] Lewes still retains something of its old character as a market town on which converged once or twice a week within a radius of 10 miles or so the inhabitants of the surrounding farms, villages, country houses, vicarages and wayside cottages, meeting after business at the market at *The Star* (on the site of the Town Hall), the *White Hart*, or one of many other numerous inns. Lewes must now be one of the most beautiful small towns in England but will it become 'chi-chi', as have the bogus towns of Surrey?

*Chapter Two*

# THE CHALK TAKES CARE OF ALL

**B**asically, the South Downs are simply a piece of chalk. It is this curious substance, almost too soft to be called a rock, that has made the Downs what they are by impressing its own particular stamp upon the enormous, smoothly-rounded curves and the rolling rise and fall of the land that are so special to downland. Chalk has other very distinctive properties: being permeable to water, chalk country has no marshes or standing water; lacking dampness, it has been famous proverbially for the wholesomeness of its air; and also for the purity of its water because, as rainwater soaks downwards into the porous chalk, dust and soot it has absorbed are filtered out in its passage. The clarity of springs at the foot of the chalk shows that the water is cleaner than the rains that fed it. Centuries-old nibbling and trampling by sheep and rabbits produced a fine short turf as smooth as a regularly-tended garden lawn.

**16**   The chalk cliff of Seaford Head. The lower capping is of a younger rock and upmost is sludged material of the Glacial Period.

Where this survives it harbours beautiful wild plants that only grow on chalk or limestone, more species than any other land surface in Britain, many so miniature that one can cover half a dozen with a spread hand. Chalk has shaped the activities of its farmers through time and its flintstone has been the traditional material for churches and domestic buildings. A ploughed hillside shows a remarkable gradation in colour, almost white at the top, where soil is thin, and darkening downwards as soil increases towards the valley floor. Chalk also imparts its own pellucid colour to the landscape, a gamut of greys and where its luminous whiteness meets the sea it seems to bleach even the colour of the sky. Thus to look at downland scenery without understanding chalk is like listening to an opera in an unknown language; one can discern the beauty but miss the meaning.

## Creation

Although the purity and whiteness of the chalk in the White Cliffs of Dover, at Beachy Head and the Seven Sisters has so long symbolised England as to have given the island the name of Albion more than two thousand years ago, the origin of the chalk is still imperfectly known. Once believed to have been built entirely from the skeletons of minute sea creatures, chalk is now regarded as largely a chemical precipitate created by the action of a particular group of microscopic calcareous algae, a primitive plant. In her evocative book, *A Land* (1951), Jacquetta Hawkes wrote that she liked to think of the seas when the chalk was forming as 'clouded with white as from a snow storm'.[1] Scientists now consider the algae as too small to fall and reckon that they first passed unchanged through the digestive system of microscopic shrimp-like creatures called copepods before becoming solid lumps of excrement which were heavy enough to settle on the seabed. This process operated over the course of more than twenty million years and to a depth of more than a thousand feet between about 97-75 millions years ago. The chalk also contains visible fossils such as ammonites, bivalves, fish, sponges and occasional corals. The characteristic bands of flint, seen when walking under the cliffs or when looking at an exposure of chalk in a quarry, are also of biological origin. It has recently been demonstrated that they were probably formed by the percolation of water charged with sulphur released by decaying organic matter which became concentrated in the burrows of scavenging sea creatures, hence the knobbly seams of flint, which itself is a form of silica. The astonishing purity of the upper layers of chalk suggests that land was far away when the sea was accumulating

**17** No more indefatigable or brilliant student than Gideon Mantell has become involved with the South Downs but his unmitigating commitment to geological and archaeological research first undermined his marriage, then his medical practice and, finally, his health.

calcareous ooze on the sea bed and that the climate was perhaps as tropical and arid as that of the Kalahari Desert today.[2]

The upper layers of white chalk are remarkably homogenous but it does display slight, but significant, variations.[3] The most conspicuous effect on the landscape of this is the so-called secondary escarpment on the Downs in the vicinity of Worthing. Standing on the crest of the main escarpment and looking seawards, the surface in most places dips uniformly to the English Channel as a long, gentle slope (a dipslope). In the Worthing district and at places further westwards, the normal smooth declivity of the dipslope is abruptly broken by an intermittent line of north-pointing, bow-like hills running east-west across the Downs, one to two miles south of the main escarpment, including Steep Down, Cissbury Ring, Church Hill, Blackpatch and Harrow Hill. These lovely little hills stand up higher than their surrounds because their chalk rock is unusually hard and so more resistant to erosion, this being partly due to a re-inforcement of exceptionally hard flint. This was so readily accessible and is of such durability and strength that it was one of man's principal sources of stone axes, scrapers and adzes as early as 4000 B.C.[4] (See fig.20.)

There is no better way for a non-specialist to begin a study of chalk than in exposures in abandoned quarries near Lewes historically associated with Dr. Gideon Mantell (1790-1852), the son of a Lewes shoemaker who became one of England's foremost pioneer palaeontologists through his knowledge of the rocks and fossils of the Downs and the adjoining geological zones in the vicinity of Lewes, to which he was confined by a demanding medical practice. Ever since, this district has been the happy hunting ground of geologists, for on the banks of the river Ouse there are more chalk pits than anywhere else in Britain and Europe on account of the river long being used for the carriage of agricultural lime. This activity has exposed the most complete sequence of the chalk rock in Europe, for which reason the Southerham Grey Pit and the Machine Pit are both designated Sites of Geological Special Interest.

Mantell's book *The Fossils of the South Downs* (1822) was the first geological synthesis of an English chalkland. He is chiefly remembered today for his dramatic discoveries made later of the giant Iguanodon and other dinosaurs then living on the margins of the Cretaceous Seas, but his brilliantly assembled collection of chalk fossils now at the British Museum of Natural History reveals how this indefatigable scientist was able to demonstrate the exceptional diversity of fossil fish. This work formed a basis for Sir Arthur Woodward's *Fossil Fishes of the English Chalk* (1902), which is still the standard work on the subject.

**18**  An engraving from Mantell's *The Fossils of the South Downs* (1822) by his wife, Mary Ann, from drawings of the author. Shown are Ammonites and Scaphites from the Chalk and Chalk Marl near Lewes, including (*top left*) Mantell's newly-discovered *Ammonites Mantelli.*

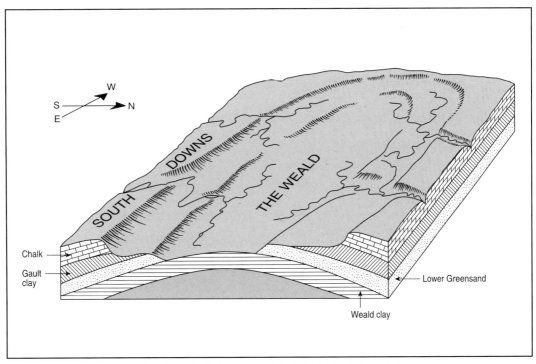

**19** The geological structure of the Weald (after Wooldridge).

Rocks older than the White Chalk outcrop at the base of the northern escarpment in a similar sequence of narrow bands to that described by Gilbert White in his famous introductory chapter to his *Natural History of Selborne*. The Chalk Marl gives rise to a slip of very stiff arable which is followed northwards by a bench of Upper Greensand (traditionally called Malmstone locally) on which most of the spring-line villages lie. This is also very calcareous and fertile. Near settlements it is often black in colour with the humus applied over several thousand years. This narrow belt of fertility is suceeded by the Gault Clay which forms low, rank, ground which is very wet and sticky and as hard as iron in summer. Farmers have normally kept this heavy land under permanent pasture. In the Chalk Marl occurs a band of harder chalk locally known as 'clunch', which was used effectively for domestic building and even for parish churches (p.27).[5]

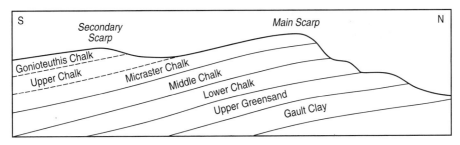

**20** Cross-section of the Downs near Worthing.

## The Shaping of the Downland

Although the South Downs are an impressive range of hills, they are a mere fragment of a vast chalk landscape that once covered the whole of south-east England. The Downs were raised above the sea when the earth's crust buckled and was thrust upwards and overturned on a gigantic scale right across Asia and Europe, so creating the mountain ranges of the Himalayas and the Alps. In this cataclysm south-east England was upheaved as one of the 'ripples of the Alpine Storm' into a dome of chalk with a crestline running east-west roughly on a line from Handcross Hill on the Surrey-Sussex border. As a result of natural processes operating over the past 75 million years, rivers and seas have eroded the central part of the dome entirely, leaving the chalk hills of the North and South Downs as an upstanding rim overlooking the Weald. The former existence of the dome is evident from the inclination of the chalk in quarries. In the North Downs the layers of chalk are tilted at a sharp angle towards the north; in Sussex (on the opposite side of the dome), the visible rocks have a seaward dip in the reverse direction. This sharp tilt of the rocks in the South Downs, and the progressively wider and deeper denudation of the soft beds of clay and sand below the chalk in the Weald explains the unusually high and abrupt north-facing escarpment of the Downs which adds so much to the beauty and fascination of south-east England.[6]

The porosity of the chalk is one of its most notable properties, for rain is largely absorbed through a microscopic, inter-connected, pore system instead of lying on the surface and forming rivers, lakes and ponds. During winter these pores become saturated with water rather like a sponge. Once saturated, water drains down through fractures to the water-table which may lie hundreds of feet below the surface. It is on account of its porosity that the natural outlines of chalk are so exquisitely smoothed and rounded into convex hill-tops and concave valleys. From a height it looks as if the whole downland was flowing in vast waves swollen to the point of breaking. This is explained by the little flowing water on the surface to erode the hills into the more varied, more irregular ridge-and-valley landforms which characterise gentle English landscape. The undulations of chalk country are thus a drama of abstract waves, not tossed about like a troubled sea in a storm, but forming sinuous, convex and concave curves, often double-curve elipses. They are as muscular and subtle as those of a classical nude and, where unmasked by trees, create a vivid sense of the 'barebones of the earth'.

Nevertheless, there is evidence of a relatively short period of normal river erosion before the smoothing action of chalk topography was again restored. This explains the deep hollows called coombes and the intricate, tree-like pattern of branching valleys, once containing water, but now dry.

The river action is attributed to the period of the last Ice Ages, to which a number of the present features of the present downland are also due. In the tundra climatic regime which then prevailed, the chalk rock would have been frozen. It would thus have been rendered impermeable and so running water in summer would have sculpted the valleys, and gushing springs would have sapped chalk hillsides headwards to form the deep depressions called coombes and also the characteristic flutings along steep slopes which represent embryonic coombes. With the restoration of a more equable climate, the rain again soaked into the chalk, leaving the present valleys dry. It becomes evident in walking the downs that the valleys are normally asymmetrical, with a steeper west- or north-facing slope, probably the result of the noon-day sun which would have warmed the opposite slope longer and so allowed more running water to erode its base and steepen the slope about it. The steeper valley sides have been generally left unploughed, or are under grass, gorse or woodland. It is thus probable that such coombes supported mini-glaciers like those on the Cairngorms to this day.

The last glacial period is also responsible for a diversity of soil types on the downland. The scouring and eroding effects of rapidly melting snow during the last Ice Age also deposited rock and soil from the hillsides on to floors of the valleys and on to the coast. Thus we find areas of chalky and clayey drift deposits caused by meltwater and hillwash at various places. In addition the streams and rivers in spate have carried down and deposited gravels and alluvium, which, like other drift deposits of an earlier age, serve to mask the underlying chalk and affect the uses to which the land has been put by plants, animals and man. These superficial deposits covering the chalk are called Clay-with-Flints, Coombe Rock or Plateau Drift. They are very variable in thickness and content, ranging from heavy clay to silty loam and from a few inches to many feet in depth. This means that even a single field has diverse soils, which can make crop management tricky. In cliff sections this material is well displayed, as in the famous Black Rock exposure at Brighton Marina and at Birling Gap.

One former layer of rock younger than the chalk has been largely stripped by these processes and this has led to the occurrence of sarsen stones. These stones, sometimes called 'Grey Wethers' because they resemble the form of a sheep lying on the ground, are a silica-segmented sandstone up to eight feet and more. When the sarsen layer was stripped away by erosion great numbers of sarsen stones found their way down into valleys. Many have been moved about by man who has used them for building and for marking the boundaries of manors and parishes as does the 'Rest and be Thankful' stone on the trackway to Thundersbarrow from Kingston and Southwick. Numerous sarsens now ornament ponds such as those at Stanmer and Falmer, or have been brought together as at the Stoneywish Country Park in Ditchling.

## Farming the Chalk

Taken altogether, chalk has been exceptionally favourable to man as a farmer.[7] Hilaire Belloc in *The Old Road* suggested that chalk should be 'warmly hymned and praised by every man who belongs to the south of England'[8] and this is exactly what farmers have done through the centuries. Its soil has been forgiving, even kindly, taking care of man, when well managed. It was William Cobbett's judgment that it seemed impossible to find a more beautiful and pleasant country than the South Downs 'or to imagine one the more easy and more happy than man might here lead'. This opinion must have been echoed by generations of horny-handed downland farmers unable to use a pen. Chalk soils are lighter than clay and have thus been easier to till. According to farmers on the difficult heavy soils of the Weald, theirs is a man's land compared with a boy's on the chalk. In winter the clay can become so waterlogged that plants have little air to breathe and when drying in the summer heat it shrinks to clods of earth that can easily break a farmer's heart. For these reasons the growing season for crops is several weeks longer on the chalk which also takes care of weather, for clay farmers are more

**21** A soil pit, revealing rubbly chalk loam which sludged down over chalk bedrock in the last Ice Age. (Kingley Vale.)

at risk from frost and other bad weather than the 'hill' farmers on the Downs who can work the land all year round except in heavy frost and snow. This advantage was greater in the past than now, but even with the use of mechanical equipment the chalk farmer retains the edge.

Many of the beneficial properties of chalk for man arise from its porosity, excessive rain being freely absorbed through the pores of the chalk instead of lying on the surface. This has been a supreme advantage to farmers in leaving the topsoil relatively dry. For this reason the chalk was immensely important to early man and it was on it that the first farmers gained one of their earliest and firmest footholds. In subsequent times it greatly cheapened the cost of arable production, as well as making farming easier, for none of the downland requires ditching and draining, an unremitting and costly task in the Weald, and nor were hedges needed, sheep being coralled with temporary fences made of hurdles. Chalk has also another important property which accounts for its ability to protect vegetation from the effects of drought. Although there may be no visible water for miles around, all except the shallowest-rooted vegetation usually survives a long, hot, summer. This is because of the huge capacity of the chalk to store water. As water is removed by evapotranspiration in the heat, so capillary attraction is able to suck up water out of the chalk to supply roots, not in abundance, but sufficient to sustain most plant life. This was understood by that great all-rounder William Cobbett nearly two centuries ago when he deduced that chalk 'seeks to absorb and retain water, and to keep it ready to be drawn up by the heat of the sun'.[9] Rigorous scientific explanation had to wait until 1982.[10]

Chalk farming did pose particular problems. A fundamental problem was the inherent lack of fertility natural to the thinnest soils of the chalk. This was overcome by a special system of farming. Sheep were used to fertilise the fields. The main method was by folding the animals on the arable at night so that they could both spread dung themselves and tread in it, thus consolidating light soil with their feet in preparation for wheat or barley. This device, probably established in distant prehistoric times, proved to be the perfect answer for chalk farming until artificial fertilisers multiplied from the mid-19th century. This symbiotic relationship between sheep and corn farming on the chalk thus depended absolutely on sheep. A chalk farmer could not grow cereals without them. Indeed, for most of the Downs' history, the main purpose of sheep was for their dung. When sheep became unprofitable from the 1880s corn farming also suffered terribly as a result.

Flint-ridden soil has always caused severe wear and tear of the plough-share and other implements. This is revealed dramatically by the trail of sparks in the wake of a plough in evening light or the noise of the share grinding against stones. Traditionally it was the task of farm boys and women and children to pick up flints by the basketful from ploughed land and to carry the stones to the edge of the field for collection by horse and cart. It was slow, heavy and back-breaking work and despite this regular 'flint-picking' the same number remained the following season, giving rise to the superstition amongst labourers that the chalk actually 'grew' flints. The phenomenon has now been explained scientifically. Each time the plough disturbs a flint, however slightly, small particles of soil fall into the cavity beneath and prevent it from settling back into its old position. In this way, season by season, the flint inexorably works its way to the surface. Moreover, for each flint 'picked', the amount of worked soil is reduced so that with each subsequent ploughing (or digging in a chalky garden) the plough reaches fractionally deeper and so reaches hitherto undisturbed flints. Even when there is no soil left the surface is never free of flints, for frost and rain will begin to expose some more. It would seem that all this labour of flint-picking might actually have reduced the productivity of the land

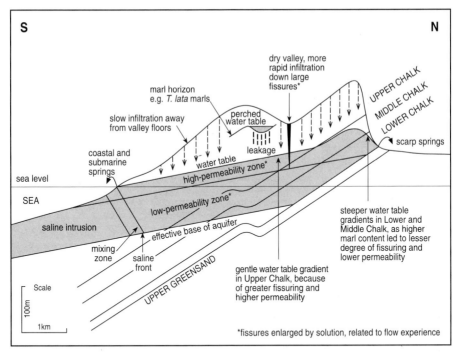

**22**    Typical water levels and flows in the South Downs chalk aquifer (after J. Thompson).

because Arthur Young's experiment, conducted on the stony chalk of East Suffolk at the end of the 18th century, disclosed that the yield of land cleared of flints was less than that left untouched.[11] Nevertheless, stone-picking continued because of its supposed benefits to the soil and for the little money it earned the farmer when the material was used for the maintenance of parish roads.

## Building with Chalk

It has been noted that 'Chalk (except for a few special varieties), cannot be successfully used in building unless it is studied and coddled, its weaknesses understood and guarded against'. Chalk indeed was usually too soft and lacking in durability to be suitable for building, at least for exteriors, in contrast to the Oolitic limestone of the Cotswolds, for example, which provides the finest of building stones. There are, however, some more compact beds of chalk at the base of the northern escarpment which contain tiny fragments of shells and other impurities which produce a more gritty texture. This is called 'clunch', a word evocatively conveying a sense of its soft, yet dense and resistant quality. Clunch is hardest in the Western and the East Hampshire Downs and was widely used for the exterior walls of farmhouses, cottages and barns in the Meon valley and eastwards along the northern escarpment towards Duncton as at Cocking, Elsted and Harting. On account of its inability to resist rainwater, clunch had to be protected by wide eaves from rain-bearing winds, and by a foundation course to keep it clear of the ground, generally a footing of sarsen stone. To a lesser extent it was used near Lewes, as in barns at Hamsey. Several church interiors are modelled in clunch, including Burpham in the Arun valley. Local builders have now forgotten how to select or handle chalk, and no longer trouble to use it, although there was a local saying, 'Find Chalk a good hat and shoe and it will serve you well'.[12]

Much more generally used, and accounting for much of the charm of the downland village, is flintstone, the characteristic building material of Chalk country for the walls of churches, farmhouses and cottages, barns, stockyards, dovecotes and around orchards and paddocks. Old flint walls make a gamut of greys a constant background colour but lichens weather them into a patina of warm orange hues and iron staining occurs when flints were collected from the top soil of a field. Flint walls are not normally straight: they sag a little here, bulge outwards a little there, and are built not only with flints but 'any old thing', such as pieces of Roman tile, stone or broken brick. Living with them is a homely and comforting experience (though expensive in maintenance).

Alec Clifton-Taylor has remarked how strange flint is as a building material. As a building stone it is quite unlike any other, and although readily portable, is not easy to handle. Taylor thought it improbable that anyone would have chosen it if any other stone had been available, but on downland there was no alternative to wood, until the advent of brick.[13] Field flints are nodules formed orginally, as we have seen, in the Upper Chalk formation and dislodged presumably during the denudation of the South Downs during the Ice Ages. Their white silica exterior is stained. They are generally sub-angular and were collected by hand from the plough land and used in the construction of walls of agricultural buildings and cottages. They are usually laid in regular courses in a strong lime mortar with an admixture of fine beach pebbles.

The special difficulty of building was that the shapes were so irregular and hard that flint did not blend so readily as brick or stone for it does not allow mortar to penetrate into its pores. This entailed a great deal of mortar of high quality. Although the flint itself is virtually indestructible, the mortar has to be renewed periodically and few present-day builders have the special skills and patience to do this. Cement pointing is wrong because it does not 'breathe' like mortar and so does not not let penetrating water dry out. Building a flint wall is slow because of the need to select carefully the right size of flints and the process requires a pause every few feet of walling to allow the mortar to set. No building can be done in wet weather and little during the winter months. A special difficulty of flint as a building material was that, as it is not found in large pieces, it was not easy to build in square shapes. This probably explains the three circular church towers in the Ouse valley, St Michael's, Lewes, Southease and Piddinghoe.

The shaping and trimming of flint to show its dark glassy insides and to offer a smooth rectangular face for a greater decorative effect is called flint-knapping. The knapper wore a leather apron and first roughly dressed the flint nodule and shaped it into a 'quarter'. The flaker then worked his way round the flint, striking off a succession of long narrow flakes using a metal tool, working it into any shape desired. If knapped accurately and uniformly they fitted like brick and needed no more than a quarter of an inch of mortar between them. Knapped flints, especially the squared variety which became fashionable in the 18th century, always give pleasure. In sunshine after rain the glassy surfaces which sparkle brightly are known as 'Sussex diamonds'.

The observer will discover many different methods of arranging and using flints in walling. They include the use of flints in rubble masonry, usually indicative of ancient building; uncoursed field flints for ordinary walling; knapped field flints in roughly uniformed courses, a superior form of work; random cobbles, boulders in random order and coursed cobbles and knapped boulders. These are all found on the Downs and at seaside locations. Knapped and squared flints, the supreme achievement of the knapper's art are only found on building of some quality. Chequered flint and stone is usually late medieval in age. Finally the use of large white flints, knapped or otherwise, set in either light coloured or black mortar is common on 19th-century restored churches and in new buildings of the same age. To many people these

**23** *(left)* A wall of St Andrew's Church, Steyning, a good example of a 'chequer-work', using stone and knapped flints.

**24** *(above)* Superb 18th-century flint walling at Boxgrove Priory.

have a hard, unlovable character and suggestive of Victorian 'killing-kindness'. Yet another version of a wall consists of squared knapped flints set alternately with stone or brickwork in a chequer pattern. This is called 'diaper' work. Amongst the earliest diaper work is the façade facing the main street at New Shoreham of the ecclesiastical-looking building called The Marlipins. The side elevation is of untrimmed flints dating from *c.*1100, the south-facing façade probably *c.*1340 is outstandingly beautiful in its pattern and demonstrates how skill in the use of flint had grown in the intervening period. It is not amiss here to mention that the walls of The Marlipins are extremely thick and composed of flint rubble bounded by large flints on outer and inner sides, the usual method of construction of ancient buildings.

To counteract the rocking of amorphous flints, a wall-builder introduced spare narrow flakes of flint upright into the mortar. This process became known as galleting, from the French *galet*. The practice goes back to medieval times and the intention was originally to provide some mechanical support to non-porous flint set in very slowly hardening lime mortar, but in the 18th century the spare flakes were used with squared flints, to give an additional decorative effect. The impossibility of achieving clean angles in flint led to the use of brick as dressings to doors and windows. The exquisite brick craftsmanship contrived with flintwork on the splendidly proportioned main front of Newtimber Place is the most aesthetically pleasing in Sussex.

**25**   A barn, *c.*1860, at Iford Farm in the Ouse valley, marking the transitional phase from flint to brick construction.

Lewes flint work is particularly instructive and interesting. In the castle keep the stone is almost all flint, most of it set in rough layers but here and there the coursing is of the herring-bone type, always indicative of early Norman construction. The early Norman gatehouse also displays large flints laid with herring-bone coursing. The flintwork on the 13th-century Barbican, the outer gatehouse, one of the biggest and finest in England, is striking. The flints have been carefully knapped and laid in fairly regular courses, a decidedly early example of this technique of treating the virtually indestructible flints. Spanning the centuries, flint work appears in many guises in Lewes. Ovoid cobblestones were used for the paved water-course that runs down the precipitous Keere Street. Local people called them 'petrified kidneys'. The town walls visible from Keere Street are now coursed with brick at wide intervals, but predominantly are of flint.

Some of the loveliest flintwork in Lewes is visible on the façades of 139, 140 and 141 High Street and on the exterior of St Michael's Church. Nearly all flints used here were knapped and mostly egg-shaped, and they are regular coursed within beautifully pointed brick surrounds. On 141 many of the flints are not only knapped but squared, a refinement permitting a reduction in the amount of mortar used, which is always the bugbear of flint. In addition, 141 has its flint set off by the elegant Portland limestone, employed for the quoins, the cornice, arch and windows and the Doric porch. Because shapes are so eccentric, flint benefits tremendously from regular coursing and, if all the flints are of the same size, so the better is the appearance.

Rottingdean has plenty of lovingly preserved buildings of flintwork in the old village street and so has Shoreham-by-Sea in Church Street and in its several delightful lanes, but it is at Brighton that English flintwork reaches its greatest development. Tar or pitch applied to make it more weather-proof is an old Brighton custom. In the Downs the best flintwork is on the landed estates of the Western Downs. Flintwork at West Dean House is a magnificent example of the galleting technique in beautiful walling. The Goodwood estate is the finest shrine to the flint-knapper's art in Sussex. The House *c*.1810 has knapped flints to a very high standard. The earlier built stables designed by Sir William Chambers are an outstanding example of knapped flint worked into a square exactly matched over its long length and so closely fitted that mortar is almost unnoticed between joints. Excellent flint knapping extends to cottages and farm-buildings on the estate, as it does on the former Lavington estate adjoining. For superior work, walls have some designed arrangement with both untrimmed and trimmed stonework. Singleton village on the Goodwood estate is one of the best places to observe several different ways of handling flint. For sheer quality, the flintwork of the South Downs is probably matched in England only by north Norfolk which has a *joie de vivre* of patterns of seaside walling and had the most skilful knappers in the 19th century. By the 1860s building in brick was replacing flintwork in both towns and villages. All the new cottages of the Duke of Richmond at Single-ton and Lavant, for example, used both flint and brick. Bricks were then sold at about 32 shillings per 1,000. Flint cost only the picking and the cartage. There was then, however, little saving in the cost of flintwork, since it required more mortar and took more time to lay than bricks. Cartage costs were growing, too.[14] An interesting transitional style for barns and other buildings before brick finally triumphed is the use of flintwork and brick courses alternately. The decline in flint building is generally apparent in restored Victorian churches, though that at Henfield is an exceptional example of traditional workmanship at its best.

*Chapter Three*

# EARLY MAN

To one walking or riding the Downs today, they seem to be almost empty of human life. One can spend hours on them without being impinged upon by another living soul and experience a feeling of deep peace. Yet all around there are ancient remains of man to remind us that the Downs were one of the cradles of civilisation in Britain. It may not be wrong to envisage around A.D. 100 a virtually continuous succession of separate farms with intermixed villages in those now emptied hills, as seems to have existed on the Wessex Downs. Instead of finding the solitude sought this century, the traveller would have encountered a bustling economy based on agriculture, forestry, metalwork and trade. Prehistoric farmers found it easier to till the light soils of the chalk than the heavy clays of the Weald and with steadily improving implements of stone, bronze and iron they progressively stripped the Downs of much of their woodland and blanketed them with their fields. It is probable that this woodland clearance was almost total in the Eastern Downs and that arable cultivation had reached a high-

**26** Reconstruction of Iron-Age farmstead at the Butser Ancient Farm.

water mark in *c*.A.D. 100 which was not exceeded until after the Second World War. The Downs in early times were relatively densely inhabited, indeed apparently more so than at any other time in the historic period and many times more so than in the 20th century, though because dwellings and farm buildings were largely of wood and earth which has perished, little is to be seen of these earliest man-made landscapes except defensive earthworks, field boundaries, burial mounds and religious sites.

Even by A.D. 100 downland farmers had learned by experiment and inherited experience over more than 3,000 years how to get the best out of the Downs. The essence of this was a particular kind of farming perfectly adapted to the thin, well-drained chalk soils. This was sheep-and-corn farming, by which sheep dunged and consolidated the light soil with their hooves for growing wheat and barley. This agriculture presumably evolved from Neolithic times, perhaps earlier than 3000 B.C., and with spasmodic shifts in the proportion of arable to sheep pasture, and modifications due to improved livestock and new crops. This was to be the farming system that continued almost universally on the Downs throughout the historic period until living memory, when it was suddenly replaced by an unsustainable system of agriculture.

It was not until two or three centuries following the invasions of the South Saxons, who gave their name to Sussex in the early fifth century A.D., that the hill country of the Downs was progressively abandoned and farms re-established mainly in villages under the Downs. There still remained a general sprinkling of hamlets and isolated farms on the Downs proper, together with a few large villages during the early Middle Ages, but since *c*.A.D. 1340 there has been a progressive contraction of the farming population on downland. Once abandoned, this downland of Celt, Romano-Briton and early Saxon was never settled again, being mainly used as sheep pasture.

Yet on account of the record on the landscape of man's habitation over a span of time reckoned in millennia, there is always a feeling of a long human presence on the Downs, even although it is now that of the invisible presence of the dead. In places the ancient dead still seem to rule the Downs. This gives many places a mysterious power, a potency that is still in the air like electricity. Such presences are hidden everywhere, as on Barlavington Down. Another is Chanctonbury Ring, the clump of trees marking an Iron-Age fort, a Roman temple, the burial place of Roman and Saxon bones, and layers of earlier and later occupation enveloped in 19th-century graffiti, all of it concealed between roots and cowslips, until trees were felled in the Great Storm of 1987. One has a kind of vertigo trying to contemplate the 40th or 50th century B.C. when the Downs were acquiring their first herder-farmers or the more than 2,000 years ago when hill-forts such as Cissbury were being erected. It is this immensely long humanising process, strange to sensibilities unused to plumbing such a deep well of uncalendared time, that distinguishes the Downs from all other districts of southern England and endows them with a particular *mystique*.

With downland, history, as it is generally defined, represents less than one thousandth part of the total span of human occupation. The recent discovery of Britain's earliest known habitation just below the chalk dip-slope of the Downs at Boxgrove in West Sussex has dramatically re-endorsed this. Since the shin bone of a tall and heavily-built man was found there, Boxgrove has become one of the most celebrated archaeological sites in the world. The site was used some 500,000 years ago by men to butcher wild horses, deer and other meat, using flint tools made from the old chalk cliffs then towering over it. Before the Boxgrove finds, it was uncertain whether humans had lived in Britain that long ago but now the several hundred beautifully-crafted hand axes and the remains of carefully butchered wild animals give us some idea of their stage of civilisation and of the impact of humankind at that time on the natural environment. Dr. Mark Roberts has already demonstrated that Boxgrove Man was not merely an opportunist scavenger, but skilfully selected his prey. 'Only hunters who were in total command of their patch could have done that and only a species capable of considerable organisational skill could have achieved that domination.' Europe's oldest human remains at Boxgrove were preserved by layers of sediment and marshy deposits which accumulated later and were finally buried by 20 feet of gravel washed down during the Ice Ages. This is evidence that subsequent nomadic hunters could only roam the Downs during spells of warmer climate known as Inter-Glacials. It was not until the final retreat of tundra-like conditions some 12,000 years ago that a continuous story of human settlement begins on the Downs. Climate then slowly improved, bare landscape became increasingly covered with trees, wild animals moved in and fish populated the rivers. For some 5-6,000 years human life on the Downs was still based on the feeding habits of wild animals. By the Mesolithic (Middle Stone Age period, *c*.7000 B.C.) people probably hunted the entire Downs and nomadic groups consisting of a score or so of people should probably be envisaged operating in hunting territories each many miles in circumference. In summer the hunter-gatherers appear to have made forays into the forested Weald, possibly using some of the later well-defined north-south trackways, but their winter quarters were doubtless on the dry soil of the Downs near their sea fishing.[1]

## Pioneer Archaeologists

The Downs proved to be a superb hunting ground for archaeologists driven to learn more about the ancient farming communities who followed the hunters. The surface teemed with abundant ancient remains such as waste flakes, occasional scrapers and other implements from the flint mines which had been little disturbed before 1939 by subsequent ploughing or building. Additionally, Col. Lane Fox (later the famous archaeologist Lt. General Pitt-Rivers) was thrilled to observe that so little soil covered the earthworks that every break on their smooth surface caused by the hand of man in past ages was preserved with a 'wonderful distinctiveness' and since the faintest traces of man's occupation could be seen for miles on the then greensward he considered that 'perhaps no part of England would more quickly repay the prehistoric archaeologist the trouble of exploring it'. The South Downs became, therefore, one of the chief parts of Britain where the pioneer archaeologist sought prehistory. He could chart human movements over several thousands of years across this particular countryside and explore the development of successive cultures contributing to the early civilisation of Britain. Before Pitt-Rivers' excavations at Cissbury and Mount Caburn in 1868-9, knowledge of the Downs' prehistory was perfunctory, confused, often bizarre. Cissbury's massive size, for example, had dominated the imagination of people for generations. Early antiquaries associated so famous an earthwork with Caesar and people at Findon in the 17th century pretended 'to show the place were Caesar's tent was'. Others found irresistible a spurious association with Cissa, a reputed son of the first king of the South Saxons. It was not until 1868 that Col. Lane Fox, as he was then known, proved by means of the first scientific archaeological excavation in Britain that neither was responsible and that the hill-fort was attributable to the Iron Age.[2]

Ever since Pitt-Rivers' astonishingly precocious campaign on the hill forts of Sussex, the South Downs have played a leading role in archaeological research and excavation in Britain. In the 1920s and 1930s the two doctors Eliot and Cecil Curwen of Hove, father and son respectively, made the Downs the model area for such aspects of British archaeology as flint mines, field systems and related settlement sites.[3] Among their teamworkers were three young men destined to become famous in British archaeology, namely Stuart Piggott, later Professor of Archaeology at Edinburgh University; Grahame Clark, Professor of Archaeology in the University of London; and C.W. Phillips, of the Ordnance Survey. From 1932 Cecil Curwen worked with an augmented team which included G.P. Burstow, later head of the junior section of Brighton College, G.A. Holleyman, who became the leading antiquarian bookseller in Brighton and Dr. A.E. Wilson, a distinguished pre-historian and historian of Brighton Grammar School and Brighton Technical College.[4] Other notable archaeologists working on the Downs in the inter-war period included L.V. Grinsell who moved to Brighton in 1925 and was so enchanted by the turf-covered vestiges of antiquity that he called the Downs a 'barrow hunter's dream'.[5] Of earlier influence was Herbert Toms who was trained by Pitt-Rivers and was appointed to Brighton Museum. In 1906 he was the principal founder of the Brighton and Hove Archaeological Club (later Society). Cecil Curwen stated: 'My father was roped in to join the Club in 1907 and this

**27** Cecil Curwen, the doyen of amateur archaeologists between the two World Wars, examining pottery from his Whitehawk excavation (1927).

**28** Cissbury Ring. The 'pimples' within the Iron-Age rampart denote debris from Neolithic flint-mines. Traces of a Romano-British field system are also visible within the fort.

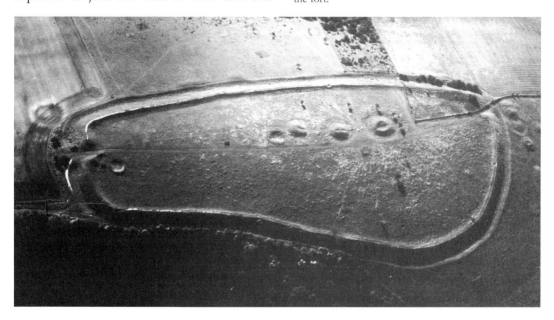

aroused my interest in turn'. Another redoubtable pioneer who was a member of Toms' Club was A. Hadrian Allcroft, a classical scholar and master at Lancing College, whose forte was field survey, not excavation, then a new approach. His love and archaeological knowledge of the Downs in such works as *Earthwork of England* (1908) and *Downland Pathways* (1924) awakened a more vivid realisation of the heritage of the Downs.

## Prehistoric Farmers

With the coming of the first herder-farmers *c.*5-4000 B.C. the life of the community was probably first bound up with cattle and pigs, simply because the first farms on the downland were carved out of woodland. Soon, however, the life of the family appears to have been centred on sheep on account of numerous sheep's bones found at most prehistoric sites. Despite the continuous changes in the farmer's routine the sheep flock has been the one constant strand until recent times. The wild sheep domesticated by Neolithic man was probably very much akin to the Moufflon whose rough coat, a mixture of hair and kemp, was shed naturally and made into felt, the earliest form of cloth. The successors to the Moufflon on the Downs now survive only as rare breeds of sheep on the islands of the north-west coast of Britain. One was the Soay sheep, the typical sheep of the Bronze and early Iron Age. These are found today in Soay, a small island to the west of St Kilda. These sheep have a woolly rather than a hairy fleece which also shed naturally or was plucked off in season before being spun into yarn and woven into fabric on a simple upright loom. By the late Iron Age the sheep were generally heavier and had woollier fleeces with a longer staple. Breeds representing these sheep are the Manx Loghtan, the Hebridian and the Shetland sheep, all typically horned and often mistaken for goats.[6]

Very few structures of the New Stone (Neolithic) Age survive as earthworks. The most remarkable are the flint mines which are concentrated in the South Downs more than anywhere else in England. These fall mainly into two groups, one near Worthing comprising Cissbury, Church Hill, Findon, Blackpatch and Harrow Hill, and the other north of Chichester (Stoke Downs and Bow Hill). Windover Hill near Alfriston has also been confirmed as a flint-mining site and a single mine shaft was found at Slonk Hill near Shoreham-by-Sea. More single shafts probably await discovery.[7]

These flint mines include the earliest recorded in Britain, Church Hill and Blackpatch both being radiocarbon dated prior to 4000 B.C. They thus represent the earliest natural resource to be exploited by farmers in Sussex. The Stone-Age men easily worked the hard glassy substance of flint into any desired shape or form. By chipping off slivers, known as flakes, and using another stone or piece of antler as a hammer, a piece of flint was shaped into robust implements such as an axe. Alternatively, the razor-sharp edges of flint when flakes were chipped off would be used as cutting tools or shaped further into knives, piercing tools, scrapers, strike-a-lights or arrow tips. There is growing evidence that high-quality polished flint axes from these mines were exported from the South Downs to the populous areas of the Wessex chalkland. Mined flint was far superior to flint nodules picked up from ploughed fields or from the boles of trees, or dug out from patches of Clay-with-Flints because these would have been made brittle by exposure. The plentiful supply of axes, adzes, sickles, knives, scrapers and arrowheads from the mines facilitated the clearance of the woodland on the Downs and the successful introduction of agriculture.

The flint mines on Harrow Hill were excavated by Eliot and Cecil Curwen in 1924/5. These lie on the isolated and conspicuous promontory which forms part of the beautiful secondary escarpment on the dip slope of the Downs where particularly hard flint reached the surface. The summit is crowned by a sub-rectangular earthwork enclosure, of early Iron-Age date, which may also represent the heathen Saxon shrine which gives the hill its name (O.E. *hearg* a shrine). On the elastic chalk turf of the hillsides are no less then 160 cup-shaped depressions marking the mouths of filled-in flint mines. There are surrounded by heaps of spoil, including 'wasters' and knapped flint flakes, often to be found in soil brought to the surface at the entrance to rabbit burrows. The Curwens selected one pit for excavation. The shaft was some 22 ft. deep and three seams of flint were discovered. The Neolithic miners had worked these by means of short galleries radiating from the sides of the shaft. When the miners had worked out one shaft they sank another close by. Buried in the shaft were found the picks used by the miners, made from the antlers of red deer and shovels made from shoulder-blades of oxen lashed to a wooden handle. The shafts and galleries were shored up with oak props. A system of ropes and leather bags brought the newly dug flints to the surface, where they were sorted for transmission to the knappers and blade-makers working perhaps inside 'camps'. To protect the fertility of the mines, effigies in chalk of an Earth Spirit together with chalk phalli were enshrined at the entrance to each shaft and in alcoves underground. Scratchings made by a sharp flint were probably tallies, but a bored miner's graffiti are reminiscent of a child's scribbling. Soot from a miner's lamp was still perfectly fresh after a lapse of some 6,000 years. The Blackpatch flint mines were discovered by Worthing postman J.H. Pull, whose ecstasy at their visible signs on the then 'wild pasture lands' in the 1920s is one of the highlights of the archaeological literature of the Downs.[8]

Other visible signs of the earliest farmers are the causewayed enclosures, of which three are large, Belle Tout near Eastbourne, and the inner ramparts of the Trundle, and Whitehawk above Brighton, but many a hill-top swells with the now grassy banks, remnants of defences of similar age long defunct by the time of Christ. It is generally agreed that they served as a focal point for local Neolithic communities. The fences of these sites are very weak. The bounds are simply marked by ditches and no attempt was made to take advantage of any natural protection afforded by steeper slopes. One recent theory is that these shallow ditches and banks defended a taboo area as in present-day Melanesia. We can also imagine these hill-top corrals being used for seasonal gatherings of flocks and herds when branding and shearing, the dispersal and slaughter of stock, and perhaps for communal lambing being a rampart against wolves.

## The Bronze Age

During the Bronze Age (*c*.1500-*c*.500 B.C.) woodland clearance and farming appear to have spread all over the Downs but little is known about the settlement and farming activities or the economy and social organisation. In the years 1949-53 the best known site at Itford Hill near Newhaven was excavated, and examined again by Peter Drewett in 1979. The removal of turf and topsoil disclosed a number of circular huts, each with a large central post and smaller posts placed equidistant around the perimeter. The roofs would have been made with boughs and roughly thatched and the walls probably made of wattle and daub. There were enclosures for cattle and the whole site was remarkably like native African villages which exist today. In the larger huts were storage pits cut deep into the chalk and the gashes made by the bronze axes were still to be seen. In one of the huts carbonised barley was found, presumably grown on the small irregular fields marked by cultivation banks (lynchets). Trackways entered the fields from the outside and 11 round barrows are sited in the vicinity. Drewett asked questions such as

29 A Bronze-Age burial mound at Bow Hill, Kingley Vale National Nature Reserve.

'What kinds of activities were practised in the huts? What social groups used them? Were the lynchets contemporary with the hut platforms?'. Drewett concluded that the proximity of huts suggests a close social relationship, a family or an extended family group with separate fenced yards for independence. Unmarried daughters may have fenced off a little of their mother's yard and constructed their own living hut and some buildings, probably shared, e.g. a kitchen hut. This type of settlement is characteristic of an extended family in a compound, e.g. in Uganda and Nigeria. The compound includes independently owned units. The huts do not appear to have been long in use for there are few replacement post-holes.

Drewett was able to identify huts used for food preparation, crafts, storage and for housing lambs or calves. Arable farming was practised and wild food was gathered in season, such as sea food, wild alowa, blackberries and hazel nuts. Sea kale would have been collected from the sea coast for cooking as a vegetable. Chickweed was also used as a vegetable, as in the Middle Ages. A similar farm is identifiable on New Barn Down near Patching, although partially ploughed down, and consisted of about six round huts.[9]

Burial mounds are ubiquitous. The earliest are Neolithic in date and are long or oval mounds flanked by ditches. There are also two well-preserved long barrows in the East Hampshire Downs near Old Winchester Hill. Bevis's Thumb at Compton, above Chichester, is the best example. It covered mortuary houses containing the bodies of the dead. Bronze-Age burial mounds are normally circular in plan and contained cremated remains in pottery vessels. They may occur singly or in groups. The plan of the burial mounds varies. Where the ditch is separated from the mound by a flat area (berm), the feature is called a bell-barrow. Bowl-barrows are closely bounded by a ditch. These are the most numerous barrows. Most examples appear to belong to the period 2400-1500 B.C. The barrows generally occupy prominent locations and are major elements in the modern landscape. Many were robbed in the 18th and early 19th centuries and this is usually indicated by a depression in the top of the mound. Their considerable variation in form and longevity provide important information on the diversity of beliefs and social organisations amongst the early prehistoric communities, e.g. round barrows on platforms (platform barrows), of which fewer than fifty examples have been recorded nationally, although they show a marked concentration in the South Downs. The barrows on Heyshott Down are amongst the finest in the Downs. They comprise a group of at least ten barrows, including one large, detached bowl-barrow. The finest group of bell-barrows is on Treyford Down, the five large and two small barrows here being known as the Devil's Jumps. Another notable group of barrows are the 'Kings' Graves' or the 'Devil's Humps' comprising two bell-barrows and two ditched bowl-barrows on Bow Hill, overlooking the Kingley Vale National Nature Reserve. The former are assumed early-middle Bronze Age in date; the latter may be several hundred years later in origin.[10]

Commonly encountered on the high Downs east of Butser are rather slender earthworks across spurs, promontories and ridges. These may be attributable to the late Bronze-early Iron Age and probably delimited grazing land on the hilly terrain. They are often associated with longer linear ditches which are thought to have bounded ranches, the arable land being generally on south-facing slopes. Good examples of dykes and linear ditches are at Belle Tout near Eastbourne, Ranscombe near Lewes, Lavington Down near Duncton Hill, Bow Hill near Chichester, and on Butser. [11]

A much smaller hill fort is the Trundle, north of Chichester, which was constructed around an earlier causewayed camp. The hill fort on Mount Caburn near Lewes is currently being re-interpreted by Peter Drewett. It appears to have been occupied prior to the construction of the first rampart in the late Bronze or early Iron Age. At some stage in the later middle Iron Age (*c*.300-100B.C.) a simple enclosure was bounded by a ditch and bank. It probably enclosed no more than a farm, possibly the rural seat of a member of the nobility who practised an economy similar to that of the famous Little Woodbury in Wiltshire. At a later date which Drewett considers was possibly late Saxon a new enclosure was built with vertical and horizontal timbering and at about the time that Lewes Castle was built in the 1070s the rampart was still further heightened.

By the beginning of the first century B.C. each block of downland appears to have possessed a major hill fort replacing many of the older forts of the Iron Age which had feebler defences such as Torberry, Thundersbarrow, the Devil's Dyke, Butser Hill and Bow Hill.

## The Romano-British Period

Cunliffe has identified agricultural settlements which had evolved continuously on more or less the same sites for well over one thousand years, as at Park Brow near Cissbury, at Thundersbarrow Hill near Shoreham-by-Sea and at Chalton near Petersfield. At Thundersbarrow a Romano-British village succeeded a hillfort community established in the early Iron Age. Its fields lay on either side of a wide ridgeway and the village was provided with at least one well.[12]

Such villages are now regarded as possibly widespread. Their houses on a rectangular plan replaced the round Iron-Age houses and were built of timber, wattle and daub. On Park Brow such houses possessed glazed windows, a clear sign of comparative affluence, and a door key was found indicating that the contents were sufficiently valuable to warrant locks.

Much of our present knowledge of Romano-British farming on the Downs has been acquired recently. When Mr. Budden of the downland parish of Chalton on the Hampshire border began to clear the scrub-covered land to the north of the village in 1953, lynchets and settlement sites were discovered. His bulldozer dragged out a beaker of the late third or early fourth century A.D. containing six toothed bronze implements. In 1956 Mr. Budden and Professor Cunliffe began a programme of intensive fieldwork in the Chalton area, as a result of which 120 archaeological sites have been discovered, including the site mentioned above which is a Romano-British village. Since villages of this kind with well-preserved earthworks are rare in southern

**30**   Buckland Bank, near Lewes, a good example of a Romano-British field system. This is now under grass but for more than thirty years after the last war cultivation severely damaged the site.

Britain, Mr. Budden decided to use the site as a permanent pasture, thus protecting the earth-works from erosion which would have increasingly accompanied constant ploughing. It is very probable that the densely wooded area of Queen Elizabeth Forest covers ancient field systems, whereas south of Chalton medieval and later ploughing has destroyed all traces of earlier field patterns but field walking over these patches has brought to light a number of prehistoric settle-ments, all of which tended to occupy positions just above the shoulder of the valley sides.[13]

Fields were ploughed with a superior and more efficient ard than that used by Iron-Age farmers, it having apparently pairs of 'ears' or ground wrests and a 'keel' like that of a small bronze model found in an unidentified Sussex barrow. The ground wrests piled up loosened soil in ridges between furrows and the keel gave greater stability, allowing the ard to be tilted so as to turn the sod. This probably made crossploughing no longer necessary and consequently a preference for a longer furrow arose.

Examples of long rectangular fields laid out in the Roman period as at Fore Down, Lullington, Windmill Hill and at Chalton may indicate the colonisation of new land. Specially constructed corn-drying ovens have been discovered at several sites, such as the Thundersbarrow Romano-British village and at nearby West Blatchington. The roasting or parching of corn must have been quite normal at all farmsteads. Among the advantages would have been the prevention of germination during storage as well as lessening the risks of rotting and spon-taneous combustion.

A new element in settlement on the Downs in the Roman period was the villa. These were richer farms than the peasants', scattered fairly evenly over the Downs and they tended to be sited on soils which were more productive either on the Malmstone bench at the foot of the

northern escarpment as at Bignor, Pulborough
and Beddingham, or on the southern fringes
of the Downs at Fishbourne, Angmering,
Southwick and Eastbourne. The latter group
were all exceptionally well-appointed villas established before the end of the first century
A.D., and each lies on a geographically distinct
block of land over which a landowning aris-
tocracy appears to have held control. If this
hypothesis is correct the pattern of large estates, especially in West Sussex, which is still a
feature of the present-day, may have originated
in the Iron Age and Roman periods. Later on
villas developed on the Downs proper: these
included the smaller corn-and-sheep producing farms in the Chilgrove valley.[14]

## Visually exploring the Downs

The ability to recognise traces of man's past
activities in the prehistoric and succeeding
Romano-British period is a way of making a
downland walk more instructive and interesting. A useful axiom is that, as chalk is naturally
smooth, any break on, or departure from,
smooth, flowing outlines is the result of hu-

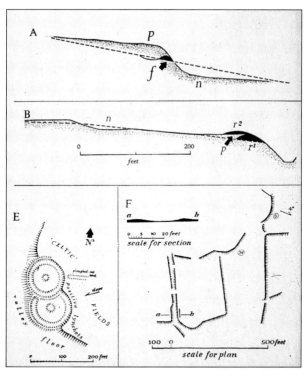

**31** The origin of prehistoric and Romano-British lynchets (after
Bowen). The pecked line marks the original land surface, p = positive
lynchet, n = negative lynchet, f marks boulders marking edge of
one farmer's field.

man interference in some form, whether ancient or modern. The dimpled surface of filled-in
flint mines, or the faint outlines of neolithic 'camps' are immediately observable from a considerable distance by those who know what to look for. The same applies to the commonest
memorials of all, the remains of ancient fields.[15]

   Once the protecting mat of vegetation was torn away from the soil by ploughing along the
contours, rain year by year washed the loosened soil downslope: the steeper the slope, the
greater the wastage, the soil always moving from the upper end of a field to the lower (the same
process can be seen operating on modern fields to this day). At the upper end of a field the
constant waste of soil downwards gradually created a break of slope which became a bank
(lynchet) rising yearly higher above the field: while below the ploughed field the progressive
accumulation of downwashed soil gradually built up another bank which also grew higher yearly.
The upper bank was created by the *removal* of soil, the lower by the *accretion* of soil and these are
called negative and positive lynchets respectively. Several sets of parallel lynchets can sometimes
be seen. Good specimens, at Buckland Bank, near Falmer, on the slopes of Chantry Hill near
Sullington, or in large areas now covered with woodland near East Dean on the Western Downs,
have the appearance of a giant's stairway (Fig.30).

   Before the extensive ploughing-up of the South Downs after the last war, the visible sign
of lynchets across the smooth contours of the chalk was one of its most remarkable features.
Where they still exist, the lynchets are all that remain to tell us what once was a ploughed field.
The height of lynchets is broadly related to the degree of slope and the number of times the

**32** Aerial photograph of the downland around Buckland Bank. Traces of former lynchets can be distinguished and the field-system is revealed with great clarity.

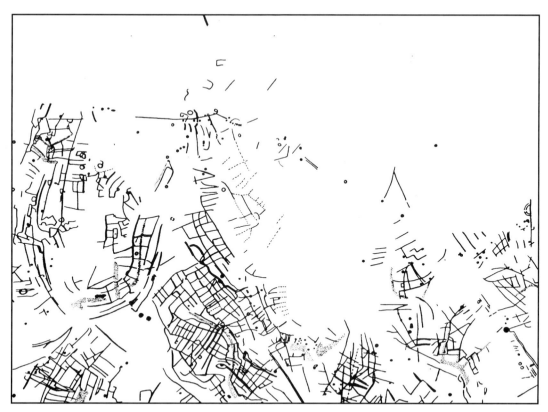

**33** Lynchet-lines still visible each year from late summer until early spring in the environs of Lewes. (East Sussex County Council Archaeological Sites and Monuments Record.) (Scale six inches to one mile.)

field was ploughed. Sometimes the lynchets are so slight as to be scarcely recognisable, though once one is on the lookout for such things they can be identified more readily.

Although most of the ancient fields were bulldozed after the last war, to a surprising degree they are still identifiable by means of soil and crop marks. Although the banks which once bounded the field are now almost flattened and scarcely recognisable to an inexperienced observer, the appearance of a freshly ploughed modern field is that of a grid-iron. The dark lines of the grid represent humus or top soil which accumulated deeply above a lynchet in ancient times (or in the trough of a fossilised ditch). The lighter lines are the remains of the chalk exposed on the bare slopes between the former lynchets.

It is thus possible by examining bands of darker and lighter soil between crops to form an estimation of the extensive ancient agricultural economy on the Downs. It is also surprising how much of the ancient rural landscape is traceable from crop marks arising from the differential growth of crops in the same modern field. Thus corn standing on a silted ditch or on the remains of a positive lynchet will probably stand taller on account of the greater depth of the soil and its moisture content than that on, say, a buried rampart or negative lynchet where it will usually be correspondingly shorter.

The patterns made by such crop and soil marks are most visible from the air. A circular ditch might become visible from the air because corn on it would benefit from the moisture and do better than in the rest of the field. Similarly, the irregular grid-iron effect of bulldozed lynchets is widespread on aerial photographs. At first sight the 'grid-irons' seem to have been imposed on the modern fields, but this is in fact the other way round. Thus the stored-up past survives obstinately on aerial photographs and by their means one can trace ancient field systems on the Downs even when they have been overrun by recent ploughing; how much longer these signs will remain now that deep ploughing is continuous is another matter.

The terraces created by contour ploughing in early times should not be confused with the very general striation of steep turf-grown slopes into diminutive terraces which serve as trackways for sheep, cattle and rabbits. These 'terracettes' form from the downward drift of soil, the formation of miniature ridges being due to soil lodging against a root or stone while the soil below is washed simultaneously downwards.

The first to use aerial photography to map traces of prehistoric and Roman cultivation on the Downs and its contemporary settlement was George Holleyman in 1935 who was inspired

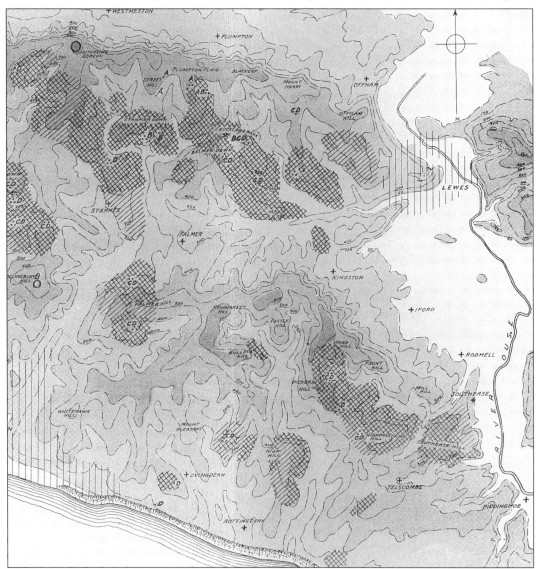

**34**   A section of Holleyman's pioneering map of prehistoric and Romano-British cultivation traced from aerial photographs. The hatched areas bore traces of field systems.

by the earliest work published on the subject, O.G.S. Crawford's and Alexander Keiller's *Wessex from the Air* (1928).[16] The picture to emerge from this major event in the archaeology of the Downs is of a densely farmed landscape laid out in blocks of Celtic fields within closely spaced settlements of varying sizes, including single farms and villages, some being as little as a mile apart. The map has an inherent limitation in that some gaps in field systems correspond to the presence of medieval villages and their fields, which obliterated early evidence of farming, while the spread of recent building along the coast has had the same effect. Nevertheless the map throws invaluable information on early man's use of the Downs, a milestone in fact, in understanding the prehistoric South Downs. A very important element in the distribution of farmsteads brought out by Holleyman's map is that they were packed closely together on the optimal sites of gently sloping spurs on the middle and lower slopes of the Downs, which had good soil and accessible water for cattle, and just below the chalkland on the crest of the Downs where sheep ran.

## The Ancient Farm Project

The important heritage from the prehistoric past makes it particularly appropriate that the Downs should be the location of a unique project in Britain with the remit of studying the agricultural and domestic economy of the late Iron Age. This is Butser Ancient Farm, originally set on a spur to the north of Butser Hill in 1972 and later on another site on Hillhampton Down on the southern slopes of Butser. The project is now sited at Bascombe Copse, Chalton, where the Romano-Celtic world was crowded with farms. Here the construction of a working farm as it would have been about 300 B.C., with livestock, crops and equipment, is being complemented with a working Roman villa similarly fitted with all its accoutrements. To many of its visitors it is no more than a delightful way of learning about the past but it is in fact an open-air research laboratory with all the rigorous scientific controls needed for archaeological experiments. Since its inception the project has been under the direction of Dr. Peter Reynolds. Amongst the questions the project seeks to answer are: what happens to an Iron-Age house over the years from rising damp, rain, wind and snow, its function in the economy of the farmstead, the level of agricultural productivity and what effect ploughing and earthworks had on the land surface. Many foreign organisations have since based their work upon the methods and techniques developed at Butser.[17]

No complete wooden house survives from prehistory but there are modern replicas at Butser Ancient Farm based on patterns of chalk-cut post-holes from actual sites, such as Longbridge Deverel Cowdown in Wiltshire excavated by Dr. Sonia Hawkes. This had no central post, yet a diameter of 50 feet and a floor area of *c.*2,000 square feet, the weight supported by the peripheral posts being about 30 tons. Examining this replica reveals the challenge of using a double-ring beam supported on an aisle of shorter uprights, all the timber being morticed and tenoned into place. Such a large house would have belonged to an exceptionally rich and powerful person and would have been furnished in an appropriate manner, but other houses were well constructed and evidently long-lasting. The word 'hut' disappears from the vocabulary. Similarly an awareness of a more flexible and successful agriculture and forestry is gained from research at the Farm. The sheer quantity of rods and stakes required for an Iron-Age farm suggests that woodland was coppiced for this purpose, the fencing being replaced necessarily at approximately the length of time it would have taken the hazel shoots to grow to the required size. Ploughing at the Farm is done with Iron Age ards drawn by medium-legged Dexter cows,

**35**  Emmer wheat (*Triticum dicoccum*) appears to have quickly supplanted Einkorn as the principal wheat of prehistory and was the traditional bread wheat of the Roman Empire. Autumn sown, a single plant will usually produce between three and nine (exceptionally even more) tillers (fruiting stems), giving an output of up to 240 seeds (each spikelet contains 36-44 seeds). Emmer wheat has double the protein value of modern bread wheat.

the nearest equivalent to prehistoric cattle. With the use of a seed-furrow ard crops are sown in distinct rows allowing the hoeing of weeds. On field area all the varieties of prehistoric wheats can be seen actually growing. The reason for studying them is their growing patterns, resistance to disease, their ability to cope with invasive weeds and to find out from long-term growing trials what levels of yields Celtic farmers might have obtained. The research to date has shown that Emmer Wheat, the most celebrated of all prehistoric cereals, yields remarkably well under different treatments, averaging one ton per acre. The Spelt wheat also appears to have thriven on less fertile soils, and sprouted tall for thatch. When milled and made into flour it is higher in protein than modern flour made from winter wheat and has a higher concentration of vitamins. A gene extracted from the threshing and storage areas of Danebury hill fort shows that it might be feasible to improve modern corn crops with genetic material from ancient varieties.[18] Altogether, ongoing research at the Ancient Farm is deepening our knowledge of the considerable achievements of prehistoric peoples on the Downs and it is unlikely to remain in the purely academic sphere.

# Chapter Four

# THE SAXON SOUTH DOWNS

## The South Saxon Kingdom

From the third century A.D. Roman Britain became the prey to attack from outside which accelerated when the army and fleet left the province unprotected at the beginning of the fifth century. A long drawn-out period of violence, raiding and settlement then ensued which ultimately brought about the total collapse of the Romano-British economy. Downland Britons saw a way of life they had taken for granted disintegrating all around them: they must have been totally devastated. This period is known as the Dark Ages because a whole civilisation, at least nominally Christian, was destroyed by pagan barbarians; dark also because our knowledge of what actually took place is very fragmented and conjectural. Yet gradually a new rural order was established and by the middle of the seventh century a degree of equilibrium had been reached.[1] This proved to be the base from which a remarkable new Saxon civilisation evolved, deeply Christian and in the forefront of European art, learning and economic development. It is on this high note when Sussex had been merged with the hegemony of Wessex that this chapter ends.

The Britons who were left to fend for themselves appear to have suffered a number of specific Saxon landfalls on the Downs resulting in permanent settlement. One of these was near Bishopstone at the mouth of the river Ouse.[2] Early Saxons, like prehistoric peoples, are known to us mainly by their burials. There is such a concentration of pagan Saxon burial mounds on the Downs between the rivers Ouse and Cuckmere that Welch has suggested that in this area, remote from Chichester, the administrative centre of the Romano-British canton, and free from large Romanised villa estates, the sub-Roman authorities may have chosen to abandon the area to incoming Saxon settlers by a treaty agreement in return for their protection from further invasion. There is a memory of such an agreement in the Anglo-Saxon Chronicle. This refers to a battle fought by the Aelle, the supposed leader of the Anglo Saxons who gave their names to Sussex, in 485 near the banks of the river 'Mearcredesburna', 'the river of frontier agreed by treaty'. In this frontier zone, at Rookery Hill, Bishopstone, is the most completely excavated site of the early Saxon period in Sussex.[3] Here the invaders laid out their landscape *de novo,* building their houses over many long-established farm enclosures and trackways without regard for them. Another settlement at Highdown, the isolated chalk hilltop near Worthing, may have been another isolated group of mercenaries placed on a strategic site within the Iron-Age hillfort. From there they would have commanded a view of the entire Downs from Beachy Head into Hampshire. A third group of invaders, possibly a tribe of Jutes, landed on the coast of the Solent and passed up the river Meon. A site at Droxford produced a gilded bronze brooch similar to one found at the old Roman shore fort of Portchester.

It is still, however, very uncertain what actually happened to the Britons in general. Historians used to conjecture that the South Saxons wiped out or drove away the inhabitants

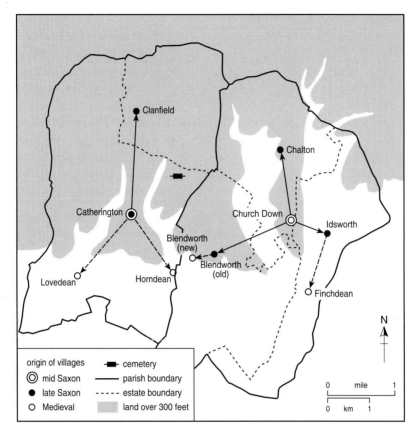

**36**   Migration of Saxon and medieval settlement in the East Hampshire Downs (after Cunliffe).

and made a fresh start with farming and settlement in an emptied landscape. It was envisaged that the invaders immediately introduced a new rural pattern based on large manors centred upon still existing nucleated villages at the scarp- or dip-foot of the Downs. What seemed to corroborate this conjecture was the abandonment of the relatively densely crowded farmsteads and fields on the Downs proper which were the subject of the previous chapter.

This theory has come under attack. The Saxons actually settling in Sussex seem to have been modest in number and the British population too great to have been massacred or driven away entirely. Stress is now laid less on cataclysm and more on continuity. We have seen how the intellectual and physical capabilities of Romanised and earlier peoples on the Downs were much greater than formerly supposed. The Downs, even in the mid-fifth century when Saxon settlement began, were already one of the longest-inhabited and populous parts of Britain with, as we have seen, layer upon layer of inherited man-made features etched into the surface over many generations. We have noted that the bare chalk greensward had come into being by the Bronze Age. The management of coppice woodland, first recorded in the Sussex economy in Domesday Book, 1086, until recently regarded as an 11th-century innovation, is now also expected to have evolved over millennia earlier. Thus scholars now speculate that the ancientness of the downland landscape is to be attributed to a continuous agricultural colonisation extending over at least five millennia.

## The New Agrarian Ground Plan

A central issue in the history of the Downs is the origin of the nucleated villages which are now such an attractive feature of the present-day scene and how they related to the emptied Downs. In the first integrated and up-to-date study of a Saxon kingdom to be published, *The South Saxons* (1978), Barry Cunliffe pointed out how a systematic campaign of intensive field survey and excavation would undoubtedly advance our understanding beyond its present limitations.[4] In reality little work in the past twenty years has been done on the question of Saxon settlement in Sussex and the fate of the British inhabitants, although Cunliffe's work in the 1960s and 1970s provided a model which can be applied to movements of population for the South Downs as a whole.

This was based on Cunliffe's work at Chalton, Hampshire which covered a compact block of land sited on the dip-slope of the Downs measuring some five miles in each direction.[5] The method of discovering new Saxon sites was to walk the fields after the ploughed land had been washed by rain and search systematically for characteristic grass-tempered pottery. This technique yielded a number of new sites including the substantial village sites on the hill top at Church Down. Nearby is another hill-top site of early occupation, Catherington. These discoveries, together with the hill-top village of Bishopstone in East Sussex, suggest that the old belief about early Saxon settlement in the valleys may not be acceptable. Church Down was probably abandoned in the ninth century, while the villages of Chalton, Idsworth, and probably Blendworth began to be occupied at the same time. These are valley settlements. Cunliffe suggests that eventually colonisation at these places, being more convenient for farming, gradually eclipsed the mother settlement and drew off its population. Catherington continues in use with a satellite, Clanfield, recorded in Domesday Book. Cunliffe suggests that Church Down and Catherington were originally the only substantial Saxon settlements on this block of Downs. He argues that the limits of their joint territory to the south probably became the boundary of Ceptune Hundred with the line of the north-south parish boundary (later dividing Catherington and Clanfield from Blendworth and Chalton) separating the two original Saxon territories. Up Marden in Sussex also occupies a hill-top site (now much reduced in population) and so does neighbouring Compton.[5] It is tempting to think that a similar evolution of Saxon settlement took place as in Cunliffe's model but no archaeological work has yet been undertaken.

It would seem that at about the same time as valley settlement developed around Chalton between the 9th and 10th centuries, a shift of population was taking place from the high downs to the spring-line villages which grew in size to around A.D. 300. These places had peasants' farmhouses lining the main street and expanding common fields (presumably to provide peasants with the means to work the sheep-walk), and they are found in Domesday Book acting as headquarters of large manors. Although the location of specific villages was controlled essentially by a convenient spring, the virtually equidistant spacing of many of the scarp-foot villages, e.g. between Bepton and South Harting, suggests the boundaries of their parishes may have been inherited from the boundaries of Romanised villa estates which lay earlier on the Malmstone bench to exploit the various resource potential of fertile farmland on the bench itself, the sheep grazings on the Downs and swine pannage in the Weald.

It would be wrong, however, to believe that the sole unit of settlement in the Saxon period became the village. Over the high Downs, especially in West Sussex, is a sprinkling of isolated farms which bear early Saxon place-name suffixes, typically in -ley, -worth or other ancient variants. These include Chilgrove, Colworth, Downley, Hylter, Locksash, Malecomb, Raughmere,

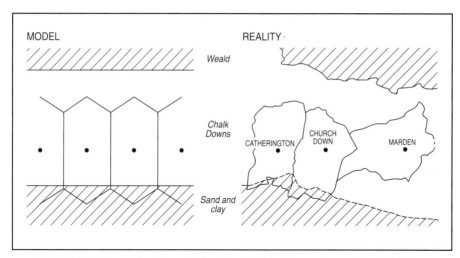

37    Model of Saxon migration applied to Marden in the Western Downs (after Cunliffe).

Stapleash and Tegleaze, the latter recorded in a late copy of an Anglo-Saxon charter purporting to be of *c.* A.D. 675. It is not yet possible to answer the question as to how many inhabitants of the dispersed farms were of direct Romano-British descent. Quite a number of them are recorded separately from the neighbouring villages in Domesday Book. An entry rubricated under Falmer Hundred reads:

> Gezeline holds I hide of William [the King]. It has not paid geld [tax]. In demesne is one plough. It is, and was, worth 20s.

This appears to be, not an ancient farm, but one of the smaller new farms being colonised on the downland waste beyond the village fields. For Up Waltham on the Western Downs there are no less than seven entries in Domesday Book of this kind:

> Arnold has 2 hides. 2 cottagers and 1 slave. Troarn Abbey has 2 hides. 3 cottagers … The Earl has 2 hides in his park. Land for 1 plough … In Lordship 1 plough, with 5 cottagers … Alfward, a free man, held one hide … Siward holds 1 hide from the Earl … Land for 1 plough.

What are we to make of these little farms which lack substantial peasants (villeins) and are in the hands of small freemen? The probability is that they, unlike the group of isolated farms with early Saxon place names, are not archaic survivals of Romano-British colonisation, but part of a much later one, as the Domesday entries hint at recent and embryonic occupation.

When the Downland emerges into the stronger light of the 13th and 14th centuries we find, in the Eastern Downs, peasants working unfenced strips of common arable and the lord's demesne invariably divided off separately, although similarly unhedged or permanently fenced. The territorial basis of the common fields was not the parish, not even the manor, but the *tithing*, i.e. the cluster of dwellings making a township (toun) for administrative purposes. Even small downland parishes such as Alciston and Bishopstone made room for a smaller, subsidiary but self-contained set of common fields (Tilton and Norton respectively), additionally to that of the main cluster of farmsteads around the parish church. The parish of Ringmer contained four separately differentiated common-field systems at each of its anciently-set hamlets of Ashton, Middleham, Norlington and Wellingham. There was no such field system at Ringmer

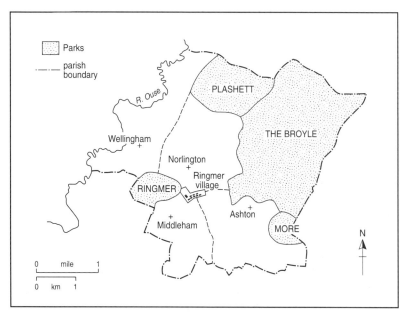

**38** *Borgs* (independent hamlets) in the parish of Ringmer near Lewes. Each had an earlier origin than the village itself.

itself which would seem to have post-dated the origin of common-fields. The nucleated village of West Firle, the 'head' settlement of the parish, had three neighbouring hamlets—Charleston, Compton and Heighton, now reduced to single farms. Burpham was composed of three tithings of Burpham, Wepham and Peppering. Offham was a separate tithing of the parish of South Stoke and Rackham, Cootham and Buddington were similarly organised within the parishes of Amberley, Storrington and Steyning respectively. It is noteworthy that several of these places are recorded separately in Domesday Book and that they all have early place-name suffixes. This multiplicity of common-field systems based on villages and on peripherally sited hamlets interspersed between them evidently represents an antiquity which is older than the institution of the parish. Some of these hamlets appear to have been specifically placed for dependent labourers on large estates. In the case of the two Charltons in the Downs one was located on the edge of the once royal estate of Steyning and the other on the former royal estate centred on Singleton. The name is derived from old English *Ceorls-tun*, 'the peasants' village'. The agrarian organisation in the Eastern Downs, and of which we have glimpses back to the seventh century, bespeaks a high level of efficiency and economically advanced achievement by the late Saxon period. It is in this Saxon ground plan that we can perceive the precociously developed agriculture of the Downs considered in the following chapter. The easy access to seaborne commerce would have removed an insuperable barrier to economic development and the rich soils of the coastal plain and the great sheepwalks on the downland would have provided one of the most favourable natural environments in England. All this would go far to explain the great concentrations of landed estates in the hands of the Crown, the great Saxon lay magnates, and the church at the end of the 11th century.[6]

We can trace the origins of some of these great grants of land in early Saxon Charters. In the seventh century, land on the Downs which had notionally belonged to the kingdom of the South Saxons was being made over to noblemen in return for loyalty and services, and the

**39** The Tegleaze signpost on Lavington Down near Duncton Hill is close to one of the earliest recorded boundaries in the Downs.

coming of Christianity also led to large grants of land in support of religious communities. These charters survive only as copies and the forgery of copyists, misreadings or misunderstandings must also be taken into account. The rambling boundary clauses in Old English are later additions and Martin Welch has remarked, 'We must accept that they represent the boundaries of the tenth and eleventh centuries rather than those of the eighth'.[7] A number of charters which seem to be reliable are of significance. The assignment of land centred on East Dean to the church by king Nunna gives boundaries which can be partially traced. Another is of the Downs at Stanmer which includes lands in the Weald, swine-pastures in Lindfield, West Hoathly and Wivelsfield. A tenth-century charter of Durrington takes us upon the Downs near Cissbury and out to detached Wealden holdings which were probably swine-pastures. Still later in date are charters relating to Annington in the Adur valley which had detached woodland pastures in Kirdford and Slinfold. Washington also had detached land in the Horsham district.[8]

Conspicuous on the boundaries of Saxon estates were the pagan burial mounds datable to the seventh century and earlier, before the valley-ward shift of population. The majority of these burial sites in Sussex are on the chalkland suggesting that the pagan Saxons were attracted to it by the light soils and the long tradition of cultivation and that they settled this first. A number of these burial mounds also came to mark parish boundaries, formalised from the eighth century, in many cases coincident with earlier estate boundaries. They were invariably robbed by the 18th- and early 19th-century 'archaeologists' when they were found to contain a skeleton facing westwards with a knife in the left hand surrounded by grave goods including gold earrings, buckles, brooches, combs, glass tumblers, boss of shields and circular urns.[8]

## Place-Names

Saxon place-names throw considerable light on the history of English settlement in Sussex and help to reveal what sort of environment was presented and how the new farmers saw the landscape. The Sussex volumes of the English Place-Name Society were published in 1929-30 and have been overtaken by radical changes in thinking. John McNeal Dodgson daringly challenged in 1966 the assumption preached for a hundred years that the numerous place-names bearing the suffix -ing (-ings, -inga) belonged to the invasion phase of Saxon settlement.[9]

This speculation has proved influential and it is now generally accepted that they belong to a later colonising stage. As Dodgson remarked inimitably, while the men whose names are immortalised in the -ingas place-names are demoted from the captaincy of armadas they are transferred 'to the leadership of the folk who made Britain England'. This new chronology fits better with the account of the settlement given on p.47. It now appears that the place-names in -ham have a better right to be considered the earliest Saxon names. These lie significantly nearer to known Romano-British or English settlement than -ingas ones.

Recent work has also brought to light some instances of the likely co-existence of an English and a British community, although the place-name nomenclature of the Downs is over-whelmingly English. Professor Coates has noted the name Pen Hill in Elsted (British penno-, a hill) which is associated with other British hill-names in the vicinity, e.g. Torberry in Harting, La Torre recorded in 13th-century North Stoke and the place Muned at Chilgrove near West Dean in 1296 which seems to be akin to Welsh mynydd, mountain.[10] Coates has also identified Ciltine mentioned by the eighth-century monk Bede as in the forest of the Weald with East and West Chiltington and suggests that the name is derived from the British -cilta, a precipice or steep hill, and is perhaps the regional name for the scarpfoot below Mount Harry and Black Cap and further west along the Downs escarpment.[11]

Other places where British and English appear to have lived contemporaneously in the same district is indicated by three place-names Wickham, each along the line of the Roman road running through Streat and Ditchling, a name derived from vicus, Latin, village, the first element and ham, OE, home, village.

Coates has also reviewed the name of Lewes and the problem of deriving it from Old English hlaew and has speculated that it might be derived from British Lexowias, slope, which, in the absence of a known pre-English settlement at Lewes, may have been another district or regional name for the eastern Downs, or part of them.[12]

Some more likely British-speaking inhabitants of early Saxon Sussex have been disinterred by the discovery by Bleach and Coates of three locations in Ringmer associated with the name Walcto and others in Warminghurst, Durrington and other places in or on the margin of the Downs. This name includes the element -walh, a slave or foreigner.[13] Coates has made additions to the heathen religious sites bearing the name Harrow or a variant, derived from OE hearg-, a pagan shrine, to include Harrow Hill in Angmering (the site of Neolithic flint-mines), the Harrows in Harting, and the two Mount Harrys, one near Lewes and one in Brighton.

Nature names incorporating elements associated with woodland such as OE leah, a forest glade or clearing, hyrst, wooded hill and graf, a grove are largely absent in the Eastern Downs but are typical of the Downs west of the Arun, which implies that the differences in primitive vegetation in the early Saxon period and later were much in evidence. The local geographer, historian or archaeologist has yet to map place-names and relate them to specific landforms as Ann Cole has done for the Chilterns and other places.[14] The place-name -ofer appears to have been used for a settlement on the top of a ridge, e.g. Southover, Windover, and bottom (botm) adopted for the trough-like floors of dry valleys. At least three names for hill are evident. Ann Cole has demonstrated that the element -ora was applied to an elongated, flat-topped hill termi-nating at one or both ends with a rounded shoulder and that the several examples of the name along the coast around Portsmouth Harbour and the Sussex inlets refer to distant hills on the Downs which would have been visible to Saxon sailors wishing to identify their position and make a landfall.[15] Hoh was used for a spur, as in Balmer Huff near Falmer. The word was apparently applied to a differently shaped hill from that of an ora, namely a rounded hill like an upturned bowl. The name 'down' given to chalk uplands as a whole was a word derived from British *-dun*, adopted as a loan word by the Saxons and meaning an inhabited hill.[16] We have earlier remarked on the two names for valleys, *denu* and *cumb* (p.9).

It is sometimes necessary to take into consideration an area wider than the Downs proper. This is the case regarding the numerous outlying pastures in the formerly forested Weald which in the light of Saxon charters and later documents are revealed as detached outliers to manors on, or at the foot, of the Downs, and along the coast. An extensive network of routes woven by men travelling to and from the principal centres of manors and their numerous outlying pastures resulted. This close net of Sussex by-roads and obsolete 'greenways' was from north to south in general direction and many of them are still traceable on maps and on the ground over remarkably long distances. The present intermittent paths or bridle-ways can be found to link up into a formerly continous track just where the compass needle points north or south according to the direction of travel. It is a road system which suggests that the local necessity of settlers on the Downs was not so much connections with neighbouring settlements as between each one and its outlying woodland pasture. They are in fact old droving roads, the old arteries through which ran Sussex life between the Downs and the Weald. Each of these droveways, used for the transhumance of people and swine and cattle, crossed the escarpment of the Downs and continued downwards by means of the inclined bostals, previously mentioned (p.17) before proceeding out into the deep Weald as a wide passage way between bordering banks. A number of these droveways are conspicuous enough to be readily identifiable. Such is that from the early Saxon site of Bishopstone which winds over the Downs to descend Bostal Hill at Alciston and then passes through the village and thence to Selmeston before

**40**   Bostal descending the Downs at Wolstonbury Hill. An oil painting by Roy Adams (1994).

passing on a now extinct course along the parish boundary of Chalvington en route for the Wealden outlier at Heathfield. Also clearly marked on the ground and on map is the ancient route from Falmer across the Downs to its former pastures in Plumpton and Worth Forest. From Kingston Buci and Southwick manors another trackway went via Thundersbarrow Iron-Age hill fort and Truleigh Hill, down the escarpment to Tottington Sands and Bilsborough, east of Henfield and thence to Shermanbury where these manors had their woodland pastures. A similar route from Portslade went across the Downs at Edburton Hill and continued northwards. Sompting, Broadwater and West Tarring manors probably used trackways converging near Cissbury Ring which came down the escarpment just east of Chanctonbury Ring and descended in a fine 'hollow way' to pass Buncton church before making for pastures in the Horsham district.

The track descending Chantry Hill, Sullington, was on the route between Barpham (in Angmering) and its pastures at Deddisham near Horsham. The droveway linking Slindon and its swine-pastures in Plaistow Woods, Kirdford, runs for more than four miles as a chalk track from the north edge of the village across some of the most deserted Downs country before dropping down Bignor Hill where it is traceable as a metalled by-way making for Stopham Bridge on the River Rother. On Graffham Down the downland track from East Dean and Singleton manors descended at the Lavington crossroads, one of the most prominent crossings of the escarpment. This route formerly linked these manors with pastures at Selham and Loxwood.

Examples of these old drove ways could be greatly extended. They still remain to be mapped definitively and they would make an appropriate project for an aspiring field worker. It

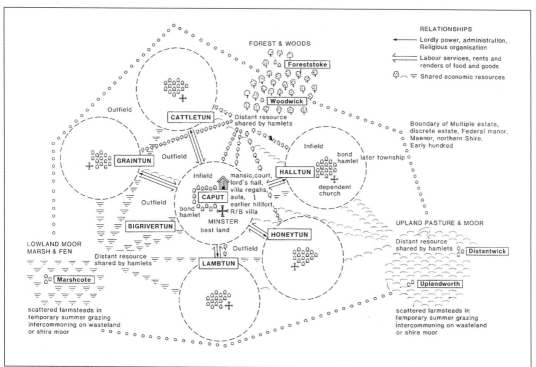

**41** A diagrammatic explanation of the territorial structure of a multiple manor based on the Downs. Shown are the headquarters village, dependent hamlets and distant resources in marsh and Weald (after Aston).

has hitherto been assumed that this system of long-distance droving roads based on scattered woodland pasture 'outliers' is of Saxon origin. One day we may be nearer to the solution of this enigma. They are conceivably older. Certainly, the Saxons formalised this use but the probability is that their origin is in the prehistoric Iron Age or even earlier.[17]

## The Domesday Survey 1086

This can be regarded as a summing-up of the wealth and development that accrued under the Saxons. The 11th-century downland and coastal plain is revealed as a land of very large, complex, fragmented and composite manors variously called federal, discrete and multiple by scholars.[18] When they can be studied in the clearer light of the 13th century they are centred upon a head village normally bearing the name of the whole manor, containing the principal church, the lord's hall and court, the demesne (home farm) and also common fields for the peasants, cultivators who performed work services for the lord. Numerous dependent hamlets, separately named, were also dispersed over the manor amidst still remaining waste in the form of wood-grazings and sheep downs inter-commoned by peasants of these settlements. The peasants in these dispersed hamlets were required to perform work services on the home farm, regardless of distance, or wherever else the lord might own land. By the 13th century some of the hamlets had acquired subordinate chapels on account of the length of journey to the main church. Droving roads and other highways crisscrossed the manor inter-connecting the various settlements.

Some of these multiple manors were huge in extent and already considerable in population. That of Ditchling, for example, held by King Edward the Confessor before the Conquest, contained lands dispersed over the parishes of Ditchling, Wivelsfield, Ardingly, Chailey, Lindfield, Worth, Balcombe, West Hoathly, Cuckfield and East Grinstead. Washington manor extended over the parishes of Findon, Storrington, West Chiltington, Ashurst, Shipley, West Grinstead and Horsham, apart from Washington itself. The archbishop's manor of South Malling, centred on the village of that name just outside Lewes, extended as a great corridor across the Sussex Weald into Kent. The manor of Singleton included land in that parish and in East Dean, Up Waltham, Graffham and Cocking together with land in the vale of Rother.

Unfortunately, Domesday was never intended to differentiate each individual settlement that was a dependency of manorial headquarters and consequently this already articulated countryside of the Downs and its borders does not figure clearly in the Survey. Thus Ditchling is credited with 111 villeins (substantial peasants) and 69 bordars (lesser peasants) and 10 slaves, representing a total population of about seven hundred men, women and children, but we have no way of knowing how many of these, and other resources such as ploughs, belonged in the Sussex Weald which we know from other documents was not completely vacant. Washington manor is credited, in all, with 159 recorded persons (which should be multiplied by a factor of four to approximate to a family), Singleton 162, and Steyning, the largest manor of all, with a recorded population of 326.

When the other resources of the Downs apart from population are considered, such as the number of ploughs in use, fisheries, water meadows (especially the Ouse valley) and water mills, it is evident that it must be regarded as one of the most developed parts of 11th-century England. Although the higher levels of the Downs are characterised by thin soils, the lower slopes and valley floors were much more rewarding to the plough and the closely-spaced, large villages along the foot of the Downs produced high densities of population. Unfortunately

Domesday adds little to our knowledge of farming types and methods. For example, the only mention of shepherds is the 10 recorded at Patcham near Brighton.

This wealthy farming system on the Downs is reflected in the prosperity of the towns. Lewes appears to have been the largest town in Sussex with a population of about 2,000 persons. There is mention of a mint for coins, of toll, and of trade in horses, oxen and slaves. Many of the surrounding manors held appurtenant *hagae* (houses and crofts). The rise in the value of the place for taxation purposes since 1066 suggests that the town was flourishing.[19] The reference to Steyning borough is brief and incomplete, e.g. there is no mention of the mint which we know was there. A hint of urbanisation is also made by a remarkable archaeological discovery. It is of a late Anglo-Saxon disc brooch of a type not normally found in rural settlements. There is a glimpse of infant Arundel, a new borough replacing Burpham across the river Arun, which had then only four burgesses.[20] Saxon churches are considered in Chapter Six.

*Chapter Five*

# Farming Communities in the Middle Ages (1100-1500)

easants and their lords practised a similar sheep-and-corn farming in the medieval period but with entirely different ends in view. To the small cultivators with family holdings occupying common fields, the primary concern was subsistence. On the other hand, the great church estates of the Archbishop, the Bishop of Chichester and the Benedictine foundation of Battle Abbey, for example, and those of great lay magnates operated large demesne farms worked by numerous dependent cultivators and engaged in coastwise trade in corn and wool. Some of the arable land like that of the bishops of Chichester at Amberley was lowly valued in the 13th and 14th centuries because it was dispersed in strips and intermingled with that of the peasants' lands in common fields. Some of it was recorded as being cultivated by the lord separately but within enclosures taken down after harvest to enable collective grazing on the fallows by both lord and peasants until Lady Day (25 March) or Easter. A third group was exclusively cultivated separately ('in severalty') and this exceeded in number and greatly in acreage the other estates partly or solely 'in common'. This segregation of the lord's fields from the common fields of the peasants, and also the distinction between the lord's sheep pasture and the tenantry down of the small farmers, permitted lords to engage in agricultural innovation which resulted in achievements greatly surpassing the precariousness which was the norm of English medieval husbandry. Thanks to mastery of the arts of sheep-and-corn farming, the Eastern Downs became celebrated by the 13th century for advanced agricultural techniques and fleeces of good fine wool which contributed to England's staple export.[1]

Almost all the peasant farmers lived in nucleated villages during the Middle Ages. As we have seen, the origin of these has been assigned to the 9th-11th centuries. The reason for this concentration of small farmers in villages and the abandonment of most of the dispersed farms on the higher Downs has been much debated. It is argued that lords created the villages and laid out common fields for the peasants in order to enhance their power and profit and for a more efficient working of their demesne. There is much to be said for this view for from the time of the earliest documents the lords' farms were grouped into extensive estates and functioned as a kind of federated grain and wool factory worked by lowly dependent cultivators, very many of whom were merely cottagers. Yet not all parts of England with strong lordship like Sussex had large villages. Another explanation for the downland village may lie in the environment. The peasant farmer with his few score sheep could not manure and consolidate his light chalk soil with these alone. By putting them into a common sheep flock guarded by a common shepherd he could command 500 or more sheep which dunged in rotation each villager's dispersed strips of arable land in the common fields. Without the introduction of the common sheep-fold peasant farmers would not have survived on the Downs. More than anything else

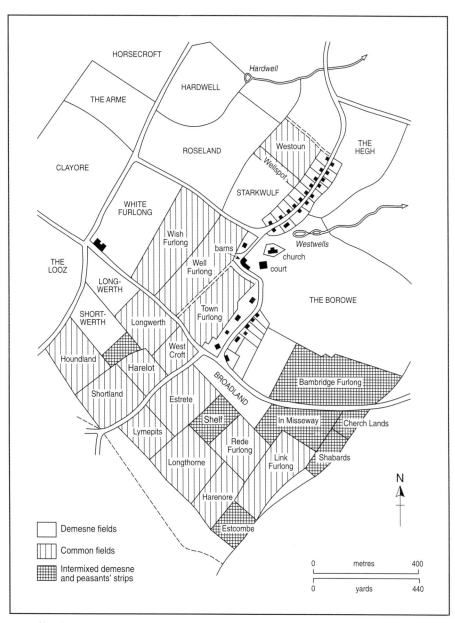

**42**  Quasi-permanent arable at Alciston manor, *c.*1440. For fuller explanation, see pp.75-8.

this institution that fed and clothed man and manured and trod his soils was as perfect for the purpose as any that could ever have been invented. While it lasted it preserved the little self-sufficient farming communities and their modest life-style. The system was gradually brought to an end with the engrossing of tenements which began in the late 15th and 16th centuries. The Tudor bishop Hugh Latimer (preaching when land speculators were depriving small family farmers of the sheep-fold) expressed the former symbiotic basis of sheep-and-corn very vividly: 'A ploughland must have sheep; yea, they must have sheep to dung their ground for the bearing of corn; for if they have none to fat the ground, they shall have but bare corn and thin'.[2] The

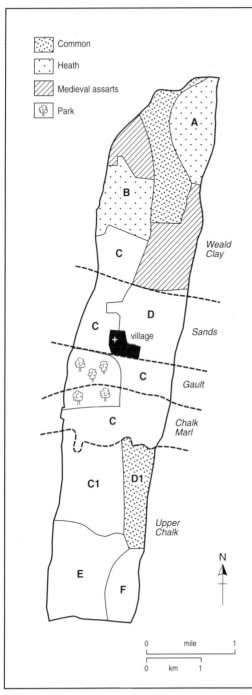

**43** Medieval Ditchling.
A and B—hunting grounds of the lord;
C—demesne arable;
D—commonfields;
C1—lord's sheepwalk;
D1—peasants' sheepwalk;
E and F—separate farms on the Downs.

practical operation of the sheep-fold would clearly have been more proficient when small farmers lived in villages rather than in dispersed farms. Peasants paid a heavy price for the institution of the common sheep-fold. Their lot was hereditary servile status and onerous obligations to the lords owning great landed estates. Peasants had also to accept agreed farming routine and common grazing on sheepwalk and on commons, and also to hold land in standard units in intermingled strips. It was a system which at least produced an equitable use of resources and put the interest of the community above individualism.

There was a recognisable division in the 13th century between peasants with 12-20 acres of arable land or more and those with smaller holdings. The former (*villeins*) could support their families with their holding. Lesser tenants, *bordars*, or *cottars*, could not and supplemented their incomes by work for wages on the lord's demesne or on the farms of the bigger tenants. Apart from managing their own holdings all peasants ploughed, hoed and harvested a given acreage of the lord's land and this meant many days' work away from their own farms at busy times of the farming year. Villeins were also required to travel frequently on the lord's business, e.g. West Dean and North Stoke tenants used pack horses or carts to take food to Arundel Castle and fetched seed corn from East Dean. By the 13th century commutation of many of these heavily burdened services was being made for cash.[3]

A man's holding was termed a yardland (virgate) in West Sussex and a wist (wista) in East Sussex. Its size was considerably less than in most parts of England but considerable wealth came from wool produced with a share in the tenantry sheepwalk on the high Downs. At Alciston, East Blatchington and many other manors in East Sussex the wist was equal to 10 customary acres (larger than a statute acre). At Brighton and Meeching (Newhaven) it was 12, at Preston near Brighton 14 and 16 at Heighton St Clair. The yardland in West Sussex was no larger. Most of the villeins' holdings were between one to two yardlands or wists.[4] Each yardland or wist comprised intermixed strips of arable scattered amongst a number of units called furlongs which in turn were grouped into sowing units comprising little strips called paul-pieces, about one eighth of a customary acre. The standard strip seems to have two pauls, a size which might have been chosen as convenient for a night's dunging by sheep in the fold and to facilitate the ploughing of the fallow.

In the Eastern Downs the common-fields were unhedged, giving rise to the 'prairie' landscape called 'champion' (after French open landscapes in Champagne) by 16th-century writers. These open arable lands were called laines (*leynes*). The few hedged or walled enclosures were always called *fields*. The common-field landscape of the Western Downs creates a distinctly different local landscape. Here the common fields were invariably made up of a group of small units called fields, crofts or *garstons*, the latter derived from O.E. *gaerstun*, usually meaning grass or meadow but in West Sussex the term was used to mean a small common-field containing arable strips. Such fields containing strips of peasant land are mentioned at Nutbourne near Pulborough, Up Marden, Sutton, West Burton and Duncton. Why the practice of hedging was mainly confined to West Sussex is not entirely clear. The probability is that the common-fields were carved out of woodland and in a wood-using district timber growing in hedgerows would have been regarded as a valuable resource. Freeholders tended to hold their lands in independently-held closes.[5]

The layout of the common-fields was quite different from that in the Midlands of England where large nucleated villages tended to lie amidst two or three large common fields with scattered strips. In West Sussex common-fields were 'irregular' by the Midlands standard, being smaller, hedged, and bounded by a labyrinth of winding lanes, patches of woodland and closes of the freeholders. This kind of countryside can be sensed by travelling along the by-way

**44**   The age-old solution to thin, infertile soils was the sheep-fold.

between Bury and Duncton below the Downs. The numerous small common-fields were joined
into groups for sowing purposes. There is no fully accepted explanation as to why a regular
Midland system did not develop in West Sussex. But Williamson and Bellamy have argued that
it may indicate that Saxon settlement was less intense and disruptive than in areas such as the
Midlands.[6]

The heyday of the downland village was in the 13th century. Earlier they had grown in size
and were sometimes reorganised in plan. Nearby villages sometimes fused: alternatively a large
village could split apart. As the village community grew in the early Middle Ages the common
fields were continuously enlarged. Such freshly cleared land was distinguised by names such as
*breche*, *-broc*, and *-rede* signifying the reclamation of downland, woodland or heath. By the 13th
century the village fields had expanded to capacity thus setting a rigid limit to population increase. From the 14th century many of the villages shrank, sometimes again changing their
shape in consequence, and a significant minority were completely deserted (p.71). Nothing was
less stable than the stable-looking downland village.

## Sheep and Corn Farming

The South Downs have been associated with sheep for centuries because, with soils generally
thin and infertile, sheep have always been their most profitable and renowned product, though
the sheep of early times were very different in form and size from the beautiful animals which
became the pride and boast of Sussex when John Ellman of Glynde and others improved them
in the 18th century. Yet sheep were indissolubly associated until recent times with the other
principal farming activity on the Downs, corn production. As chalk soils are light and friable
they readily lose plant nutrients in the top soil by the free drainage of rainwater so that they
needed in past times a special form of arable farming which involved sheep (pp.26, 33).

Consequently, the downland farmer traditionally lived by his sheep, his aim being to keep
as many as possible. His farming year began when he put the ram to the ewes and he counted
time by the main events in the flocks' year, lambing, shearing and the fairs. The medieval farmer
worked from a farmhouse lining the village street and the ideal environment for sheep-and-
corn farming provided him not only with arable and sheepwalk but water-meadows (brookland)
also shared in common. Brookland was indispensable for giving an 'early bite' of grass for the
lambs in spring when the grazings on the Downs were at their poorest. This access to water-
meadow was most freely available in the Eastern Downs, particularly in the estuary of the River
Ouse, but also in the Cuckmere and Adur. Large blocks of western downland were deficient in
water meadow and this had an adverse effect on the numbers and quality of sheep.

As we have seen the linch pin of the sheep dunging system for corn production was the
sheepfold. At night the shepherd would bring down the lord's flock and the common shepherd
drove the tenants' flock from the hillpasture and 'folded' them separately each on their own
fields, herded them tightly into a part of a fallow field or on fodder such as tares, depending on
the season, and fenced off the sheep with temporary wattle hurdles. On the following morning
the wattle fold would be dismantled, re-pitched on a fresh patch of fallow and the flock was
driven up on to the downland turf to graze again. As the sheep were closely packed and walked
about a great deal there was considerable treading of the soil, so producing a tilth better than
any implement could then produce.

The yield of corn depended upon a number of variables including the weather, but also
directly on the number of folded sheep. But the flock a farmer maintained throughout the year

depended on how many sheep he could over-winter. This was the key problem which concerned a downland farmer from ancient times and it was only successfully resolved by the introduction of new fodder crops from the 17th century. It follows from the critical need of sheep folding for corn that the principal purpose of keeping sheep until early modern times was for the dung of the sheepfold, and that wool was secondary. Little attention was given until modern times to the carcase either of ewe or wether sheep or lamb. The folding determined that sheep should be short-woolled, for only these could be folded because the heavier wool of other breeds would have been soiled and rotted. Moreover, the sheep were specially bred for folding. This meant that they were bred to walk daily from hill pasture back down on to the deeper soil in the coombes. Sheep had to be light in weight to be naturally active and agile climbers. The old native breed of Southdown, as well as the chunky, box-shaped, improved Southdowns of John Ellman and others, were bred to pass with ease up and down the hills that separated the nightly fold from their daily pasture. The old native Southdown of the Eastern Downs was a strong, healthy, and intelligent animal, well suited to the conditions on the Downs, but although a greedy feeder was slow to fatten and the fleece, although white, fine and of medium length, weighed only about two pounds. Thus both the old Southdowns and the improved breed in no way resembled the large, fat heavily-woolled Leicester and similar cross-breeds replacing them since 1945.

The earliest documentary reference to the exceptional importance of sheep farming on the Downs is the mention of the 'tegs' leaze' (pasture for tegs, one-year-old sheep) in a charter purporting to be that of Northey, a king of the South Saxons in A.D. 698, but with place-names added later. This was on or near the present site of Tegleaze Farm, near Duncton Hill.[7]

Domesday Book of 1086 is tantalisingly short of information on sheep, the only mention of shepherds being 10 at Patcham near Brighton previously mentioned.[8] In the early 13th century there is more confirmation of the importance and skill of sheep farming on the Downs in letters of the steward Simon of Senlis to his lord, the Bishop of Chichester:

I will, if you please, commit the custody of your manor of Bishopstone to Henry the sergeant of *Burn* [Eastbourne], especially on account of the sheep which I keep in your hands, seeing that I believe the said Henry will devote himself well and ably to the matter ... to Richard, whom Thomas of Cirencester sent you, I have committed the

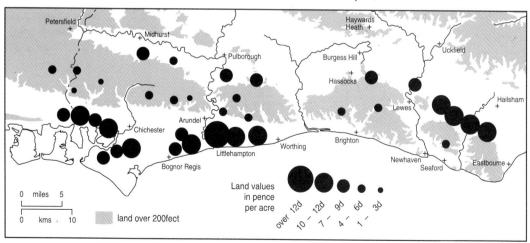

**45**   Land valuations: evidence from 14th-century *Inquisitiones post mortem*.

keeping of your manor of Preston [near Brighton] since I think he understands the cause of sheep ...[9]

The bishop obtained sheep from ecclesiastical estates in Lincolnshire, Gloucestershire and Worcestershire, keeping their shepherds in each instance, which suggests a dearth both of good sheep and shepherds.

## Medieval High Farming

For the early 14th century the geography of sheep farming on the Downs can be worked out in outline from surviving documents. A most illuminating record is the *Inquisitiones Nonarum* (1340-1) (Nonae Rolls) which for taxation purposes gives one-ninth the value of corn and fleeces, and explains any major differences from the taxation of 1292.[10] In some parish returns the ninth of corn, adult sheep and lambs is not separately distinguished; in others sheep and lambs are combined, though this is easier to disentangle for the price of a sheep's fleece was valued at 2d. and a lamb's at 3d. Using this data for downland parishes, and bearing in mind the limitations of the statistics and the fact that these probably are underestimates, the distribution of sheep on the Sussex Downs is remarkably interesting (Fig.46). The special importance of sheep in the economy is evident but the distribution clearly shows a special development of wool-growing on the Eastern Downs, for of the 23 downland parishes listed with exceptionally large flocks, only four of these are west of the river Arun and only eight west of the river Adur. The huge flocks at Eastbourne, Piddinghoe, Alciston and Lullington are particularly remarkable.

Further useful information about sheep farming is obtained from inquisitions of landed wealth of Thomas, Archbishop of Canterbury and the Earl of Arundel in 1397.[11] This reinforces the marked preponderance of sheep on the Eastern Downs. The records also disclose that it was on the Eastern Downs that sheep farming was most efficiently organised. There the lord's flocks were invariably run on private sheepwalk separate from that of the tenants' flock, and so stocking rates could be altered at will, whereas on many of the manors on the Western Downs the lord's sheep pasture was the harder stocking there, for constant grazing by big flocks would have suppressed coarse grasses, bramble, bracken and shrubs and produced a dense turf. Another important piece of information about medieval sheep farming arises from other sources. It is evident that the value of a fleece on the Eastern Downs was usually higher than that from the West. The best prices of all were apparently received by the monks of Battle Abbey at their manor of Alciston and Lullington, their higher quality wool doubtless being the result of better flock management.[12]

The part of the Downs producing the finest wool in medieval times broadly coincides with that in Arthur Young's day at the end of the 18th century, although by then the amount of sheep kept was about treble the number in the 14th century. The question arises as to whether the 26 miles of downland from Eastbourne to Steyning has always had this pre-eminence in wool-growing. Gilbert White, writing in 1773, drew attention to a difference in breed between sheep grazing on the two sides of the Adur valley:[13]

One thing is very remarkable as to the sheep: from the westward till you get to the river Adur all the flocks have horns, and smooth white faces, and white legs; and a hornless sheep is rarely to be seen; but as soon as you pass that river eastward, and mount Beeding hill, all the flocks at once become hornless, or as they call them, poll-sheep; and moreover black faces with a white tuft of wool on their foreheads, and speckled

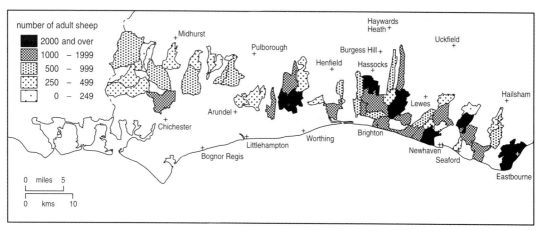

**46**   Sheep flocks by parishes, 1340.

and spotted legs; so that you would think that the flocks of Laban were pasturing one side of the stream, and the variegated breed of his son-in-law Jacob were cantoned along on the other. And this diversity holds good respectively on each side from the valley of Bramber and Beeding to the eastward and westward all the whole length of the downs.

In White's description we can recognise the old long-legged sheep on the Western Downs that were replaced by the improved Southdowns from the end of the 18th century and also what was almost certainly the parent stock of the Southdowns on the Eastern Downs improved by John Ellman and others. The downland farmers of the 19th century used to say that the 'Southdowners'[14] had a 'pedigree older that the peerage'. The parent stock appears to have been indigenous to the dry chalky hills of the Eastern Downs where doubtless they had grazed for centuries whereas the taller horned sheep would have done better on the heavier soil and more wooded Western Downs.

Here common pastures were normally different in character. Much of the sheepwalk was not the characteristic springy turf which has already been described but a coarser, more varied, and, on the whole, less nutritious grassland. This is because many large Forests and some deer parks had an economic role, being in effect sheep runs as well as hunting grounds. Other sheep runs were in common woodlands. Parts of Arundel and Charlton Forests were commonable to peasants in Bury, Eartham, East Dean, Singleton manors on the Downs and to Strettington and Woodcote on the coastal plain.[15] In the large Forest of Stansted the manors of Westbourne, Compton and Marden had common pasture as did some of the tenements in Marden, in what is now Hampshire, but the county boundary of this heavily wooded country was long indeterminate.[16] West Dean manor had 250 acres of woods used as common sheep pasture and East Dean had several copses for the same purpose. Eartham also had common woodland.[17]

These common woods or wood pastures were an attempt to combine multiple uses of woods. In the medieval period regulation of community rights would have been difficult, especially when different manors had common in the same woodland. We can probably envisage woodland being increasingly degraded to open common or heath. The equilibrium was restored in the 16th and 17th centuries with enclosure (p.94). We are probably correct to assume that these pastures were generally inferior to those of the Eastern Downs.

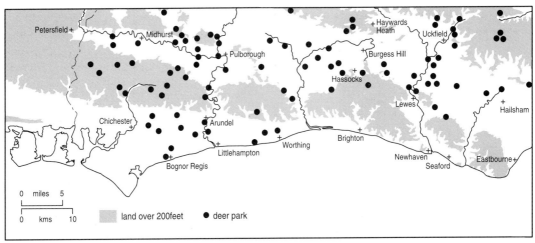

**47**   Medieval deer parks in the Downs and southern Weald.

Apart from wood-commons much of the wood pasture on the Western Downs was en-closed in deer parks for the exclusive use of the greater lay and ecclesiastical magnates. A deer park usually contained areas of woodland, some divided off for timber growing, and grassy *launds* or lawns.[18] Such parks were expensive to construct and maintain because deer required more effective enclosure than sheep or cattle. An outer fence or pale consisting of a strong palisade of cleft oakstakes over six feet high was surmounted on a bank. In contrast to wood-boundary banks this was inside the bank and designed to keep animals in rather than out. These defences were so formidable that the banks and ditches commonly survive. The optimum shape of a deer park was circular or oval giving the maximum internal area for the minimum length of fence. Most medieval parks did have this outline and subsequently such a space devoid of old farm buildings and other settlement can often be regarded as *prima facie* evidence on maps of the possible site of a medieval deer park. The Archbishop of Canterbury's deer park at Slindon is detectable in this way. The size of parks varied substantially. Areas as small as 25 acres would have housed up to 40 fallow deer. The average-sized park was about 100-150 acres, but downland parks were invariably larger. Parks were impaled in part by customary tenants living up to twenty miles away, though probably the most distant of them commuted their obligation for a money payment. The archbishop not only made his tenants enclose his parks but required them to assist with the hunting for 6-12 days annually. Domestic animals were consistently agisted in parks during summer, though never in the 'fence' period, i.e. usually for a period of one month at midsummer following the fawning season. Sheep were commonly excluded from parks be-cause their grazing habits interfered with the keeping of deer but on the Western Downs the hunting grounds were so extensive that lords conceded common grazing in default of other pastures. The Earls of Arundel in the 13th and 14th centuries had 12 Forests and 11 deer parks on the Western Downs (Fig.47).

An important feature of sheep  management was long narrow buildings housing ewes or wethers, up to several hundred in each. The shepherds probably lived with their flocks, perhaps in lofts above. The cotes presumably lay near the main barns for the sheep were folded on fallow whenever the weather made it possible. Thus medieval sheep were presumably less hardy than present-day ones. Fed on a 'starvation-diet' in winter, they would have been in rather poor condition at lambing time.

As to arable farming in the Downs during the Middle Ages, at first sight the thin, stony, alkaline soils of the high Downs look very unpromising for corn production and this was the assessment of medieval farmers. 'Dry and stony' arable on the high Downs was valued lowly, as in Findon and Sompting.[19] But there were especially good opportunities for tillage in the narrow belt of soil derived from the Malmstone which lies at the foot of the chalk escarpment and receives added downwash from the chalk. This was heavy land to plough and inherently very fertile, highly valued in the 14th century and regarded by Arthur Young's son, the Rev. Arthur Young, in 1813 as one of the richest soil belts in England. Other rich lands were the fine red loams in the floors of dry valleys and on the seaward flanks of the Downs. West of the Findon dry gap the soils tended to be derived from Clay-with-Flints and associated deposits. They were sticky, leached soils, that were difficult to cultivate and have for centuries been largely under woodland.

In the 13th and 14th centuries the Eastern Downs would have had heavily-grazed sheepwalk and great expanses under corn. The marked degree of intensive arable farming by lords of the great estates that characterised the downland and its borders is reflected in the tenemental organisation of that time. Intensive sheep-corn farming required large numbers of tributary tenants who performed onerous work services on the lord's farms. A special feature was the large number of cottagers (cottars) who had tiny holdings and worked as wage labourers.[20] After the Black Death in 1348/9 the commutation of work services became general and the critical seasonal labour problems that arose on big corn-growing manors were resolved by hiring labourers who migrated from the Weald as reapers for about five weeks at harvest.[21]

This practice of hiring forest peasants became general in the late 14th and 15th centuries, e.g. at Glynde, and at Alciston and Lullington, both manors of Battle Abbey. Occasionally pestilence disturbed the flow, as in 1426, and in rainy weather the carts provided to take the reapers' corn allowances back to their villages of Framfield, Heathfield, Hellingly, Waldron and Walberton had difficulty negotiating the Wealden byways. In times of low wheat prices, as in 1463 and 1464, these itinerant labourers were powerful enough to withhold their labour until an agreement was reached to substitute generous board 'at the lord's table' for their traditional allowance of corn.[22] These men were put up in barns during bad weather. At Alciston, where the great medieval barn remains, the accommodation can still be seen at the south end where there is a flight of stone steps on the outside.

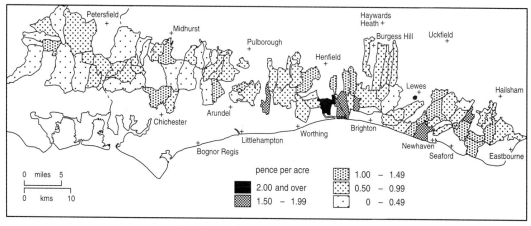

**48** Sheep and corn tithe valuations, 1340.

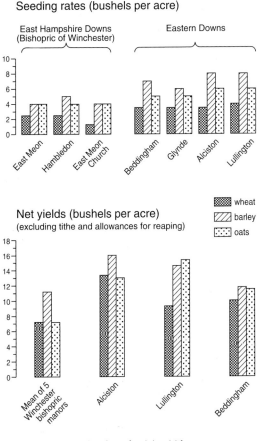

**Seeding rates (bushels per acre)**

East Hampshire Downs
(Bishopric of Winchester)　　　　Eastern Downs

wheat
barley
oats

**Net yields (bushels per acre)**
(excluding tithe and allowances for reaping)

**49**　Agricultural productivity, 14th century.

The Nonae Rolls of 1340-1 throw as much light on arable farming as on sheep production. To those accustomed to think of the Downs solely or mainly as a sheep-raising area in the past the information is a surprise. R.A. Pelham expressed this when he first used the returns in 1931, which showed a preponderance of corn-growing in the Downs and that the value of corn on downland manors exceeded that of sheep in every instance.[23] If we take the information in the Rolls further than he did, it becomes apparent that of 38 parishes on the Downs, 21 had above average acreages of corn and were located east of the Adur, which we have seen was the principal wool-growing area. The discrepancy in values between the Eastern and Western Downs would have been still greater but for losses of arable land to flooding and raids by the French in the former district. In the case of the scarp-foot parishes between Harting and Eastbourne, of 15 with above average acreages of corn, 10 are east of the Adur. There was a special development of corn growing in this belt between Lewes and Berwick on the edge of the Cuckmere valley, including Glynde, Beddingham, Alciston and Lullington, the two last being manors of Battle Abbey so proficient with sheep. Bearing in mind that the yield of corn depended, in the main, on the number of sheep kept in the fold, the preponderance of sheep in the Eastern Downs would lead one to expect greater acreages of corn and higher yields there.

The Nonae returns tell us that this is correct with regard to acreages. To find out whether the arable farming was proficient we have to turn to other sources. Until recently medieval agriculture has been in low repute and long-held assumptions about it went unchallenged. One of the old heresies was that the corn yields were derisory by modern standards and that the practice of husbandry varied little throughout the country. Schoolchildren and university students alike conjured in their minds a farming system in which either half or one third of the arable land was left fallow each year, the lord's strips of corn being intermingled with those of the peasants. It is now accepted that medieval farming was more diverse and complex than formerly thought and that, where the location, soil conditions and social circumstances were suitable, a relatively advanced and productive agricultural system in the van of its day could be, and was, established.[24] The Eastern Downs was one such district.

The key location of innovation was the scarp-foot zone on the rich soil of the Malmstone. Here with easy access to market by sea via the ports of Seaford and Shoreham a highly developed form of arable farming emerges in the 13th century. This inestimable advantage stimulated lords and other larger farmers to break decisively with the limited round of agricultural techniques that prevailed. By the 13th century the Downs had thus become an area in which, on the better soils, various soil-renewing crop rotations were adopted and systems of continuous cultivation evolved which superseded some of the traditional fallowing which, with the large sheep flocks yielding superlative wool, placed them firmly in the vanguard of the English economic development of the time.

One of the striking innovations was the prodigious quantity of legumes (peas, beans and vetch) raised, in place of fallow. Spring-sown vetch was fed off by ewes and lambs as a standing crop when nourishing grass was scarce and was a useful standby for feeding livestock in times of fodder shortage, particularly in long, hard winters, when it was used to give energy to the plough-oxen, cart-horses and to fatten swine. Beans and peas were also new field crops which were fed to horses and also used for fodder, but mainly for human diet as potage. These nitrogenous crops were part of a cycle of new rotations which suppressed most of the traditional triennial fallow (Fig.51). Theoretically the extensively sown legumes helped to restore nitrogen to the soil, thus increasing both soil fertility and corn yields. This is what broadly speaking seems to have occurred, although, of course, the capriciousness of weather sometimes prevented it happening. The unusually dense sowings of corn per acre, comfortably surpassing sowing rates adopted in much of England, were presumably adopted on fertile soils by landlords aiming to produce a substantial surplus of grain for the coastwise trade as a practical farming tactic. This dense sowing was needed to overcome some of the technical shortcomings of medieval agriculture such as the need to smother weeds and offset the large amount of broadcasted seed lost to birds or which failed to germinate in the rougher seed-beds produced by the rudimentary farming equipment available. Another characteristic of downland farming was the skill of its cultivators in the protracted care of the soil. The preparation of a bare fallow for wheat, an operation very expressively called a 'season', involved three ploughings, and often more, using a yoke of eight oxen. The turn-wrest plough (a wheeled plough on firm ground and swing type on the soft marsh soils in the chalk valleys) had a deeper and more pulverising action than most medieval ploughs and so produced a finer tilth and better seed bed. It was fitted with a detachable mould-board and so was well adapted for turning a furrow on the side of a hill.[25]

Epitomising the flexibility in crop rotations in the management of arable in the scarp-foot zone of the Downs at the end of the Middle Ages is a lease of Heighton St Clair manor in West Firle dated 1517 which prescribed the regular folding by 600 wethers and a three-course rotation of wheat, barley and legumes. Fallow (18 acres, about 10 per cent of the estate), arable to lie *lay* (i.e. as recuperative pasture) and land 'which has always been saved to sow barley' (doubtless a heavily-manured parcel capable of producing high-quality malting barley) are also mentioned.[26]

Thus, thanks to the mastery of the arts of sheep-and-corn husbandry and other farming techniques the Eastern Downs became one of the few parts of England—others being the coastal plain of Sussex, north Kent and part of Norfolk—which became a byword for advanced agricultural development far ahead of the norm of its day. It is also apparent that the Eastern Downs stood apart from the rest of the South Downs as a distinct region in this period as in all the various times in its history.

One of the most striking differences in the agricultural techniques practised in the Eastern Downs compared with the Bishop of Winchester's estates including East Meon, East Meon Church, Hambledon, Beauworth, Cheriton, Sutton and Alresford in Hampshire is the much greater variety of auxiliary crops sown in Sussex, especially the prodigious quantity of legumes

**50** A reconstruction of the Hangleton medieval cottage at the Weald and Downland Museum, Singleton, the foundations of which were discovered by Eric Holden in his excavation of the deserted village.

raised there. The density of seed sown per unit of land in East Sussex also comfortably surpassed those on the manors of the Bishop, which broadly corresponded with the sowing rates advocated by the anonymous author of the 13th century *Hosebonderie*.[27]

This brief examination of arable farming near Lewes in the 13th and 14th centuries shows that when Arthur Young and William Marshall praised the progress of husbandry of the Eastern Downs at the end of the 18th century, they were praising a district with a tradition of advanced agriculture which dated back both to changes in the 13th century, and almost certainly to innovations in the centuries before that.[28] The scarp foot of the Eastern Downs, in fact, has long been known for corn as well as for sheep. Since the Elizabethan writer Camden observed of Sussex that the 'fat chalke or kind of marle' yielded corn abundantly,[29] a succession of writers has confirmed that in their day the district contained some of the best cereal-growing land in England and, with the sheepfold, better management efficiency and thoroughness in cultivation, it produced yields amongst the highest recorded. To this day the largest, most efficient and productive arable farms in Sussex have been in or at the edge of the Downs. As we have seen its comparative excellence as a corn-growing district was even in the 13th century established in the Lewes district on the basis of husbandry little modified in the centuries to come.

## The Downturn: Deserted Medieval Villages

There is another aspect of cultivation which is rendered clearer by the Nonae Rolls. It was assumed until recently that the downturn in the agrarian economy of England generally took place after the appalling mortality of the Black Death in 1348/9. The Nonae Rolls, however, provide evidence of a considerable contraction in arable land on the Downs between 1292 and 1340, when 32 downland parishes reported lands untilled that had been cultivated at the earlier date. The explanations given for the decline in arable are several. Some parishes reported exhausted soil (*debil*); in others, the hard winter and extreme drought of 1340 are adduced as explanation. At Ovingdean it was said that land had been devastated by escaped rabbits from Earl Warenne's warren. Floods occasioned by 'tempestuous seas' account for coastal losses. In numerous others the poverty and 'impotence' of peasants is mentioned, and other places lacked tenants.[30]

The Nonae returns seem to indicate that the clear and undisputed age of expansion in the English economy which characterises the 12th and 13th centuries was over, and that the flow of economic activity was no longer in full flood so that some lands, perhaps the most marginal, were falling out of production. It is evident that much of the abandoned land was still vacant in the late 14th century when it is referred to as *barren* in inquisitions and the probability is that it lapsed back to poor downland pasture and gradually recovered its old turfy state.

In the later Middle Ages deserted and shrunken villages are the most permanent memorials of severe population decrease from pestilence, famine and other causes. All over the downland the observant traveller will discern the visible evidence of settlements which have dwindled to insignificance, and a long-since deserted farmhouse or hamlet in a beautiful valley never fails to exert its magic. The dearth of Decorated or Perpendicular church architecture itself suggests a 'poor folk and a few' in the later Middle Ages and the many shrunken and rudely repaired churches indicate reduced congregations over many generations. In some cases a solitary church may suggest vanished homesteads, as at Beddingham, Hamsey and Warminghurst. At others vanished chapels tell of decline, as at Balmer near Falmer and at Old Erringham. A very general phenomenon on and near the Downs is the shrunken village. Berwick near Alfriston is only a fragment of a large medieval village and Allcroft noted that 'under its grass fields you may see the steads of a multitude of buildings … that have vanished'.[31] These are still traceable in fields north and west of the church and in a field at the northern end of the village. At Arlington the fields south and west of the church bear traces of unexamined earthworks which were probably the foundations of cottages and the Lydds in Piddinghoe is possibly a deserted site also still awaiting archaeological excavation. At Botolphs, which has dwindled to four houses, the foundations of former homesteads are still visible in a field opposite the church. This settlement lies in the Adur valley and the surviving earthworks around every farm and church in this part of the downland indicate that the valley once teemed with country folk in contrast to its present empty state. Coombes demonstrates this very well. At present it simply comprises a tiny 11th-century church, a 14th-century clergy house, a handful of old cottages and a single large farm all nestling into the great fold of the chalk which gives the place its name. These buildings overlook the sites of homes that have long since disappeared.

Documentary and field evidence also amply attest to the dwindling of innumerable settlement sites to an isolated farm today, often

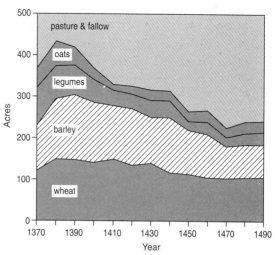

51   Decline in arable farming on the Alciston demesne in the later Middle Ages.

**52** Litlington church and manor farm in the Cuckmere valley. A typical shrunken settlement in the Downs.

the old manor house, and at most a cottage or two, where in medieval times communities of land-holding peasants co-operatively farmed the arable and had grazing rights on the sheep downs and commons. With the exception of a few farms on the Downs in the neighbourhood of Brighton, such as Mulstan, Hotsgrove and Patchway, and a few others in similar remote and lofty places in the Western Downs, also probably never anything more than single farms in the distant past, the vast majority of old farms on the Downs have gradually absorbed all the little peasant holdings that formerly existed there. The medley of rambling farm buildings—some probably dwelling houses at some time—helps us to visualise the scene of peasant cots and little farmhouses with their attendant walled gardens, tofts and crofts, often gathered about a small green. Not all these decayed townships were small. Few visitors to Glyndebourne would suspect that at the nearby farm were 14 peasant holdings in 1462; that Sutton and Chyngton near Seaford, now two large farms, had 39 householders between them in 1327; and that Winton in Alfriston, now a mere hamlet, had a minimum of 25 peasant holdings.[32]

The decline of most of the settlements discussed above was gradual and proceeded through the 14th and 15th centuries into Tudor and Stuart times. In certain cases, however, the economic and social forces responsible for depopulation occurred during the medieval period. As we have seen, the retreat of rural settlements apparently began even before the Black Death. The number of sites actually deserted or reduced to extreme decay during the later Middle Ages amounts to about seven per cent of the vills enumerated in the tax schedule of 1334—a much smaller proportion than in the Midland counties but appreciable enough to suggest changing social and agrarian circumstances.

At Hangleton it is probable that the Black Death was the turning point in the fortunes of the village. At the Poll Tax of 1377/8 only 18 persons over the age of 14 paid tax compared with 25 contributors, presumably households, to the Subsidy of 1327.[33] Only two householders were recorded at the village in 1428.[34] West Blatchington nearby had a similar story. In 1340 it had lands untilled and mustered only 16 persons to the Poll Tax of 1377/8.[35] In 1428 the parish was completely devoid of inhabitants and in 1596 the church was reported disused and there was only one dwelling in the parish.[36] Evidently the parish had become co-extensive with a single sheep farm as only two houses are recorded at West Blatchington in the Hearth Tax of 1664. Sutton-next-Seaford and Chyngton on the flanks of the Cuckmere valley have long been represented on the landscape as large single farms but they formerly constituted a populous parish with its own church at Sutton. The 1296 Subsidy bears no less than 58 names drawn from both villages.[37] The 1327 Tax roll credits Sutton with 18 and Chyngton with 21 taxpayers. In 1340 Sutton was one of many downland parishes reporting substantial acres of untilled land and in the 1428 return of parishes with less than ten houses, no dwellings at all were recorded in Sutton.[38] In 1509 the parish was combined with Seaford because '... the church is utterly destroyed and [there are] no parishioners, save a few neat herds ...'.[39] Another downland village that completely disappeared is Exceat, also in the Cuckmere valley. The Nonae Returns of 1340/1 are silent on trouble at Exceat but it is highly unlikely that it would have escaped the damage from the French inflicted on neighbouring Friston, East Dean and Seaford.[40] In 1460 it was stated:

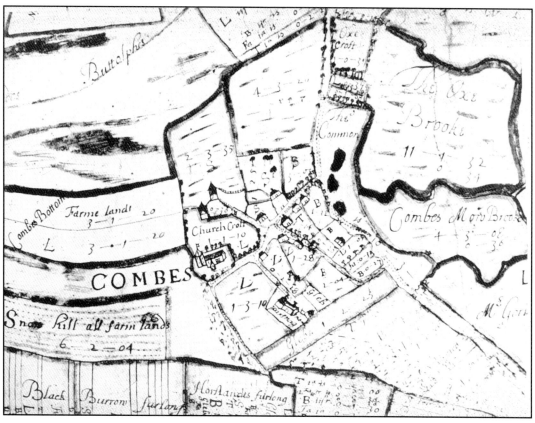

**53** This map of Coombes in the Adur valley, dated 1677, is indicative of the shrunken nature of the rural settlement by this date. The drawing in perspective of the church is important because it shows that a tower existed at the west end, of which little evidence remains.

The parish church of Exceat has long been, as it now is, destroyed, utterly fallen to the ground and its materials torn up and carried away; and there are only two inhabited houses within the parish ... There is no hope in the future of the rebuilding or new construction of the church of Exceat itself, or likewise or bringing back the parishioners ...[41]

The church, once a prominent landmark from the sea, was ploughed over in the last century and all traces of it disappeared. The foundations of the church were later discovered and the lonely site is now within the Seven Sisters Country Park.

Of much interest is depopulation in the present-day parish of Angmering which was formerly divided into three separate parishes, each served by its own church, namely West Angmering, East Angmering and Barpham. The ruined church at Barpham had unmistakable Saxon origins (p.81). It lies in a small field known as Chapel Croft lying immediately westwards of Upper Barpham Farm, across the track from Angmering to Lee Farm, via New Place. The tax payable in respect for Barpham in 1296, 1327 and 1332 suggests that population was declining even before the Black Death which presumably hastened further depopulation, and the living of the church had become a sinecure before the Reformation. As for the church of St Nicholas at East Angmering, virtually nothing is left above ground today. There was a burial recorded there as late as 1559 which suggests that the church was still in use at that time but it had presumably fallen into disuse by 1593, as no incumbent is recorded after that date. The decline of the parish probably followed a similar pattern to that of Barpham. West Angmering also saw considerable decline in the Tudor period.

To the inexperienced or untrained eye, the remains of a deserted medieval village are vestigial in the extreme. Grass covers a tangle of humps and hollows, concealing stretches of tumbled flint-walling, hollowed out lanes, house-platforms, and small farm buildings. Yet this was sufficient for a skilled map surveyor to locate accurately the 'Site of Ancient Village' at Hangleton. This is the only Sussex Deserted Medieval Village which has been comprehensively excavated. The bleak and windswept site, higher than that of the church, appears to have declined gradually in the 14th century. Eric Holden's excavations revealed that cottages were built very close to one another, but at varied angles to the line of the street, and were very shortlived, sometimes only lasting for a generation or so before being rebuilt, when the orientation often changed.[42] Makeshift repairs were often called for, such as buttresses to support collapsing walls. The earliest houses were probably constructed of timber wattle and daub but in the mid-13th century the villagers replaced their timber framing with flint walls 4.5 feet high. These were built with random flints and so usually had rounded corners. Apertures with wooden shutters served as windows. The cottages had only one or two rooms and a single door-way off-centred on one of the longer sides; they were unfloored and little attempt was made to level the chalk before construction started. The cottages, probably thatched, were extremely cramped by modern standards. One of the best preserved examples has been reconstructed at the Singleton Weald and Downland Museum. This had a tiny interior measuring only 21 by 13 feet divided into two by a wattle and daub partition. The larger room had a central hearth, the smaller an oven. Some of the dwellings had farm buildings associated with them. Two houses may have been 'long houses' with a main living room and inner room and a third room used for animals which fed from a cross passage. All the furnishings have perished but they were probably very sparse and consisting of a three-legged table, a few stools and truckle-beds, a storage chest or two and a few pots, pans, pitchers and wooden platters.

It is possible to visualise the indubitable marks of decay in following centuries at these Deserted Medieval Villages. As the population fell, the few inhabitants left—men, women and children—could have sat at their ease with plenty of room in the chancels of the decaying churches. In each decayed or shrunken village tumbledown buildings would have been general, with former houses in use as barns or cattle byres. In some villages houses with rotten thatch, broken windows, rotting door-sills and all threatening to fall remained a dwelling of a ragged family of labourers which William Cobbett thought might be the grandchildren, perhaps, 'of a decent family of small farmers that had formerly lived very happy in that very house'.

## A Chalkland Village in the Later Middle Ages

Finding a typical chalkland village would have been as difficult in the Middle Ages as it would be at the present day. Alciston is not put forward as such a village. It has been chosen for detailed study because of the large quantities of medieval documents relating to it that still survive and because many of the buildings in use in the medieval village are still recognisable today at what is a very large modern farm. In some respects Alciston can be regarded as an archetypal chalkland village. Its spring-line site below the escarpment of the Downs between Lewes and Eastbourne, the lay-out of the fields and the history of the village itself, which grew in the early Middle Ages and then contracted—these are classical in character. Yet in other respects it is exceptional. Its lords were monks of Battle of the Benedictine order, a community famed throughout England for the excellence of its sheep-and-corn husbandry. As we have previously noted, here, and on the monks' subsidiary granges of Lullington and East Blatchington, downland farming reached its apogee in the Middle Ages. For a fuller picture of medieval agriculture we must turn to the demesne for this was conducted on a much larger scale than those of the monks' tenants and it is much better documented.

**54** The enormous barn at Alciston Court Farm, formerly property of the monks of Battle Abbey.

At the comprehensive survey made in 1433 there were 31 dwellings lining both sides of the village street.[43] These fell in two groups: the larger constituting 'North Town' (*toun*, a village) was older, being nearer the springs that give the village its water and by the parish church. Dwellers here could also service the demesne better from here (p.59). The smaller group of houses was called 'South Town'. This lay among the common fields and had shown signs of decay by the end of the 15th century. This 'polyfocal' origin of an English village is not unusual. The southern group (separated from the northern houses by the manorial farm buildings and manor court) is probably to be explained by population pressure in the early Middle Ages. The old idea that a village was stable in plan must be discarded: on the contrary, villages were constantly changing shape and size during the Middle Ages.

Comparing the extensive demesne with the small scale of the common-fields, one recognises that this manor, like so many other great estates in the downland, functioned as a 'federated grain factory' and dominated the downland economy with the great scale of its wool production. The core of such an estate was the great demesne farm worked by large numbers of dependent cultivators who had small shares in common-fields. This explains the small extent of common-fields, in aggregate only *c.*190 statute acres. It would appear that the monks had been unable to let some lands in the common-fields after the population declined in the 14th century, notably after the Black Death (1348-9) for villeins rented dispersed strips in addition to their holdings leaving a residue of strips which the monks in 1433 had to keep in hand.[44] This common-field land lay up against the escarpment and was dissected by markedly asymmetrical dry valleys with steep sides invariably left unploughed. Although the fields are divided into three 'leynes' for sowing purposes, their acreages varied from year to year according to weather conditions and particular requirements and thus it was not unusual for selected furlongs in the common-fields to be sown with a succession of corn crops and for fodder crops to replace fallow on some of the land not used for corn. This flexible system in varying degrees seems to have operated all over the Eastern Downs by the 14th century where the intensive use of the sheepfold provided dung for exhausting crops such as wheat. In addition to land in the common fields tenants could put 30 sheep for every wist on to the tenantry Down and three cows on the common.

The demesne lay on the best farmland. The peak of sowing in the later Middle Ages was *c.*420 acres in the 1380s which declines steadily through the 15th century to about 300 acres in 1500. In most years wheat was the largest crop. The stiff chalk marl was ideal for it. An important feature was the extent of legumes (vetches, peas, beans, tares) sown on the fallow.[45] The amount of fallow on the more or less permanently arable part of the demesne was never more than about one fifth of the total acreage in the period 1375-84 and in several years less than 15 per cent. This intensity of arable production distinguishes the downland and the coastal plain of Sussex from the rest of the county. Besides this core of permanently arable land there was a group of intermittently cultivated fields in the northern part of the manor which lay on the Upper Greensand and Gault Clay formations on which there was little permanent arable in the later Middle Ages. The fields were too damp for the sheep fold and were tilled intermittently until they 'ran out', when they were put down to pasture again. The port of Seaford was used to export corn and fleeces and to transfer stock and seeds to Apuldram near Chichester, another manor of the monks of Battle Abbey. The monks' magnificent old aisled barn is of such great length, width and height as to be the largest traditional Sussex barn. It lies on medieval foundations and part of the roof trusses and piers are of medieval date. The great roof was originally thatched and appears to have been relaid with tiles in the late 17th century. This barn is often

**55** The stone arch at Alciston Court Farm and another at the opposite side of the medieval hall now continues into rooms later lofted over the hall, probably in the 17th century.

**56** A unique cross-passage surviving at Alciston Court Farm. The door on the right led to the medieval hall; to the left doorways gave access to service rooms.

casually called a 'tithe' barn: instead, it was built by the monks for storing their immense amount of wool, hay and corn. An old ox-stall housing the plough-oxen has only recently fallen into dereliction. An unusual dovecot lies nearby with two chambers. Alciston Court Farm, the old manor house, is a fascinating building of various periods of which the kernel is a medieval hall house which, uniquely, contains 14th-century masonry of windows which, before bedrooms were inserted, extended the full height of the walls.[46] A cross-passage extending the whole width of the house is also an exceptionally rare survival (p.77).

*Chapter Six*

# THE SAXON AND EARLY MEDIEVAL
# DOWNLAND CHURCH

The chief characteristic of the downland church is its utter simplicity. Coming to mind is a little squat building with a high-pitched roof and a diminutive shingled tower (a Sussex cap) nestling toy-like in a fold in the Downs against a hillside, often alone in an atmospheric churchyard amidst fields. It normally has a simple single or double chamber and, commonly, Early English lancet windows and an interior as ascetic as a dissenters' chapel lacking chamfered arcades, corbel heads, aisles, transepts, roof bosses, rich Jacobean furnishings and has few noble monuments. Small and undistinguished, it also tends to be narrow and tall, which Pevsner's *Buildings of England* volume for Sussex observes is 'a literal reaching up to God which still moves the visitor wherever it survives intact'.[1] Great lords did not have Caen stone carted into the obscure hillsides nor did foreign masons come to carve elaborate capitals. The sole building materials were the local chalk villagers hacked from the ground and flints collected from the fields, mixed with some Roman tiles. Such churches were built, and repaired, in effect, for the people, by the people with their own sweat. An unusually large number were built by Saxons or early Normans in the period *c.*1050-1125, known as the Saxo-Norman overlap, and many have remained substantially unaltered. Many more are of 13th-century date, generally on earlier foundations, and centuries have passed these too with a minimum of change. These tiny downland churches are thus hallowed by hundreds of years of prayer and worship, of births,

**57**  The Old Rectory, a late 15th-century flint house with a hall and solar on the first floor adjoins the broad tower of All Saints' Church, West Dean, near Eastbourne, with its unusual half-hipped spire.

marriages and death, of giving thanks, and of doing business and swearing on oath in the porch. The simple architecture of these little stone cells has a remarkable power to move the spirit of believer and unbeliever alike. They also have a special appeal by so completely embodying over centuries the identity of such small and simple village communities.

When their churches were built, numerous downland communities were poor and unimportant and remained so for centuries and this poverty and small population is the background to the modest little churches with their simple, austere, interiors of, for example, Idsworth in Hampshire, the three (formerly four) at the Mardens, and Hardham, Didling and Up Waltham in West Sussex. Other communities, although relatively well-populated and prosperous in the 11th century through sheep-and-corn farming, salt making and maritime activities, tended to dwindle steadily in population from the later Middle Ages, if not before and subsequently became poverty stricken and small. In such places decay often meant that rural communities could not maintain the fabric of their parish church which became ruinous, and curtailed from the 14th and 15th centuries. Damaging raids by the French also account for the decline in population in coastal districts from the 14th century and the engrossing of holdings from the late Middle Ages was another factor in reduced congregations and absentee landlordship. For these various reasons the repeatedly enlarged church, elaborated according to the architectural fashion of the day to meet the needs of an expanding congregation, as, for example, at Fletching, Cuckfield, Thakeham and Rudgwick in the Sussex Weald, hardly exists. A comparison with Cotswold churches is also instructive. The downland churches were 'sheep' churches as were the latter but they saw little of the wealth of wool because parishioners were wool *growers* and wool shepherds, not wool *merchants*, and thus a rich patron to rebuild a nave, add a great tower, endow a chantry, or be commemorated with his good name carved in stone was rare. Also generally lacking are the great Norman churches with sumptuous detail which distinguishes several of the old Sussex seaports like Steyning and Old and New Shoreham. The East Hampshire Downs have a different pattern of church building from that of the Sussex Downs with a higher proportion of complex medium-to-large churches, for example, East Meon, on an estate of the Bishop of Winchester, Hambledon and Buriton. The very bad state of repair of downland churches in the 18th and 19th centuries meant that several were totally rebuilt in Victorian times and many others restored with varying degrees of 'killing kindness' but because the Downs remained isolated from the growth of coastal resorts and railway towns, and consequently was unfashionable amongst *nouveaux riches* country house owners, the large Victorian church in imitation of the greater medieval churches is absent.

On account of the history of the South Downs there is a higher proportion of churches containing surviving features of Saxon workmanship in their existing stone fabric than in most other districts of England. What is also significant is that recent research has made evident that in addition to this observable, visible, evidence of Saxon work in the exterior of many existing churches, there is also often a Saxon element underlying, and influencing, present structures which date from after the Norman Conquest, as at Findon and at Hambledon, Hampshire. Thus the Saxon element is even more ubiquitous than was first thought and there is probably a wealth of Saxon church building awaiting discovery.

H.H. Taylor's list of Anglo-Saxon churches in England numbers 267, of which 18 and possibly several more are in the Downs.[2] E.A. Fisher regarded the 'probables' of Taylor as certainties and added 20 more, mostly downland churches.[3] The great disparity in numbers between these two lists arises from the difficulty of dating precisely many of the ancient churches. Most of them are built of flint rubble with a minimal use of dressed stone, and they have round-

**VI** *Arundel Castle* by G. Vicat Cole. Oil on canvas, dated 1877. The earliest depiction of autumn tints on the beech trees. The hanger was devastated by the Great Storm of October 1987 but has been replanted.

**VII** The tiny unspoilt Up Waltham Church in the Western Downs. Before his conversion to the Roman Catholic faith, Cardinal Manning was an Anglican curate here. He recalled the setting 'rising up to one like the background to some sacred picture ... the Downs seem to be only less beautiful than Heaven'.

**VIII** The present-day aspect of Plumpton Place, home of Leonard Mascall in the 16th century. Early in this century it was the home of Edward Hudson, proprietor of *Country Life*, and Edwin Lutyens designed the music room shown.

**IX** View across the Weald from Firle Beacon, 1994, by Alan George.

headed windows, single-splayed openings plain chancel arches. Such churches could belong either to a period when Saxons were busy building new flint churches to replace earlier wooden ones or to the Early Norman. The Domesday survey is no firm guide since many known pre-Conquest churches are not recorded, presumably because they produced no revenue. Examples of churches difficult to date are Hangleton with 'herringbone' masonry in the 11th-century nave and the three remarkable circular church towers in the Ouse valley, at St Michael's, Lewes, Southease and Piddinghoe, where no stone quoins were used so that the walls were rounded.

It takes time and patience to discern this Saxon and other early workmanship in downland churches and to unravel their history. The oldest buildings have an interesting story to tell of the earliest developments in Christian worship and organisation. Local churches on a parish basis did not exist for two or three centuries after Christianity was re-introduced into Sussex by St Wilfrid in the 680s. In this early phase of religion minsters were founded which supplied itinerant clergy to surrounding districts. Singleton near Chichester, Lyminster near Arundel, Findon, and Bishopstone near Seaford were minster churches of this type.[4] The clergy may have been actually housed in the church itself, as is suggested by evidence of an earlier upper floor at Singleton which ran through the tower and above the present nave floor. From the 10th century Saxon lords were beginning to build churches on their estates and to appoint priests to serve them. The plan was generally irregular, the two sides not exactly parallel and the two ends not exactly at right angles to the sides. There was no structural division into nave and chancel and the altar was placed in a central position to allow the priest to celebrate the mass facing the congregation (an arrangement re-introduced into all Roman Catholic and many Anglican churches since the 1960s). An important feature of a Saxon church was the *porticus*, or side-chamber used for special services. Sometimes there were two of these, on either side of the nave. The chancel was usually rounded in the form of an apse.

On Barpham Hill, on the Downs above Angmering, lie the surviving foundations of this earliest kind of church.[5] Around it are the pits and mounds of a medieval village which has been totally abandoned, apart from a Tudor farmhouse and a great thatched barn, doubtless built to serve the sheep farm that replaced the peasants. The Barpham church site also reveals church building of later periods up to the 14th century. The earliest church had an apse at its western end and was tiny, less than one-third the size of the church at its fullest extension. Whether it represents the first of a series of Saxon churches or had an even earlier origin in Roman Sussex is unclear. This church was succeeded by another in later Saxon times, a two-cell structure with nave and chancel clearly differentiated. This in turn was re-built, also in Saxon times with nave, central tower and rectangular north and south *portici* and with a chancel of unknown plan. Other stages of church building took place in post-Saxon times. The excavation of the church of St Nicholas, Angmering, also revealed a comparatively small late Saxon church with very slight evidence for an even earlier Saxon phase.

These sites are invaluable as a reminder that the visible Saxon work in present churches may have been the last of a series of earlier church constructions. The change from a small single-unit church to a two-cell one reflects a fundamental change in liturgy throughout Christendom *c.*1000, when mass began to be celebrated by the priest with his back to the congregation and a chancel for the priest was built. A small chancel arch was placed to separate the sacred part of the church from that part used by the people.[6]

A few existing churches have retained the simple single-cell structure of Barpham with little change to this day, including Warnford in the East Hampshire Downs, and East Marden, North Marden, Didling, Greatham, Wiggonholt, Buncton (West Sussex), Denton and West Dean

**58** The Saxon arch in Corhampton Church in the East Hampshire Downs.

in East Sussex. Excavation or detailed survey of the church fabric has revealed that Bishopstone, West Blatchington, Findon and Botolphs, for example, were originally single-cell structures like the first church at Barpham.

Tiny, rather later, two-cell churches are relatively common. They include Chithurst, mentioned as a little church (*ecclesiola*) in Domesday Book which remains almost exactly as it was nine centuries ago. St Botolph's, Hardham, also preserves this simple form, apart from the addition of a porch to protect the north door. St Peter's, Westhampnett has a like form, with a liberal admixture of Roman tiles laid in herringbone fashion in the nave wall, the arched head of the chancel also being wholly built of Roman tiles. Greatham is another little two-cell church overlooking Pulborough brooks in the Arun valley, as is Up Marden, with one of the loveliest interiors in England, Corhampton and Idsworth in the East Hampshire Downs and Selham. The latter is a gem. There is 'textbook' evidence of Saxon workmanship in this tiny church in the form of long and short quoins, herringbone masonry and the tall, narrow door. The chancel arch is an enigma because the Saxon workmanship incorporates stone carved in a Celtic manner which has been re-used from an older church. At numerous downland churches the Saxon work remains substantial despite later re-building. At Jevington, Sullington and Singleton, Saxon west towers survive of *c*.1040-60. Sompting, with its Saxon tower of about the same date, is one of the most famous Anglo-Saxon churches and the only surviving example of a steeple of the 'helm' type, derived from churches in the Rhineland, which may have once been quite common; inside on the chancel arch are capitals carved by Saxon masons in crude but reverent imitation of older and dimly-understood classical models, which have a moving, child-like innocence about them.[7] Botolphs in the Adur valley has clear Saxon work in the south wall of the nave, the chancel wall and the chancel arch. A north aisle was built about 1250 when it was still a flourishing farming and sea-faring community. With the silting up of the river Adur the settlement almost entirely disappeared and the aisle was pulled down when its upkeep could no longer be afforded. The finest Saxon work is at Bosham,[8] important place of the Godwin family, where the chancel arch, which Pevsner regards as 'speaking a completely developed architectural language', is a grand sight giving tremendous scale to the interior. At Stoughton, where the height and narrowness indicate Saxon workmanship, the chancel arch is similarly assured. St John sub Castro at Lewes was totally rebuilt in 1839 but the Saxon chancel arch with its restored inscription in Lombardic script commemorating a Magnus of royal Danish stock, who became an anchorite there, was placed on the exterior of the south side. This inscription was noted by William Camden, the Elizabethan antiquary, and is the sole illustration in his

**59** The famous Saxon tower of Sompting Church with its plinth course, pilaster strips and long and short quoins is unique as the sole surviving example in England of a 'Rhenish helm' cap. The dainty and elegant design of the church is a refreshing contrast to the standardised Norman church in the vicinity. The present wooden structure of the spire is 14th-century in date.

*Britannia* (1586)[9] which distinguishes it as the first published illustration in British archaeology. Bishopstone is the finest example of the process by which a fairly simple Saxon church was transformed during the Middle Ages. Saxon work includes the early eighth-century porticus with a sundial inscribed 'Eadric' on the gable. The original west doorway was blocked by Norman builders prior to the addition of a tower at the west end. In the 12th century the pre-Conquest chancel was demolished in order to extend the nave eastward. Later in the period of transition to Early English style, the chancel was extended still further eastward and a north aisle added to the nave. Finally, in the 13th century the chancel arch and the north arcade seem to have been rebuilt in the Early English style. This exceptional enlargement and alteration may be attributable to its being a possession of the bishops of Chichester.[10]

After the Norman Conquest came a wave of new church building in Sussex and Hampshire wherever rich patrons existed as a 'sort of steam roller that obliterated everything that was there before'. Even before the Conquest, King Edward the Confessor had begun to link the Sussex downland with Normandy and this was reinforced strongly under Norman rule on account of the close military and trading ties between them. This influence was still further strengthened by the division of land between leading families previously settled in Normandy. Earl Roger de Montgomery, to whom the Conqueror gave Arundel and Chichester Rapes, had his home near Lisieux where surrounding villages bear his name to this day. The de Braoses took their name from the small town of Briouze in Calvados, and amongst knights the de Coverts of Sullington can be traced to Couvert near Bayeux, the de Bucis of Kingston Buci near Shoreham-by-Sea to the village of Boucé near Briouze and the de Says of Hamsey (ie. Ham Say) to Sées near Argentan.[11]

This cultural influence stemming from Normandy is evident in the similar architectural style of churches in the Downs and across the English Channel. The apsidal church of Newhaven has similarity to that of Yainville-sur-Seine. The collegiate church at Steyning, one of the finest specimens of 12th-century architecture, was built under the supervision of the

**60** The modest church dedicated to St Botolph, the patron saint of sailors, at Botolphs in the Adur valley with the blocked-up arches of its former north aisle. Populous and prosperous with fisheries, salt-making and farming in the early Middle Ages, it now stands in a flint-built hamlet depopulated since the 14th century.

monks of Fécamp and its nave has a strong resemblance to the Romanesque churches of northern France.[12]

Old Shoreham is a good example of Norman architecture imposed on a Saxon structure. The western part of the north wall of the nave is Saxon, as is the narrow blocked-up door. The sheer height of the church is also attributed to Saxon builders.[13] The rich de Braose demolished the rest of the church, including a probable tower at the west end, and positioned a large tower centrally with an apsidal chancel and transepts elaborately carved with the conventional decorations of dog-tooth, lozenge, beakhead and billet, together with sumptuously sculpted capitals holding up the roof.

Churches which were not re-built in the Norman period tended to be so *c.*1200 or shortly afterwards. These like the simple churches built earlier, were also basically modest and have always had small congregations. Barlavington is a good example of the utter simplicity of these little 13th-century village churches. Its aisles were blocked up after the Middle Ages, the north aisle being unblocked in 1874. The exterior has been thoroughly restored but the interior is surprisingly unaltered. Litlington is even simpler and hardly changed over centuries until restored in 1863 when the original rood screen and stone tympanum in the chancel arch were removed.

The traditional Saxo-Norman or early English downland church has its own local proportions and simple lines. It tends to be a tall and narrow building with a length of 60-70 feet (excluding the west tower), about three times as long as its width. More than thirty downland churches have these same approximate dimensions which tend to make them visual 'look-alikes'. Examples are Pyecombe, Hangleton, Tarring Neville, Selmeston, West Dean (near Eastbourne), Friston, Folkington, Telscombe, Rodmell, Heyshott, Bepton, Elsted and East Marden. A memorable feature of such churches devoid of airs and graces is the work of local village craftsmen. This is often endearing in its homely rusticity, such as the axe marks of Saxon masons in Friston church; the stone ledges lining the walls of Wilmington church on which monks of the Priory sat; the slightly off-centre chancel arch of Tarring Neville; the re-used Roman tiles around a Saxon window at Arlington; the arches not quite in line at Iford; the crudely-fashioned Saxon tub font and plain, 13th-century bench ends in the 'Shepherds' church at Didling, a 'sort of architectural attic'.

Several of these re-built churches are on or against burial mounds raised imposingly by pre-Christian Saxons to guard the bones or ashes and preserve the memory of heroes, as for example are Hamsey, Piddinghoe, Southease, Tarring Neville and Berwick. Evidently they were such impressive symbols to the early Christians that they continued to invest them with such sanctity as to build their churches on the same shrine. It appears to have been the policy of missionaries from A.D. 597 onwards to Christianise pagan culture rather than destroy it.[14]

Some churches suffered severely at the hands of the French. At Rottingdean, the south aisle appears to have been burned down, for stone rendered pink and split by flames was discovered in the restoration of 1856.[15] Ovingdean church is mentioned as a 'little church' in Domesday and lies lofty and narrow with numerous lancet windows up against the steep hillside of its dene. A two-bay south aisle built in the 13th century was destroyed by French raiders and stone bears witness to this. A curious feature is a blocked arch cut into by an 11th-century window and including a lancet of the same date visible in the north wall of the chancel. 'How can that be?', asks Pevsner.[16] A probable explanation is that perfunctory repairs were made after an enemy attack.

Amongst the simplest and most moving churches are those of the Mardens in the emptiest country in the Downs. They are amongst 18 parishes in the archdeaconry of Chichester containing fewer than 100 inhabitants. At one, it was said, cows were apt to follow the congregation and join in the hymn singing in the 1960s. The church at East Marden has suffered from restoration but the single apsed room of North Marden without any addition (probably one of only four single-cell apsidals in England), and the 13th-century Up Marden, of which Ian Nairn has written 'it is incredibly moving whether one is Anglican or not, whether one is religious or not' are unspoiled.[17] Simon Jenkins, also inspired by the lovely plain interior and exceptional atmosphere of Up Marden church, noted that the Middle Ages might have been just left for the night 'and that ghosts of rough gaitered peasants were cursing the Earls of Arundel and squabbling in a thick Sussex dialect over the empty benches'.[18]

Exceptional in downland are the large and elaborate churches typical of more populous and prosperous parts of Sussex or Hampshire. Poynings and Alfriston, both 14th-century rebuilds, and the splendid cruciform church of Harting, are almost the sole examples. In both cases a patron enriched with loot acquired in the Hundred Years' War modernised the churches to ransom their own souls. A specific new ecclesiastical building of the early Middle Ages was the isolated chapel provided for worshippers in hamlets a long distance from the parish church. The chapel at Old Erringham Farm in the Adur valley, subordinate to Old Shoreham, partially survives as a storeroom. Half the former chapel at Balsdean Farm, two miles from Rottingdean church, was a stable in the 19th century. There was a medieval chapel at Norton in Bishopstone parish, another at Northease in the parish of Rodmell and one at Wootton in Folkington.[19]

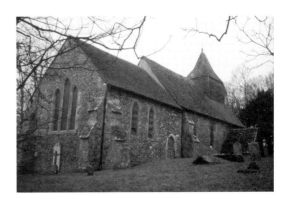

**61** The 'family' of 13th-century downland churches. Clockwise from top left: Tarring Neville, Pyecombe, Folkington, Hangleton, Kingston-by-Lewes, Hamsey.

## Medieval Wall Paintings

A number of the modest downland churches have remarkable works of art in the form of medieval wall-paintings.[20] These wall paintings comprise the finest in Great Britain and are unequalled in northern Europe. Their survival is largely attributable to the relatively unrestored condition of churches of parishes which became impoverished with population decline from the late Middle Ages. Another reason why the wall paintings are in a better condition and more complete than in most country churches is that the paintings are not on good building stone which was successively scraped, but on clunch, rubble and flint, so making it more difficult to efface the murals. Amberley, Arundel, Boxgrove, Preston, Trotton and Hangleton are amongst village churches which have good survivals of medieval paintings. More are probably to be discovered: those of Up Marden were not found until 1994 when re-decoration followed considerable restoration.

The most complete paintings are at Plumpton, Clayton, Coombes and Hardham. Hardham, exceptionally, has paintings over almost the entire wall surface of the church. The Coombes paintings are in some ways the most remarkable of all because they have a special vividness and freshness of colour and a dramatic verve in execution. These were retrieved by E.C. Rouse in the 1950s.[21] As Milner-Gulland notes, they 'can make the unprepared visitor gasp with surprise, scarcely able to believe that some nine centuries have passed since they were made'. The method of painting in this group of churches is true fresco, pigment applied day by day to freshly-plastered sections of walls before it had dried out. This technique rendered the painting exceptionally durable and brilliant. Such a method of painting was rare in medieval England.[22] The riddle of their dating and stylistic affinities is still unresolved. Clayton holds the key to the dispute in dating. The most dramatic part of the composition is the massed Apostles approaching Christ in glory above the chancel arch. There are similar motifs in each of the churches in the 'Clayton' group, e.g. in posture, gesture, facial-type and the rendering of outer garments as a series of longitudinal folds. Expert opinion has focused upon the priory of St Pancras at Lewes, the original and greatest Cluniac foundation in England, as the source of wall-painters, since Clayton, Hardham and Plumpton churches were connected with the Priory. The more

**62**   The interior of Up Marden Church.

**63** The wall paintings in St Hubert's Chapel, Idsworth in the East Hampshire Downs, dated *c*.1330. These in the little church isolated in a field are unusual in completeness and quality. Most of the paintings relate to successive stages in the life and death of St John the Baptist. In Cocking Church a splay painting of *c*.1220 depicts an angel pointing to the Star of Bethlehem and visiting a shepherd and his boy. The shepherd's dog is barking furiously at the angel.

**64** The representation of a man holding up the arch in Coombes Church in the Adur valley is one of the most vivid depictions in medieval church frescoes.

recent discovery of the Coombes paintings, which do not appear to have had any link with the Priory, has greatly weakened the suggestion of Cluniacs drawing upon Burgundian artists, and the very early style of the Hardham paintings is now regarded as having been uninfluenced by Cluniac art.

The paintings reveal what Christian message the congregation would have been expected to comprehend. At Hardham is the complete story of salvation 'clearly and systematically presented'. Clayton has the Last Judgment represented above the chancel arch with Christ, sitting in Judgment, as the central figure with processions of adoring figures on either side. On the low zone of the north wall is represented the Resurrection. On the upper part of the north wall the paintings refer to the end of the world and the Last Judgment, the figures shown in the procession being saved. The symbolism of this painting is unique in the medieval art and literature of the western world.[23]

The consensus on the dating of these wall paintings has hitherto been early post-Conquest. Baker and others favoured the turn of the 11th and 12th centuries. Recently there appears to be agreement that Clayton church and its paintings belong to the period 1050-1100. More will be learned when the chancel arch is cleared of rendering. Meanwhile, Milner-Gulland has asked, 'Could it be that these churches give a glimpse of how the South Saxon in the eleventh century saw Christianity?'. It is a most exciting speculation.

In the East Hampshire South Downs Corhampton has notable medieval wall paintings and Catherington has a remarkably well restored wall painting *c.*1350 representing St Michael weighing souls.

Victorians regarded the simpler downland churches as 'uninteresting', 'mean', 'rude' and 'barbaric' and despised their builders as 'ignorant' and 'primitive'. The judgment of the present generation is decisively different. The concentration of early church building in the South Downs, almost unique in England, is now increasingly valued as a spontaneous expression of religion in a very simple and moving 'language', all but destroyed elsewhere by more sophisticated architecture and ritual. Simon Jenkins, for example, has remarked of this, 'You can go to Iona, to Cornwall, or to the Welsh Marches and you will not find a more moving witness to early Christianity'. To Enoch Powell's heterodox way of thinking, these simple village churches were one of the secrets of England's charm, offering encoded messages of an unlettered people's way of life, beliefs and thought through a span of a thousand years, so binding him to them and helping him form his idea of England.[24]

# Chapter Seven

# SOWING THE SEEDS OF CHANGE:
# THE 16TH AND 17TH CENTURIES

## A Buoyant Economy

In these centuries the Downs emerged from the medieval to the modern world. The dissolution of feudal ties between lord and man was completed and the pace of economic life so quickened that market forces permeated more deeply and widely than ever before. Population again increased, corn prices rose more or less continuously and wool exports, raw or manufactured into cloth, paid for the goods that the landed classes bought in greater profusion as the price of land and rents rose. The demand for land encouraged well-to-do lords of the manor to convert customary (i.e. former peasants' land) into a source of greater income by means of sales licences for the creation of freeholds. as well as through fines for unlicensed breaches of manorial custom. These legal changes made the land market more flexible and facilitated the role of the encloser, engrosser (an amalgamator of tenancies) and depopulator and so strongly worked against the small family farmer, who steadily declined in number. Large holdings and speculative land ventures were favoured and these lie behind a number of innovations in farming which were to lay the foundations for the 'Golden Age' in downland agriculture in the 18th and 19th centuries.

**65** The Old Parsonage, Old Town, Eastbourne, a 16th-century house of rubble and flint with transomed three-light windows on the ground floor. The hall has a fine fireplace. Another fine survival is the Jacobean Manor of Dean below the Western Downs in Tillington.

One of the most illuminating records of the period is the meticulous transcription of manorial customs and land surveys dating back to the first year of Elizabeth's reign (1558/9) by John Rowe, a lawyer and antiquary of Lewes by which he marked his retirement in 1622 from his 25 years' stewardship of the Sussex manors of Lord Bergavenny.[1] Rowe's compilation, 'undertaken to the uttermost of my skill and understanding for the benefit(t) of posterity' is laconic and rather dry in itself but it is invaluable in taking us to the regular business of the manorial court where changes in land holding and farming practices were upheld or initiated and which led to a sequence of social and land use changes which we can sometimes trace in succeeding documents or in the landscape itself. Thus Rowe notes tersely that the lords of the scarp-foot manors of Keymer, Houndean and West Chiltington were enclosing the commons with the agreement of their tenants and his brief entry for Ditchling, where this was also happening, reads:

> Licenses granted to enclose part of the commons with the consent of the tenants, 6 Jul. Eliz 5 (i.e. 1563); March 9 Jas I (i.e. 1612); Oct. 10 Jas (1613); 28 Jul. 13 Jas (1616). The tenants contradict such grants II Jul. 14 Jas (1617)[2]

**66**   A facsimile of John Rowe's transcription of manorial customs and land surveys.

Behind these terse entries lies a record of communal unrest, going back to the reign of Henry VIII, extending over more than eighty years in which the farming system disintegrated and some tenants felt threatened or aggrieved enough to tear up hedges around new allotments from the commons, complaining that other tenants had enclosed more than their due, and engaged in various other contentious issues.

Rowe has also much information on customary tenancies, i.e. those mainly held by genuine peasants, descendants of the medieval villeins and cottars. A number of these are described as 'Gentleman' or 'Esquire'. Some of these gentlemen copyholders are clearly engrossers, holding as many as three or more tenements once held singly by lowly persons such as John Frere, 'gentleman', a customary tenant of Balsdean in the deep downs near Rottingdean, who held three tenements, two cottages, 16 yardlands and pasture for three horses, eight oxen, eight cows and 680 sheep, on 1,000 acres of pasture.[3] This entry marks the end of a hamlet once harbouring a group of small family farmers. At Portslade and Plumpton, Rowe shows that a further stage had been reached. At Plumpton land in five instances was held by 'gentlemen' which was enfranchised copyhold.[4] This is significant in that it marks the first step on the loosening of the old routines of traditional co-operative husbandry. No sooner did a man hold freehold land than he lost interest in sticking to a system which scattered the land of his farm in intermixed strips and gave him a share of grazing on the common. With the low level of rents and prices of land prevailing in the 16th century, they made profits out of the growing competition for land, whether they had lands on easy terms or not, and, encouraged by the authors of farming manuals, made the most of their opportunities by experimenting with new systems of farming and new crops.

The history of land at Plumpton illustrates what was happening in the downland generally. John Mascall paid £54 for the demesne of the manor in 1555. Forty years later it was leased to Philip Bennet of Wiston for a yearly rent of more than one-third of the purchase price of forty years before. One parcel of copyhold, some 33 acres (three yardlands) with a share in the sheepwalk on the Downs and known as 'Wales' was converted to freehold in 1559 for an annual rent of 10s. It was sold in 1599 for £165. In 1619 it fetched £340, and in 1655 £437 10s.[5] Even allowing for the fall in the value of money, these prices show an astonishing rise in land values which were more or less typical of what was happening all over the downland. Clearly Plumpton no longer functioned as a medieval village and its 'improved' farmland was an appropriate setting for the farming textbook of Leonard Mascall, who inherited Plumpton from his father.

Not all downland, however, proceeded to change at the same rate and the same time. Pockets of traditional agriculture prevailed, especially where there had been no freemen, probably because none of the tenements were thought by potential buyers to be worth the cost and trouble of enfranchising. The lands on the manor of Southease and Heighton are an example. Rowe springs a surprise by mentioning that boon works and services were apparently still being performed by customary tenants to the lord of the manor and that allowances of food and drink were being made to them apparently as late as 1623.[6] When reaping, tenants were allowed 'two drinkings in the forenoon of bread and cheese' and a dinner at noon 'consisting of roast meat and other good victuals meet for men and women at harvest time', and two more drinkings

67 The splendid 17th-century monument to Sir Thomas Selwyn and his wife in Friston church. Other lavish memorials of the same period to the Stoughtons of West Stoke and to William Thomas at West Dean (near Eastbourne) signify the advent of local landed gentry in Tudor times. Their great memorials contrast with the smallness and simplicity of the churches themselves.

in the afternoon. On the first Sunday in Lent the lord gave each tenant six good herrings and 1½ loaves of good wheaten bread. The Heighton reapers had to report at Stockferry, the river crossing of the Ouse, at sunrise and they did not leave off work until sunset. They made do with 'four wholesome herrings in Lent' but had the privilege of cutting hay on part of the brookland before Lammas (1 August). Here, clearly, genuine descendants of medieval villagers still continued to farm as if the chronometer had stopped three hundred years earlier. The gifts of herring presumably began more than five hundred years earlier (for they are mentioned in Domesday Book), when the community comprised farmer-fishermen. The homespun repairs to the parish church were in keeping with the simplicity and impoverishment of the inhabitants (p. 61) and a collection of ancient customs showed how very 'backward' these places remained in 1848.[7] Amberley is another example of a downland community which changed much less than others (p.124). What are we to make of this? Perhaps not all peasants wanted liberating. Others may have held lands not worth buying and so they were not bought out.

**68** Southease Church in the Ouse valley with its distinctive round tower is truncated from its medieval plan. The collapse of the stone chancel arch was resolved by a wooden structure constructed by local carpenters. Contrast Elizabethan work at Harting Church after a fire in 1576 where the aisle walls were raised to twice their previous height and a magnificent hammer-beam roof provided for the chancel.

## The Enclosure of Common-fields

The forwardness of the Downs in agriculture had important consequences for common-fields. As we have seen, particularly in the Eastern Downs, the common sheepfold had a crucial role in the creation, extension and maintenance of peasant farmers. Where small occupiers remained, the land was still worked in common for the sake of sheep's dung. In the Western Downs there was less reliance on the sheepfold and small cultivators with family farms with relatively low inputs and high costs began to seek ways of diversification in cattle raising, dairying, orchards and timber production. A major process in this diversifying was the enclosure of the common-fields in the Western Downs. As early as 1428 leave was granted to a tenant by the lord of the manor of Wiston near Steyning to enclose eight acres in one of the common-fields.[8] Piecemeal enclosures by tenants evidently followed because in 1466 it was said that a tenant 'was wont to pasture upon his own proper soil [in the arable fields] and to keep it towards that of others'[9]; that is, stubble was not common to all the village farmers when crops were lifted off, as in the common-field system. The 15th-century process of enclosure is detectible at Graffham. Unencumbered by ancient tradition, strips of intermixed arable land were gathered into bundles by means of exchanges between lord and tenants. These bundles were hedged into a galaxy of tiny fields called crofts.[10] The process continued into Woolavington, in the same lordship. Here most of the common arable appears to have been enclosed by 1574 but it evidently did not meet with unaminous approval for in 1579 several tenants were presented (i.e. fined) at the manor court for tearing down neighbours' hedges.[11] By this time the enclosure of common-fields had become a general movement in West Sussex. It was, however, mainly a 'silent revolu-tion' unacknowledged in detail in surviving documents, coming to notice principally by the endless difficulties and disputes that necessarily arose. Fortunately, estate maps of the 17th and 18th centuries have much to tell. Typically the new fields were small because the standard holding of fifteen to twenty acres was often divided on enclosure into three arable fields, with an additional field proportional in size to the common rights exercised over common meadow. Another field was added to replace similar common rights on the common if this was enclosed. These enclosed small bundles of open field strips resulted in a 'long close', often a furlong in length and curved in the inverted-S shape acquired by arable that was ploughed with heavy ox-teams. High massive hedges were planted, not only to shelter and provide good browsing for stock but also in contemporary Fitzherbert's phrase 'to nurse up great quantities of timber', not the least of the advantages of enclosure.

When manorial evidence is deficient, enclosure can be detected by means of descriptions of endowments belonging to the Church known as Glebe Terriers. These were required of incumbents and churchwardens of each parish in the Diocese of Chichester in 1615, 1635 and 1675, and at various other dates in the 17th century. The 1635 terriers are particularly useful for each holding of glebe (formerly intermixed strips in common-fields) is precisely identified. The returns for 1635 thus bring to light parishes where active piece-meal enclosure had occurred. From this source of information, and manorial documents, it is evident that the enclosure of common-fields had been completed by 1635 at Harting, Treyford, Heyshott, Didling, Bepton, Elsted, Cocking, Barlavington, Parham, Steyning, Keymer, Ditchling, Hurstpierpoint and Streat in the scarp-foot below the Downs and also on the downland itself at Compton, East Dean, the Mardens, Stoughton and Singleton in West Sussex and at Pyecombe and Litlington in East Sussex. The glebe terriers of 1635 also confirm that common-field agriculture was still firmly entrenched in East Sussex. It is a great loss that we know so little of the nature and scale of the

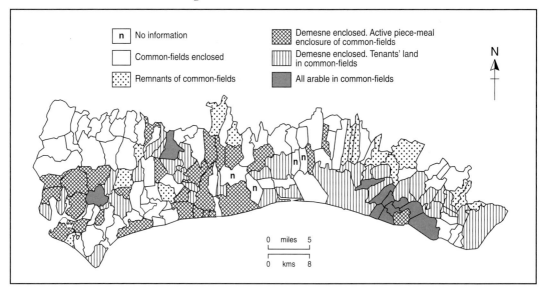

**69**   The progress of the enclosure of the common fields, *c.*1600.

social problems which must have arisen amongst the poorest classes as a consequence of enclosure.[12]

Although evidence has been cited above that most of the common-fields had not been enclosed in the Eastern Downs, important changes were occurring which undermined their function. The most pressing restriction on the initiative of common-field farmers was the necessity to observe the time-honoured three-course rotation. If demesne land still lay dispersed among that of the tenants, the lord could introduce flexibility into the rotation by consolidating his land into compact fields apart from the rest of the common-field arable. This solution had been generally adopted at least from the 13th century and there is evidence that this was effected in the 16th century on virtually all of the remaining manors with dispersed demesne. It is not surprising that some of the most progressive tenants were also chafing under the traditional system of leaving one-third of the common-field fallow each year, but in their case there was no simple remedy. The urge to break away from the medieval cropping had apparently led to a break-down of traditional cropping practices at Jevington before 1584 for in that year an order was enrolled:

> That all the tenants observe this ordinance in ploughing and sowing the common fields, one year with wheat, another year with barley and the third year they should not sow the said common fields or any of the field called the lanes [*leynes*] of this manor contrary to the ancient custom, but shall permit the fields ... to be each third year unsown according as they were used before.[13]

In this instance we are not told what crops the tenants were sowing on the fallow but the information is sufficient to show that even without enclosure more progressive agricultural innovation was taking place in East Sussex than has been formerly realised.

## The Management of Downland Manors

Meadow was in such short supply in downland that it was the subject of particularly severe conservation. In the river valleys crossing the South Downs the common meadows were known as brooks, no doubt because they were under water for much of the year. In 1086 the whole width of the valley floor probably formed a tidal inlet along the edges of which were poised settlements at the very margin of the waters engaged in salt-making and fishing in addition to agriculture. By the early 14th century highly prized meadow had been inned and embanked but its value for cattle and sheep was increasingly reduced by recurrent inundations during the later Middle Ages. Despite the raising of the river banks, winter floods were common; frequently the flood waters remained throughout the summer on the lower meadows and, occasionally, submerged crops on the bordering flanks. In 1422 a Commission of Sewers was appointed to restore the banks and drainage of the river Ouse between Fletching and Seaford which suggests that, as elsewhere along the Sussex coast, the valley was devastated by the great flood of 1421, which also wrought much havoc in the Netherlands.[14]

By the early 16th century the drainage of the Ouse and Laughton Levels had virtually collapsed. It was reported in 1537 that 'all the Level upwards of Seaford lay in a marsh all the summer long' and this is confirmed by other accounts of 'great rewyn' and that 'when abundance of water cometh by rain or other floods of the sea it is yearly drowned and overflowed with water'. The extent of the land liable to this annual inundation in the early 16th century was more than 6,000 acres from which we may infer that the whole valley from Seaford to Sheffield

**70** An extract from the map of Old Erringham Farm in the Adur valley by Robert Whitpaine in 1687. The map reveals a diverse land use including arable, abandoned arable (*gratton*), sheepdown, meadow, seasonally flooded brookland (*salts and sleeches*), cow down and a rabbit warren.

Bridge in the north and to Laughton along the Glynde Reach flowing in from the east was generally a lake for most of the year and useful only for fowling and fishing. Even the *Ries*, little islands of Gault Clay rising above the flood level, were almost valueless because of their inaccessibility and merely supported the rabbit-warrens of Lewes Priory. The Archbishop of Canterbury had earlier turned 400 acres at Broadwater in Southerham into a lake for pleasure purposes.

The seasonal inundation was doubtless due to the very sluggish flow of the river Ouse below Lewes which resulted from such a slight gradient seawards that parts of Lewes were actually below high tide levels. The gradual raising of the river bed would have been aggravated also by hindering of the discharge of upland water by the growth of a sandspit which deflected the mouth of the river eastwards, so damaging the port of Seaford. That the condition of the Ouse Levels had much deteriorated since the 13th century is indicated by the fact that Laughton manor grew crops on alluvium which was regularly flooded in 1538.

About 1540 a new scheme for the drainage of the Ouse and Laughton Levels was brought into operation. The Prior of Lewes and the nobility and gentry with landed interest in the Ouse valley had earlier consulted Dutch engineers and the successful reclaimer of St Katherine's Marsh at the Tower of London. The main problem was how best to increase the rate of flow of the Ouse to the sea. In the scheme finally adopted, the chief proposal was to cut a new channel to the sea through the shingle spit which diverted the mouth of the Ouse to Seaford Haven and checked the flow of fresh water from inland. This was probably accomplished in 1539, making the improvement of the Ouse one of the earliest canalisations in England, preceding similar proposals for the Arun and the head of Chichester Haven.

As a result of the new direct cut there was a considerable improvement in the condition of the alluvial meadows. The 400-acre Broadwater was drained and parts became good pasture. The general availability of the brookland is also evident from manorial customs. The meadows were stinted generously enough to allow each holder of a yardland between four and 12 beasts and followers. Parts were allocated for mowing by an intricate arrangement and divided into shares known as lots, doles, hides, or clouts. Lots were cast each year for strips of meadow on 10 July and by an old custom a piece of meadow fell to the holder of each yardland in turn to raise money for the festivities after the hay-making. These were called the Drinker acres at Southease and meadow at Southease was made available to downland farmers at Telscombe who lacked meadow. Generally speaking grazing was prohibited after harvest until the end of August when it was available until the end of November. The availability of these rich summer pastures permitted a beautifully balanced farming economy which would have comprised store cattle on the meadows nearest the river; dairy cattle near the barns; corn on the valley flanks; and sheep walks on the higher Downs.

The drainage improvements, however, again deteriorated in the 17th century. The villagers at Iford, for example, were once again raising and strengthening the river banks each September early in the 17th century and at Firle the tenants scoured the sewers in a vain attempt to keep the meadow from floods. In 1648 the Ouse outlet was reported 'no ways fit to sewer the level or for navigation' and in 1664 the Levels were again said to be 'hurtfully surrounded by water and urgently in need of drying'. Despite this, nothing, in fact, was done effectively to ameliorate the condition of the Levels for more than a century. Throughout the 18th century the Ouse valley was regularly inundated in winter and was often still flooded throughout the summer.[15] Less evidence for the state of the Arun and Adur valleys has survived but it is consistent with that further east. The sea is reported to have encroached on the Arun fisheries in 1478 and the Adur valley was repeatedly inundated in the late 14th century. In neither valley were major attempts made to relieve the situation in the 16th and 17th centuries.

As we have seen, the vast flocks of sheep on the Eastern Downs led to high yields of corn for productivity depended in the main directly on the number of sheep kept in the fold. This in turn depended on the amount of feed available during the winter. One way of keeping flocks large was the traditional practice in Sussex to over-winter tegs (sheep one year old) and lambs on farms in the Weald, distributing them at rates of 30-50 amongst the small clay farmers. The other way was to increase sowings of fodder and new grass crops. The principle of sowing leguminous fodder crops to provide winter food had been introduced during the Middle Ages. This practice was greatly expanded by the 17th century with the introduction of sainfoin and clover which was sown on cultivated land as part of the arable rotation. Tares (of the leguminous family) continued to be sown as a double quick-growing fodder crop, prior to wheat, an admirable practice which the 18th-century observer, Arthur Young, said was worth going 500 miles to see.

This increase in the use of fodder crops, which permitted heavier stocking of sheep, was largely at the expense of the traditional sheepwalk. For centuries little in the way of its breaking up could be undertaken because it would have harmed 'the run of the sheep'. In the early 17th century, when there were still many small producers on the Downs, the sheepwalk was so highly valued for sheep that stringent manorial regulations protected it. At Preston near Brighton tenants were fined for ploughing beyond the ancient bounds[16] and at Houghton even the encroachment of a rood on to the Down earned a penalty.[17] Sheep were the only animals allowed on the tenants' Downs during the winter from St Andrew's day (30 November) to some date in March. The Down was often rested for two months in spring as at West Blatchington where the sheep down was not used from March to May or at Eastbourne where the common sheep down was rested from Candlemas (2 February) until Whitsun, to allow the herbage to recuperate. Ewes and lambs were then grazing in young grain in the arable fields. On manors which lacked

**71** The probate inventory of John Browne, yeoman of Amberley, 1677. The record of produce suggests that Browne was sowing rotational grasses, probably clover or sainfoin, and continued the traditional practice of sowing vetches and peas to supply fodder and nitrogen. Many of the village farmers had more substantial possessions and their former thatched farmhouses spread closely along the narrow, winding street are still identifiable although now modernised residences. When, exceptionally, its common fields were enclosed by an Act of Parliament in 1803 a large and flourishing community of small corn-and-sheep farmers worked the land in the traditional manner. Streets would have been full of farm carts, livestock and dung, and echoing to voices of agricultural labourers and their children. In this century it has come to be accounted the loveliest of downland villages and 'as good a specimen of the traditional English village as one could wish to see', obsessively painted by artists, most famously Edward Stott, A.R.A. This had serious implications for those who cared for the village and the different kinds of countryside around it (see pp.66, 207).

early, well-drained grass, such as downland manors, it was a general practice to put ewes and lambs into the young corn until about mid-May. Eighteenth-century writers deplored this practice because it inevitably delayed the harvest. The same writers also argued that the side shoots (tillers) which grew from the grass as a result of grazing reduced the value of the crop but Downs farmers saw this as a way of increasing grain yields.[18] In summer both cattle and sheep were pastured on the common (tenantry) downs and at some places, as at Portslade, special Cow Downs were set aside. Wethers were kept only on manors such as Falmer and Preston which had exceptionally extensive pasture.

In winter about one ewe per acre was kept in the 17th century but as many as 780 ewes were kept on 231 acres at Northease,[19] 900 ewes on the 292 acres of Milton tenantry down,[20] stinted according to the amount of arable a farmer held. In West Sussex where pressure on the commons was less, as many as 40-60 sheep could be pastured for each yardland of arable (about 14 acres). In East Sussex between 25-30 sheep could be pastured for each yardland. Such stints of course were the maximum permitted to be stocked on the tenantry down and not necessarily the actual numbers grazed. Yet the constant complaints to the manor court concerning the over-stocking of the Downs and the repeated fines levied leave us in no doubt that copyholders generally pastured their maximum stint and even more if they could get away with it.[21]

The actual number of sheep stocked on the turf pasture of the Downs was crucially important because of the need to run the farming system sustainably. Stocking too hard would have degraded the herbage and thus depleted the quality of the wool. Yet without a full stock of sheep grass would have been so coarse that sheep would as soon have starved as eat the grass. Discovering the correct stocking ratio was one of the hardest lessons farmers learned from experience. In the first half of the 17th century there was evidence of widespread reductions of sheep stints on sheepwalk which suggested that the increase in flocks during the Tudor period had led to an impoverishment of the sward. At Offham, for example, the 14 farmers using the tenantry down agreed in 1632 to reduce the sheep stocking by one-fifth because the tenantry down would not 'keep the whole sum of sheep that are now laid'. There is also evidence of a widespread reduction of the stint on East Sussex manors in the first half of the 17th century.[22]

From the mid-17th century the introduction of new fodder crops permitted for the first time the breaking up of a 'maiden down', the term for the traditional sheep walk. At this period breaking up was called 'denchering', a term frequently encountered on maps of the South Downs (although sometimes wrongly rendered in the modern spelling of 'denture'). The word 'dencher' was a Sussex form of 'devonshire', that is to reclaim unimproved ground by the method of Devonshire farmers of the mid-17th century. This involved paring off the turf and burning the ashes which were ploughed in for extra fertility. Denchering permitted more arable cropping and the sowing of artificial grasses in the crop rotation. This is so at Alfriston where it occurred before 1690. At Telscombe also it is likely that fresh arable had been taken in from the down shortly before 1701 for a re-division of land was then made. Ninety acres of sheep down were added to the common-field arable at Kingston-by-Lewes in 1705 and the 'account of the denshire' shows that it was ploughed in three places and divided into dispersed strips like the rest of the common arable. The location of this innovation is still identifable on current Ordnance Survey 1: 25000 maps where 'denshire' is shown to have been corrupted to 'denture'.[24]

## The Western Downs

It is in the 16th and 17th centuries that differences in the management of pasture in the West and East Sussex downland become more apparent. A large amount of commonable woodland on the Western Downs was enclosed in the 16th and 17th centuries with the intention of intensifying commercial forestry at a time of acute demand for iron- and glass-working industries. Malecomb and the Middle Downs near East Dean were enclosed shortly before 1637 and over 400 acres of Singleton Forest and 600 acres in Charlton Forest were enclosed between 1558 and 1640.[25] Extensive areas of this enclosed land were planted up with beech in the 18th century, as was a good deal of sheep pasture in more open areas such as Up Marden, Woolavington and Cocking Downs. This process of enclosure can be seen as part of the rise of economic individualism at the expense of the more communal basis of peasant life in the Middle Ages. It also indicates that sheep farming for wool had become less profitable compared with cattle fattening, dairying and mutton rearing.

Moreover, in West Sussex the medieval practice of swine-fattening on beech mast on the wooded dip-slope of the Western Downs continued. In the parishes of Singleton and East Dean, beset with beech woods, 'hogg common' as well as pannage (fattening on beechmast) was claimed in part of Arundel Forest at the rate of 15 hogs for each yardland and five for each cotland (the holding of a cottager), in addition to 60 and 25 sheep respectively. At Offham in the Arun valley tenants could keep in common[26] 160 swine as well as 300 sheep on the woody pasture. Thus in actuality the wooded parts of the Western Downs were still functioning like a miniature Weald. The poorness of the sheep pastures in these wooded parts can be easily imagined and this resulted in a poor native breed of sheep. In summer great numbers of pigs were pastured in the Arun valley brookland. This practice continued into the late 18th and early 19th centuries when it surprised William Marshall. He had not encountered in any other part of England pigs grazing on marshes as between Pulborough and Arundel and also along the Western Rother. Beside their own stock the farmers of the Arun valley took in additional pigs for fattening. In a dry summer young hogs put on much flesh from nutritive plants but in a wet season many of them died of rot and survivors made little improvement. Hogweed (*Heracleum sphondylium*),[27] was well known as a nutritive food for swine as well as for cattle. Marshall remarked of the Arun valley:

During the spring and summer months, every labourer, who has industry, frugality and conveniency sufficient to keep a pig is seen carrying home, in the

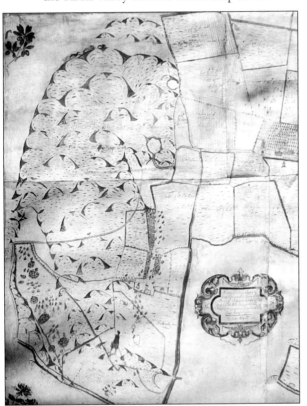

**72**   An extract from the map of Wolstonbury Hill, Danny, Hassocks by Robert Whitpaine (1666). Depicted, bottom, is a man shooting rabbits and (extreme top) greyhounds chasing a hare.

**73** Open-range grazing by pigs on the Western Downs, at Clapham Woods in 1983. It still continues at Tegleaze Farm.

evening, as he returns from his labour, a bundle of Hog weed … Children are sent out to collect it, in by roads and on hedge banks.

On the Downs fuel became in such short supply that it was the subject of stringent regulation. Manors where wood fuel had become seriously scarce by 1600 included Houghton and Amberley. It may seem strange that these places in the more wooded Western Downs should suffer in this way. The explanation seems to be that the iron- and glass-working industries in the nearby Weald had a destructive effect on common woods which forced up fuel prices to such an extent that the wood commons were being plundered illegally. At Houghton even the brushwood growing on the lands-ends of common-fields had to be brought under manorial regulation: cutting was permitted at specified times, provided that no oak or beech sapling fell to the scythe. Holm oak, Whitethorn and Blackthorn were pollarded for fencing and implements and beech was carefully preserved. Tree planting at Houghton even extended into gardens for each tenant early in the 17th century was required to plant 'four young ashes, elms or walnuts'. At Amberley the shortage of fuel put pressure on alternative sources, namely peat taken by regulation from the Wild Brooks and furze cut on the Downs.[28]

# Chapter Eight

# THE 'NEW FARMING' (*c.*1780–1880)

Over the one hundred years from about 1780 to 1880 sheep-and-corn farming on the South Downs was in its heyday. It helped to feed and clothe the sharply rising population which Gregory King estimated in 1688 to have been 5½ million in England and Wales but which rose to 9 million at the first census in 1801 and to 16 million in 1851, so assisting, by greatly increasing the supply of home-grown food, to relieve the threat to national security from rising food imports and the danger of famine in years of dearth, as in 1796 and 1800. As the Kaiser's submarines were to do a century or so later and as did Hitler's threatened blitzkrieg, so did Napoleon's aspirations reinforce official policy towards farming. John Holroyd, first Lord Sheffield, of Sheffield Park, Sussex, and a President of the Board of Agriculture, expressed this by committing support to larger farmers on the presumption that these 'mostly introduce improvements in the practice of agriculture, and uniformly grow much greater crops of corn, and produce more beef and mutton per acre than others of smaller capital'.[1]

William Cobbett expressed his abhorrence at this official suppression of the small farmer in clear, bell-like sentences. Much of his invective was addressed to the Ellmans, especially to John Ellman, junior, who farmed near his father at Southover, near Lewes, whom he called an 'agricultural ass' for allegedly calling small farmers 'peasantry'. He grieved that 'large farmers grew over the small farmers by degrees until they totally destroyed them, just as regularly as the strong plants overtop and finally kill the weak ones'. The new tenant then made the old his labourer, added another hundred a year to his profits, and reduced the farmer and his family to the labouring poor'.[2] He attacked the 'Scotch economists' and influential farmers,

**74** William Cobbett, the most pugnacious of mortals, was untiring in his defence of the small farmer and agricultural labourer.

such as the Ellmans, who accepted falsely, Cobbett thought, that large farms produced more in proportion than smaller ones. He noted that, indeed, a large farm of 1,000 acres with 50 labourers and 50 horses would produce more marketable food than 10 small ones of 100 acres each but 'if we consider that on 10 farms there are 10 wives and 40 children, all bestowing labour, and poultry and other livestock cared for by them, not omitting bees and eggs, the small farms far exceeded the output of the larger 'even leaving out the good living of the 10-farm system'. Cobbett added that, even if it were true that large farms produced more than an aggregate of small ones, 'what a mighty mischief' had been caused by adherence to the doctrine, which would have been unthinkable to the more caring society, of forty years earlier.[3]

While Cobbett raged at this in his *Political Register* and in speeches up and down the country, hundreds of small renting farmers had already fallen in the Downs and more were to follow. It was an issue which led to a memorable meeting between Cobbett and local farmers at Lewes in 1822. The doughty defender of the small farmer advanced their case in a speech in a building opposite the *White Hart* inn. On his arrival, it was moved that Cobbett should be put out of the room, whereupon the free-speaking man arose 'That they might see the man they had to put out. Fortunately for themselves, not one of them was tempted to approach me. They were like the mice that resolved that a bell should be put around the cat's neck'.[4]

Yet the vigorous attempt to save the small farmer on the Downs was to be one of Cobbett's many glorious failures. On account of government policies, and various social and economic factors, small farmers were squeezed out of their share of the Downs. In most parts of England, development along these lines hinged on the central issue of enclosure and the General Enclosure Act of 1801 was designed to hasten the desired changes in land occupation. In Sussex, as we have noted, such changes had occurred much earlier. Almost all the common-fields with small intermixed strips had been brought under individual occupation from the 15th century by agreement. The main period of consolidation had taken place in the 16th and 17th centuries. The final *coup de grace* for the little farm, which had earlier provided a living for a single family for centuries, occurred when the capitalist farmer with new ideas of farming was turning himself into a mass-producer of wool and food for the big towns. In this process from the 1780s many rural communities were finally decimated and the Downs turned into a factory for bread, meat and wool.

This was accomplished mainly by the enlargement of tenant farms on estates progressively built up by greater landowners,

**75** John Ellman, the leading improver of Southdown sheep, farmer at Glynde near Lewes.

generation by generation, as opportunity arose. Eventually such grandees became the sole, or the leading landowner of whole parishes. The Abergavennys of Eridge Castle promoted for years their 'invasion' of the Ouse valley south of Lewes. Simultaneously, the Pelhams of Stanmer purchased successively parts of Falmer and Plumpton, and the Trevors of Glynde Place ultimately became the owners of several adjacent parishes. Further west, the Earl of Egremont greatly enlarged his estate, purchasing farms, for example, as far east as the Adur valley and Brighton. The Dukes of Norfolk also engaged in territorial expansion as did the third and fourth Dukes of Richmond, though in the Western Downs the harsh commercialism of the Eastern Downs was less evident.[5]

A most important consequence of the rise of the great landed estate was the rapid disappearance of the last remaining small farmers, some of whom still occupied rather fragmented farms as a relic of the common-field system. Landlords systematically enfranchised the small copyholds and added them to larger tenancies, the aim being to create tenant farms of at least 300 acres, rising to 700 and more.

76   Arthur Young.

This lurch to big-scale farming on the Downs contrasted with the fate of the Weald which, in the main did not appeal to the capitalist farmer. The Sussex Weald was handicapped by a lack of good roads, land too hilly and broken for large-scale tillage and the heavy, tenacious soils. The farming system was not fully commercialised and remained a way of making a living directly out of the soil rather than a business where the farmer thought in terms of cash, profits and losses. Whereas the Downs' farmers had for several centuries an eager acceptance of innovation in farming, the Weald retained its age-old character of ill-managed, heavily wooded, wet land, broken up into small fields shaded with oaks on an unkind soil. The under-stocked and under-worked farms had depressed observers from Gervase Markham in 1638 onwards. In 1798 the agriculturalist William Marshall thought the 'roadless' Weald 'disgusting to ride over and most discouraging to farm on'. Riding in the Petworth district he saw scarcely a head of livestock worth looking at and declared the farming misapplied, crying out, 'What a field for improvement!', a cause which few thought economically worthwhile to carry out.[6]

## 'Long live the Southdowns'

The great landowners had a ready acceptance of improvement in farming techniques and products and a long-term vision of prosperity based on their wealth and political power. As in the 13th and 16th centuries, so in the late 18th and 19th centuries, downland farmers were again in the vanguard of the agricultural practice of the day. One of the most spectacular changes was the improvement of the indigenous Southdown breed of sheep from about 1788 which became preferred to any other Down breed of sheep in Great Britain and ultimately internationally renowned. The Sussex farmer who was the leading instigator of this remarkable achievement was John Ellman, a tenant farmer on the Trevor estate at Glynde. He was born at Hartfield, on the edge of Ashdown Forest, in 1753, the son of Richard Ellman. Typically of Wealden farmers who had experience, initiative and capital, his father moved to Glynde for a larger farm. John Ellman succeeded to his father's tenancy and progressively took on additional land, eventually running a farm of nearly 1,200 acres centred on the fine complex of buildings in the fold immediately west of Glynde Place.[7] Before Ellman's efforts at improvement there were apparently two distinct breeds of sheep on the Downs, separated by the Adur valley (p.65).[8] The agriculturist William Marshall corroborated Gilbert White's remarks, noting 'a wild-looking, base-bred' sort of sheep on the Western Downs 'having the same mongrel appearance as the mountain sheep of the West of England'.[9] He concluded that these were one of the old native breeds and then peculiar to the Western Downs, inferior to Southdowns because of poorer chalk grassland intermixed with woodland and scrub and the want of watered meadows, which was greatly to the advantage of the Eastern Downs. East of the Adur the Southdown breed was in exclusive possession. Although Ellman lacked education, social standing and hereditary connections, he transformed his flock of Southdowns between 1788 and 1829 from merely a folding animal into one giving an improved fleece and better mutton, so attracting widespread attention.

Sir John Sinclair, President of the Board of Agriculture, considered that the perfect sheep should have the fleece of the Spanish Merino, the carcase of Bakewell's Leicesters and the hardiness of the Southdown. No such animal being available, he pronounced the Southdown as the next best.[10] Ellman was particularly pleased to have bred Southdowns to bear wool more nearly like Merino than any other English breed. Its high quality wool

**77** Successive stages in the improvement of Southdown sheep. *Top*: the unimproved native Southdown; *centre*: a Southdown of Ellman's breeding; *bottom*: the Southdown of the 1930s. The Southdown breed is now an endangered species, barely one thousand being in existence.

gained favourable publicity when Sir John Throgmorton dinner-dressed in a coat which on the same morning had been wool on Southdowns' backs, it being sheared, woolwashed, carded, spun, woven, scoured, fulled, sheared, dyed, dressed and then tailored into a coat between sunrise and seven p.m. on the same day![11] It is fascinating to examine successive illustrations of rams and ewes bred by Ellman. By selective breeding they had become plumper and woollier by 1788, when Arthur Young first mentioned them enthusiastically, but they retained their speckled face and legs.[12] Twenty years later the sheep were tending to the grey, stocky, box-like appearance of today and their fleece had become thicker and finer. After Ellman's death the breed continued to evolve.[13] The speckled face and rather long legs went and sheep took on the now familiar pale-brown colour of Mrs. Coleman's Sompting flock or that of the Humphries' of East Dean near Singleton.

Apart from Ellman, who was presented on retirement with a silver tureen surmounted by the figure of a Southdown sheep by 186 noblemen and landowners from all over Britain, many agriculturists did much to raise the standard of the Southdowns nationally. Arthur Young junior mentioned Tyrrel of Landport near Lewes who sent the breed to Norfolk in 1791 and Young's father thought Miss Hay's flock at Glyndebourne as amongst the finest he had seen. Among other notable breeders was Thomas Ellman of Old Erringham Farm, Shoreham, John Ellman's cousin. Further afield, Thomas Coke, of Holkham Hall in Norfolk (afterwards Earl of Leicester) was outstanding, as was the Duke of Bedford at Woburn and, from the 1830s, Jonas Webb of Cambridgeshire.[14] The 4th Duke of Richmond, later President of the Royal Agricultural Society, had a prominent role in raising the breed and the patronage of King George III, 'the farmer king', who bred Southdowns at Windsor, was crucial to its success. Lord Sheffield, who had a model farmery at Sheffield Park, was also a great stalwart: he initiated the Lewes Wool Fair in 1786 and was its President for many years, an office later taken over by the 4th Duke of Richmond. The involvement of so many great landowners with the Southdown breed conferred from the very beginning a certain social status on flockmasters.

From the successive editions of the county agricultural reports published by the Board of Agriculture may be traced the triumphant progress of the handsome little Southdowns at the expense of other native breeds all over England. Marshall noted in 1798 that the breed was 'contending for the possession of the enviable heights of the Wiltshire Downs'. By 1811, when he again made comment, the old Wiltshire horned breed had been completely ousted by their rivals:[15] 'One may travel fifty or a hundred miles across them [the Wiltshire Downs] without seeing any other breed of sheep'. One farmer near Salisbury took the drastic step of slaughtering his whole native flock and flinging the bones down a well.[16] Vancouver reported in 1805 that the Southdowns had overrun Hampshire and were beginning to occupy 'even the remotest heaths' of Surrey. They had also overrun Kent (except Romney Marsh which was too wet for them). Mavor's *Berkshire* (1813) mentioned that they were 'very properly' gaining ground there and Arthur Young noted that by 1813 the breed had 'become fashionable' in Hertfordshire. He also claimed to have

**78**   Shepherd's hut, Weald and Downland Museum.

introduced the first Southdowns into Suffolk in 1784 where they ultimately supplanted the native Norfolk breed, although patriots considered him an enemy for 'changing the best breed in England for a race of rats'.[17] This native breed was no less fortunate in Norfolk itself. It was an ancient breed of hardy, long-legged animals, semi-wild, and ideal for foraging the poor bleak heaths for which it had been evolved. Once the heaths were enclosed and intensively cultivated with succulent root crops and grasses, the native breed gave way to Southdowns eagerly introduced by the greatest landowner, Thomas Coke. His column at Holkham, a monument to his high farming, contains low reliefs of Southdown sheep at its base. Eventually Norfolk Horns became no more than local curiosities. Marshall has recorded that when he left Norfolk in 1782 'the Norfolk breed was in full and quiet possession of the country … As to the Southdowns they were then grazing peaceably on their native hills … I was not aware of the existence of such a breed'.[18] By 1804 the triumph of the breed was complete, but Marshall, although always highly impressed by them as arable upland folding sheep, contended that the improvement of the Norfolks which had long been naturalised to the soil and climate, would have been a better proposition:[19] 'Had the same exertions, the same talking, the same bragging, the same puffing, the same showing, and one half or a much smaller proportion of the expense that has been bestowed on Southdowns and Leicesters had been judiciously laid out in improving the native breed'.[20] Wade-Martins has recently filled out more of the story of the Norfolks' demise by demonstrating that pure-bred Southdowns were mainly confined to eastern Norfolk on larger

**79** Farmer W.D. Passmore with his winning flock of Southdowns, in 1938 at Applesham Farm. Lancing Clump is on the horizon.

estates, whereas the run-of-the-mill farmers tended to improve their flocks by the cheaper method of half breeds, of which the Southdowns-cross-Norfolk was the most successful.[21]

Although the Southdowns were becoming the progenitor of all the other English Down breeds and famous for revolutionary sheep improvements in New Zealand, Australia, the Argentine, Canada and the USA, not all agriculturists were convinced that their improvement made them superior to the old native breed or to other old established ones. Marshall observed that 'For the profitable purpose of browsing bleak, barren hills by day and manuring arable lands by night, their fitness is no more. It were as fitting to put an Arabian courser into the shafts of a dung cart as a delicate, high-blooded, fashionable 'South Downer'[22] into a sheep fold.' Vancouver argued that the taller, long-legged sheep of the Western Downs coped better with the coarser pastures than the improved Southdowns which were shorter and stockier.

Many breeders of Southdowns were also prominent in the improvement of the native red Sussex cattle. John Ellman, for example, was one of these, as was the 3rd Earl of Egremont at Petworth. Several farmers in the neighbourhood of Eastbourne, blessed with access to the Pevensey Marshes, were also notable. Breeders of Sussex cattle acknowledged that they ranked below Devons and Herefords in esteem and responded to the challenge of improving them to the standard of their sheep. This was not to be realised. In the depression following the end of the Napoleonic Wars, the breed failed to sustain the attention it had enjoyed earlier. The dual purpose of the breed was the major obstacle. Traditionally Sussex cattle had been put under the yoke for ploughing at about three years of age, worked for four years or so and then sold off to a grazier for fattening. The re-emergence of the breed in the 1870s was largely due to the decline of oxen as beasts of burden. Edward Cane of Berwick then made a great name for himself as a breeder of Sussex cattle as well as for sheep and Alfred Henson of Angmering took over on Cane's retirement. The revival was again checked by the long farming depression in the late 19th century but James Gwynne of Wootton Manor was still keeping a notable herd into the 1920s.[23]

## Arable Farming

When the Rev. Arthur Young wrote his *Agriculture of Sussex* in 1813 he observed the great increase in the number of sheep being kept on the Downs between Lewes and Eastbourne.[24] He assessed the total number of adult sheep in the whole of the Sussex Downs to have been about 240,000 and of this number he estimated that about 150,000 were kept on the Eastern Downs between Steyning and Eastbourne. This vast flock in the Eastern Downs was at a stocking rate of about 1½ ewes per acre, which he thought to be the highest in the United Kingdom and 'one of the singular curiosities in the husbandry of England'. This district had not only the finest wool production on the Downs but the immense numbers of sheep led to higher yields of corn, for, as previously mentioned (p.62), this depended in the main directly on the number of sheep kept in the fold. This in turn was dependent on the amount of feed available during the winter. This was facilitated by the sowing of new grasses and the general introduction of the turnip in the 18th century, and also the growing of other fodder crops, such as lucerne, which was extensively cultivated around Eastbourne. Each of the new fodder crops tended to encroach on old chalk grassland. This led to a lively controversy as to the amount of down that could appropriately be broken up.

Mavor considered that unimproved down in Berkshire should remain at its existing extent and warned that indiscriminate ploughing-up would reduce farms to utter ruin after the first

**80** Sussex oxen on the Downs at Southwick, late 19th century. An etching by Col. Goff, R.E.

seven years or so with falling yields.[25] A similar line was taken by Thomas Davis of Wiltshire who supported the breaking-up of down on strong red land, i.e. on soil from deposits lying on the chalk itself, but deplored the general breaking-up for higher rents.[26] Vancouver, author of a Hampshire agricultural report, was of the same opinion.[27]

The most important contribution to the debate from a Sussex landowner came from Charles Goring of Wiston, famed as the boy-planter of Chanctonbury Ring.[28] Writing a Prize Essay to the Board of Agriculture at the height of the food crisis of 1801 he urged the intensification of arable on existing farmland, rather than the reclamation of wastes which would have no immediate effect on food production. As to old chalk grassland, he emphasised the extreme length of time that would be needed for old turf to restore itself once it had been broken up. He regarded the chalk sward as a sacred possession not to be violated 'to gratify an idle curiosity or risk a visionary experiment' and thought that the old farming lore delivered down from father to son from time immemorial should not be disregarded.

Despite Vancouver's and Goring's advice extensive areas of the sheep walk were ploughed up in the East Hampshire Downs and Sussex in 1800 and 1801 when wheat was at an unprecedented price, though most of this was laid back to pasture when prices fell sharply when the war ended in 1815. Even after the lapse of thirty years the sward was valued at only half its original price, so slowly did the thyme rich turf recover that had taken centuries to evolve. More than half a century later, the distinction between the original down and former fields was still clearly apparent. W.H. Hudson could still identify derelict ploughland which shepherds avoided as it had been colonised by grasses which had not formed the original, close-knit, nutritious sward:[29] 'This kind of land, spoilt by the plough, is said by shepherds to be "sickly"; and the grass that grows on it, little in quantity and poor in quality, they call it "gratton" grass'. To this day, in low evening light can be seen on many downland farms traces of plough lines on exceptionally steep hillsides that have never been ploughed since the Napoleonic Wars. With the recovery of agriculture from the 1840s down was again broken up. Lord Gage at Alciston was active in this as were the Gorings of Kingston-by-Lewes, but it never reached the extreme scale of Wiltshire or Dorset, presumably because the down was much more heavily stocked with sheep than in those counties.

The most successful ploughing-up was on red loam soils occurring on top of the chalk, as at Applesham Farm north of Lancing where the tenant Francis Gell was responsible for converting much of the sheep down to arable at the beginning of the century.[30] Much of the old chalk grassland on heavier soils plastering the Downs was acid and had to be improved by chalking to mellow and sweeten it for corn production. The scrub was first grubbed up and the surface chalked in the autumn. The raw chalk took over a year to dissolve, sometimes longer, before it could be ploughed into the soil. Chalkers dug pits some 20-30 feet deep, chambered at the bottom, the tops protected by brushwood and hazel rods. The chalk was raised in buckets by means of a simple winch operated by means of a cart wheel. Gell at Applesham laid on the exceptionally large amount of 16 barrows to a square perch (the equivalent to about 160 cartloads to an acre) on as much as 150 acres over a period of twenty years. A single pit would have chalked between four and five acres. On the present-day landscape the sites of Gell's old chalk pits still survive as large circular hollows on these 'redlands', showing up like little green islands in a sea of corn. Similar groups of old pits are observable at numerous other sites in the Eastern Downs as on the Alciston and Berwick Downs. The efficacy of this long-term improvement is illustrated at Applesham by recent soil analyses showing that the beneficial effects of liming were still apparent in the 1960s.[31]

The Ordnance Survey plans of 25 inches to a mile from *c*.1875 mark the end of prosperous arable farming on the Downs. A series of bad harvests and an increase in the import of cheap cereals was followed by the catastrophic fall in the price of corn and wool. Sheep folding continued, but whereas in former times it had been mainly on fallow, by 1850 it was on green crops or roots, so that sheep depended much less on the traditional down herbage for nourish-

**81** Improving fertility of acid soils on the chalk by applying large quantities of raw chalk has left abandoned chalk pits dotted over the surface of the Downs, which in summer are fascinating little green islands in a sea of ripening corn. This scene at Applesham Farm near Lancing is reproduced all over the higher downland.

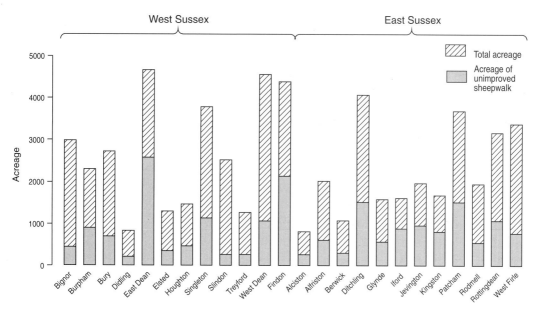

**82**   Unimproved downland by parishes. Dates based on Tithe Maps (1838-1844).

ment, consequently permitting still more arable cultivation on the Downs. The last wave of improvement on the Downs before 1939 resulted from the introduction of basic slag.[32] W.J. Passmore at Applesham, who had tenanted the farm from 1901, experimented with basic slag on 40 acres of poor downland pasture, drawing on its successful use at his former farm at Stratford-on-Avon, where supplies from chemical works were freely available. He eventually adopted an application of basic slag and kainit (chloride of potash) and treated all his downland in turn. The outcome was that so many cattle galloped over the rich herbage instead of poverty-stricken grass that it was reminiscent of American ranches. Professor Somerville, of Oxford University, also carried out successful experiments with basic slag imported by ship from Middlesbrough on 500 acres of down at Poverty Bottom at Denton near Newhaven just before the First World War.[33] Technology and chemistry were thus at last increasing man's power as never before to re-shape the appearance and texture of the Downs. The introduction of artificial fertilisers in the form of basic slag, and earlier of guano and kainit, proved to be the death knell of folding, which died out abruptly after a usage of several millennia. The disadvantage of folding from a butcher's point of view was the deterioration in the condition of sheep braving bleak hills by day and manuring arable lands by night after long journeys up and down the hills. By the mid-19th century it was accepted that the cost of the deterioration exceeded in value the return of manure. Sheep were uncomfortable when folded densely, especially on a second night needed for a 'good dressing' of manure.

Lewes, the chief market town of East Sussex, was in many ways the centre of the 'new farming'. Around 1800 the town filled to capacity on market days with farmers, their families and their animals and produce, and at the great events in the farming year every inn was full of leading farmers, landowners and distinguished visitors from all over England and abroad. The greatest occasions were the Lewes Wool Fair founded by Lord Sheffield and the sheep and cattle fair of the Sussex Agricultural Society, largely instigated by the 3rd Lord Egremont, which Young noted was junior in England only to the agricultural societies of London and Bath.

Prizes presented by Lord Egremont and other landowners were enthusiastically competed for by Sussex farmers, judged by an elite of 'improvers' including J.P. Gorringe of Kingston Buci, an esteemed breeder of cattle, W. Borrer of Hurstpierpoint, J. Farncombe of Stoneham, N. Hall of Southwick, F. Gell of Applesham and G. Payne of Lewes.[34] Gracing the events would be Lord Egremont and several other nationally-famous persons such as the Duke of Bedford, Lord Russell and Thomas Coke, Earl of Leicester. Arthur Young was a frequent attender and Sir John Sinclair, President of the Board of Agriculture, and Sir Joseph Banks, the distinguished botanist, put in appearances. Such great annual gatherings were in the presence of the Prince of Wales, or other royalty, and eminent foreign visitors including the Stadtholder of Germany. So little had improvement pervaded the Weald that hardly a single Wealden farmer competed for prizes or was a member of the organising committees. After judging was concluded, up to 200 or more persons would dine at the *Star Inn*, the oldest inn in the town (its grand staircase from Slaugham Place survives in the Town Hall subsequently built on the site), or at the *White Hart*, the *Bear* and other inns. The excited talk of the day included John Ellman's regular prize-winning successes (the rules of the agricultural society had to be framed to allow other farmers to win against his sheep), or of reports of prodigious yields of grain in the Downs such as the 40 loads of wheat produced by a tenant from 31 acres on Lord Pelham's farm at Bishopstone which earned him £700 profit. He took another six fine wheat crops off this land before sowing with peas to clear weeds in readiness for the next wheat crop. Although such yields were exceptional, all farmers (but not labourers) could look forward to higher productivity and increased prosperity.[35]

**83** The demolition of *The Star* inn has left *The White Hart* as the one survivor of the greater Lewes inns. The Georgian front disguises an ancient half-timbered structure most evident on the topmost floor (*c*.1868).

Pride of place as promoter and enabler of agricultural reform in Sussex is held by George O'Brien Wyndham, 3rd Earl of Egremont (1751-1837). According to Arthur Young, his greatest admirer, this remarkable man, 'of the highest rank and fortune', conducted his own estates during his long life 'upon the great scale in the highest style of improvement'. He also expended much energy and money in financing canal navigation, improved roads, livestock innovations, extending knowledge of new plants and implements and generously helping people in all walks of life. At his sole expense Lord Egremont made the river Rother navigable from its junction with the Arun as far as Midhurst and by a branch to Petworth, so opening up a large tract of land which could be supplied from the lime pits at Houghton and Bury.[36] Under him Petworth House was like a large inn with agricultural writers, breeders, yeomen and gentlemen farmers meeting under the same roof, coming and going as they pleased. Ellman repeatedly had assistance from Egremont in establishing the Southdown breed of sheep.

**X** The Findon Wattle House on Nepcote Green was built in 1803 to store wooden hurdles and wattle fences used for constructing sheep folds at the historic annual sheep fair. Cottage tenements occupied the ends of the building and the upper storey. A charitable trust has been formed with the object of preserving the Grade II listed building and turning it into a community centre.

**XI** The Palladian-style brick box of Fox Hall at Charlton near Singleton, the original home of the famed Charlton Hunt, was probably designed by Lord Burlington's architectural assistant, Roger Morris, for the Duke of Richmond in 1730. It functioned as a club for hunt members. A small, elegant hall and staircase lead to a magnificent dining-cum-bedroom above. The Landmark Trust has rescued and restored this building and lets it for self-catering holidays.

**XII** The Cuckmere valley, painted by Dennis Rothwell-Bailey. (See pp.125-6 for a distinctly different atmosphere at Alfriston.)

**XIII** A symbolic landscape of the Eastern Downs by Rowland Hilder, 1955.

## Barbarity

Despite these many innovations and experiments, downland farmers also adhered to farming techniques and equipment which had changed little over centuries. The reason for such survivals was more than mere conservatism: it reflected long-tried ways of farming. Most of the ploughing and other farm tasks continued to be performed by oxen as they had been from time immemorial, though during the 19th century the native Red Sussex breed was gradually replaced by Welsh black runts bought from drovers, or by horses. Richard Jefferies wrote that there was hardly a 'more imposing spectacle than of these quiet beasts of burden stepping slowly forward before the plough, against a background of grey sea and sky, their huge horns sweeping forward in generous curves'. Scarcely less impressive was the way they toiled up and down the cornfields dragging behind them the huge, lumbering, blue wagons heaped high with sheaves or stood immovable beside rapidly rising stacks. The illusion of ancientness that came from the dignity and kindly strength of the working ox produced a kind of scriptural simplicity, an effect heightened by the sight of

**84**　George O'Brien Wyndham, 3rd Earl of Egremont.

the primitive wooden yoke and the bent ashen 'bow' which passed under the animals' throat and the long iron chain connecting the yoke to the plough or whatever machine was in use. As these patient creatures came homewards at nightfall down the grassy slopes with noiseless feet, the only sounds of their progress were their soft breathing and the not unmusical cadence of the swinging chain. Not until the end of the 19th century were oxen gradually replaced by horses; the last team of oxen was working at Exceat as late as the 1930s. Their cheapness to feed, followed by sale as meat, and their ability to pull the plough steadily uphill and downhill at an even pace without pause, unlike horses, accounted for the long-standing preference for oxen.

Something of the individuality of the Downs preserved in the working oxen was also to be found in the type of plough they dragged. Richard Jefferies noted that the South Downs plough could scarcely have been invented: it must have evolved bit by bit. It was similar, with regional differences, to the Kentish turn-wrest plough. There was perhaps towards the end of the 19th century not another home-made implement of Old English husbandry still in use in England. It was made of many different pieces, chiefly wooden, shaped by hand by the ploughwright in his own workshop on the farm, and not 'struck out a hundred a minute by irresistible machinery ponderously impressing its will on iron as on a seal on wax and all exactly alike', but shaped by eye and hand and by long experience of a craftsman.[37]

The perfect adaptability of the plough to the curved lines and smoothness of the Downs was seen as a perfect example of man's adaptation to the land. The fields it had to work in were for the most part on a slope, often thickly strewn with flints which jarred and broke wood or fractured iron. The soil varied in depth from two or three inches on upper parts, scarcely enough to turn a furrow, deepening to nine inches on the 'bottom' land so that the ploughshare had to be set for these various depths of soil. As the soil was so well drained, no drain furrows were needed, nor was it necessary for land to be thrown up in 'lands' as in the clays of the Weald, that is ploughed in a series of drain furrows and ridges to throw off surplus rainwater. All these conditions were met by the wheeled turn-wrest plough which turned soil over the same way both uphill and downhill, so leaving the sowing surface perfectly level, which later suited the threshing machines better than the 'ridge and furrow' of the Weald. The forewheels (with spokes of wood with an iron rim) kept the plough more stable on slopes. When the oxen arrived at the top of a field they stopped while the ploughman lifted off the rhode bat (curved ashwood) that held the coulter in position and removed the tuck bolt holding it firmly in place to the other side. When the rhode bat was in position again the ploughman held the coulter on the opposite side of the share, so that it turned the soil the same way back as on the previous furrow.[37] This only took a few moments. The process was repeated at the end of the next furrow, and so on.

So perfect was the handiness of this plough that South Down farmers such as John Ellman of Glynde rejected criticisms of it by the Rev. Arthur Young and other agricultural writers and claimed that no new iron plough could beat it.[38] South Downs farmers were, however, apparently guilty in using the same ox team of six or eight oxen for pulling even a light wheel-less plough or when thin soils were ploughed. Young also considered that the ploughs were unsuitable for the tenacious soil on the scarp-foot bench, where they worked with such difficulty that the soil adhered almost like pitch. Here, wailed Young, farmers work with a turn-wrest and with ten or even twelve oxen and two drivers and sometimes cannot plough more than half an acre a day. On Ellman's farm he found heavy weights had been hooked to the tail of the plough so that it could be used for deep ploughing. This he denounced as barbarously unmechanical.

**85**   The Sussex plough.

## The Water Problem

Although downland turf made prime grazing for sheep, there was one major defect: a shortage of water on account of the lack of surface drainage. This was resolved by means of artificial dewponds constructed with great skill, of which the tradition has been almost lost. These are of uncertain age but it is probable that they have been on the Downs ever since they were first grazed. A saucer-like depression was scoured out, up to eight feet deep. The chalk removed was built up around the pan to form a slight lip. The floor was then covered in straw alternately with puddled clay brought by wagon from the Weald, each layer being thoroughly beaten down by pushing heavy beaters over the clay until a smooth surface was obtained. Two inches of burnt lime followed, to prevent worms puncturing the clay, and another layer of straw added. Finally, a layer of rough local earth was piled on top. This was thought to cause condensation of dew or mist, although actually the main source of water appears to have been rain. Care was taken that cattle and horses did not use the pond and break the lining. Dewponds intended for cattle had a layer of flints to prevent this. Restored dewponds are now usually made with a concrete base, as at Newtimber, where the National Trust are restoring three dewponds to their former glory as good habitats for the great crested newt and other rare amphibians. The warden tells of the shepherds' jealous guard of their dewponds: one in a row with a neighbouring shepherd took an axe to another shepherd's pond and it has been dry ever since.[39]

**86** *Top*: the village well, East Marden (depth to water: 100 feet); *middle*: the village well-house, Up Waltham (depth to water approximately 98 feet), constructed of flint and galleting; *bottom*: the donkey wheel at Saddlescombe Farm near Brighton (well 150 feet deep). A similar donkey wheel existed at Stanmer drawing up water 252 feet below.

# Chapter Nine

# TRADITIONAL FARM BUILDINGS AND RURAL LIFE
## (*c.*1780–*c.*1880)

The many ancient farm buildings on downland farms are richly eloquent of old rural ways of life. Amongst the most prized are the great old aisled barns such as those at Alciston, Sullington, Charlton, near Steyning, Glynde, Hamsey and Saddlescombe, north of Brighton. Such barns have thrown open their large side doors to tens of thousands of wagons drawn by oxen or horses, laden with corn sheaves, pockets of fleeces, sacks of turnips, potatoes or fertiliser. Their old beams have echoed to the thump of countless hand flails on the wooden threshing floor, blackened with age and polished by the beating 'till it had grown as slippery and as rich in hue as the state-room floors of an Elizabethan mansion'. They have witnessed uncountable shearings, harvest suppers and other special occasions such as weddings

**87**  This model range of farm buildings was erected in the early 19th century on Applesham Farm when it was tenanted from the Leconfield Estate, Petworth, itself the possessor of a famed model farmery in Stag Park.

in days when almost the entire population of a village was employed on the main farm in some way or another. They have also sheltered generation after generation of swallows from South Africa. Some of these great barns are medieval in age and have a ground plan resembling a parish church and vie with it in antiquity, though the barns are much larger. The roofs are braced and tied in huge timber collars, curves and diagonals. They are far more boldly cut and intricate than in modest downland churches and are supported by great wooden piers resting on masonry or brick, whilst the flintwork walls are perforated by lancet openings to give the right amount of ventilation.

A number of downland farms have particularly good groupings of old buildings. At one, the further door of the 17th-century aisled barn opens out into the old shearing-yard and to an early 19th-century round-house originally containing a horse-wheel which was used to drive a chaff-cutter and, later, an early threshing machine. On its other side is a long-range of purpose-built buildings, erected by the Petworth estate, containing the wheelwright's shop, the carpenter's shop, the wheelwright's, the smithy and stores for implements, sacks and hurdles. At the far end of this range, once a model of efficient design, is an old wagon lodge beneath a granary, where we have to imagine rows of blue-painted wagons and tip-carts, brought in nightly to protect them from the rain which rotted and warped their timbers. The granary had pulleys and levers to wind up sacks from the ground but it was usual for the farmer and his men to carry the corn harvest on their backs in a long succession of four bushel sacks up a long flight of steps. Opposite was another range of buildings housing the cowshed, ox-stalls, fatting-pens and byres for Red Sussex cattle. The flintstone farmhouse itself is a fascinating place with stone

**88**  Saddlescombe Farm in the saddle of the Downs north of Brighton. *Background:* stable and granary, mid- to late 18th-century; *left:* corn barn, 18th-century (Listed Building, Grade II); *right:* upstairs granary and cart shed barn (Listed Building, Grade II).

**89**   John Ellman's Barn, Glynde.

window frames under a centuries-old high-pitched roof in Horsham stone with antique gables. Entering by the side entrance we find its former kitchen still largely furnished with traditional plain deal furniture where smock-frocked farm labourers clumped in with their loud-sounding hobnailed boots and dined cheerily at the tables up to the late 19th century, just as their predecessors had done for centuries. The brick wing, added to the farmhouse in the late 19th century by the Petworth estate, looks south towards the sea and overlooks a smooth lawn, flower-beds and a large walled kitchen garden, altogether a comfortable and dignified home for a well-off yeoman or gentleman tenant farmer in the heyday of farming in the South Downs. Such farm complexes give an agreeable sense of careful planning and contrast in beauty and character with the haphazard concrete and asbestos buildings which have replaced them.

The farmhouse, which gives indications of the standing, prosperity and comfort of the occupying farmer and his family, can be regarded as representative of the larger traditional downland farmhouse. Other examples come readily to mind, such as Upper Stoneham Farm near Lewes (painted by Grimm when it wore a quite different appearance) and Milton Street Farm, or Court Farm, Alciston. Newhouse Farm near West Firle (famous for taking Duncan Grant and David Garnett as agricultural workers in the First World War) takes its name from the large mid-Victorian building added to the more modest older parts. All over the downland, in fact, are signs of a great rebuilding of farmsteads on more elegant and comfortable lines in the first half of the 19th century.

Arthur Young helps to fill in details of the style of life of a Sussex downland yeoman farmer at the rather earlier period of the late 18th century. There was a large, roomy, clean kitchen with a rousing wood fire on the hearth and a ceiling hung with smoked back and hams. A small room for the farmer and his family opened on to the kitchen, with glass on the door, or the wall, for seeing that things were 'going right' in the servants' quarters. When company was in the farmhouse, the fire was lit in the well-furnished parlour. At table was a great plenty of plain things, with a bottle of good port after dinner and at least a hogshead of it in the cellar. The bailiff, if one was kept, also dined at table with the family. In the stable was a nag, for the farmer's own riding, but not good enough for hunting. For carriage, he and his wife used a one-horse chaise. On the bookshelf were some books of piety and a little common literature. Young's periodical, *Annals of Agriculture*, was not there as often as he thought it ought to have been. The downland farmer at this time would thus appear to have lived comfortably, but modestly.[1]

High Farming on the Downs has also left a remarkable legacy of flint-built barns and other buildings on the remoter parts of the great farms. These distantly-built barns are little used now and are falling into dereliction. They resulted from the breaking-up of old sheep pasture and usually bear the name of the parent farm on the centuries-old arable in the valley below. When erected at the end of the 18th century or in the early to mid-19th century the barns were busy places for sheltering cattle, especially oxen who worked the downland then being reclaimed for arable, it being too distant for them to plod up and down, to and from the farm below. They also stored the heavier corn harvests and provided the new lands with a return of their own dung and saved the carriage of corn to the distant home barns. They tend to conform to a standard pattern of an enclosed yard where cattle ate barley and oat straw in winter, and 'hovels' at the side for shelter. From these hilltop barns one would have had a good view of the many ox- and horse-teams ploughing, harrowing or gathering in the harvest, the sight that so gladdened the eyes of William Cobbett.

Not all the remote barns were built for oxen. Some were built for 'cotting' sheep in bad winters (a practice which improved the fleece), and for lambing, shearing, foot-paring, culling and selecting. A fine example, built in 1845, is New Barn on Housedean Farm near Falmer. It comprises a hay barn for winter feed, two sheep pens with shelters and a stone-built shepherd's hut provided with a chimney. It has recently been excellently restored by Brighton Council.

At the main farm itself, new buildings also became necessary owing to the growing scale of farming operations. Granaries were especially built as small rectangular buildings which stood on mushroom-shaped 'steddles' to protect the grain from rats and mice. The increasing numbers of cattle fed on fodder in winter were housed in open yards sometimes provided with 'hovels'. Some of the earliest threshing machines were worked by circumambulatory horses

**90** A purpose-built sheep fold and barn with shepherd's dwelling (note the chimney) erected on an outlying part of Housedean Farm near Lewes in 1845.

which were housed in circular or polygonal houses with conical roofs. Sometimes a factory-like chimney still exists, marking the short-lived phase when stationary steam-engines were used for threshing. Despite such new technology old and trusted ways continued. At Saddlescombe the old well house is of great interest. This contained a huge broad wheel in which a donkey, pony or man stepped on 'like a squirrel in a cage', bringing up from 150 feet below the pure water on which 11 households depended for drinking in the mid-19th century. Over the massive oaken beam which formed the axle of the wheel was a single chain and at each end a large oaken iron-bound bucket holding about twelve gallons, the empty one going down when the full one came up.[2] A similar device survives at Stanmer.

## Rural Communities

By the end of the 18th century there were two distinctly different kinds of rural community in or at the margin of the Downs, which are termed 'open' or 'closed' parishes, the difference depending upon the degree of economic and social control exercised by the landowner. A 'closed' village or parish was usually ruled by one landowner, whilst an 'open' one was normally a community of owner-occupiers with their attendant farm labourers and local craftsmen. Where the suppression of small occupiers was most complete, a village commonly became an 'estate' village, virtually owned by a single great landlord such as at Folkington, Berwick, Alciston, Bishopstone, Tarring Neville, Rodmell, West Firle, Stanmer, Falmer, Glynde, Coombes, Wiston, Parham, North Stoke, South Stoke and Tillington. In such instances the landlord could control the entire population of the parish and normally restricted growth so as to keep the Poor Rate deliberately low. Such villages tended to have a 'feudal' character with small populations, large farms, few shops and inns and strong Anglican church following. The 'open' communities, such as Ringmer and places in West Sussex like Henfield, Amberley and

Graffham, were invariably larger and had many small proprietors and tenant farmers, diverse rural handicrafts, more numerous shops and inns. There was often a desperate impoverishment and a sturdy radicalism and independence reflected in politics and in nonconformity in religion. The lack of an overall control on population and housing usually meant that population growth was more rapid than in 'closed' villages and that the Poor Rate fell upon the shoulders of many small farmers whose financial circumstances generally led them to set a low level relief. This tended to cause poor housing conditions, high unemployment and under-employment and pauperism in the first half of the 19th century. Old Shoreham in the Adur valley is an example of a 'closed' community. It is now difficult to recapture its extreme isolation in former times because three main roads converging on the village were not built until modern times. The

**91** A shepherd's cottage erected at New Barn on the high downs of Cornish Farm near Eastbourne is another example of new buildings created by 19th-century 'high' farming. A well-preserved dewpond also exists at the site.

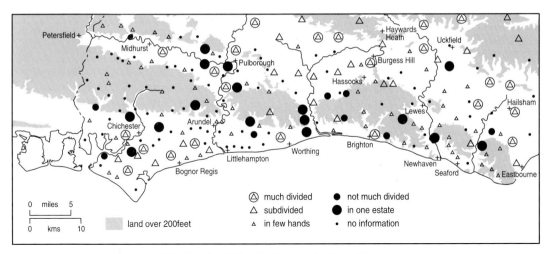

**92** 'Open' and 'closed' villages in the Sussex Downs.

A283 road following the valley floor from Steyning was not constructed until 1828; the river Adur was crossed by ferry until 1768 when a wooden bridge was built; and the A270, which cut the village street in half, dates from 1934. For centuries the old way to London involved a stiff climb by a flinty track up Mill Hill and thence over high downs before dropping steeply down Beeding Hill. Socially, Old Shoreham was for centuries a little world of shepherds, agricultural labourers and carters, followed in the mid-19th century by seed drillers from Norfolk and market gardeners.[3] The rural community was led by the squires Bridger who resided at Buckingham House for more than two hundred years. Three large farms had each their supporting labourers living in tied cottages on the farms or in the eight ancient thatched cottages in the village itself. Farmers included Thomas Ellman, a cousin of John Ellman of Glynde, and like him a notable breeder of Southdown sheep. Amongst the shepherds was Michael Blann, who wrote down his songs in his own handwritten notebook kept in the Barclay Wills Collection in Worthing Museum.[4] The squire's servant household c.1890 was the subject of George Moore's celebrated novel *Esther Waters* (1894). Graffham was in several respects a different downland community. It was such a large strip parish that the census enumerator had to make a round journey of over thirty miles between the first and last households he had to visit and his ride traversed the highest part of the Sussex Downs as well as lowland heath, woodland and marsh. As at Amberley in 1851, he encountered one large and numerous small farms, but also many craftsmen engaged in wood-using industries, coppicing, the making of baskets, trugs, hoops and hurdles and also leather. This was an occupational pattern found throughout the Western Downs.

Another skilled craft that lingered here until the mid-19th century was that of lime-burner, a craft usually handed down in families from one generation to the next. The oldest way to burn chalk for agricultural lime was to use faggots of broom or furze, but wood, and increasingly coal, was also used. The large public kilns which had been grouped on navigable water, as at Houghton, Amberley and Bury, eventually made smaller and less accessible kilns uneconomic. By the 1860s Graffham and neighbouring parishes were feeling the pinch of the deteriorating farming situation, rather earlier than the more prosperous farms in the Eastern Downs where big farms were still taking on extra hands in the '50s and '60s and building new cottages to

**93** This ruinous lime-kiln at the base of Duncton Hill was once an unusually large enterprise of Lord Egremont of Petworth until the opening of the Rother navigation created rival limeworks on the waterways.

house them, as at Applesham. Of the 1,245 acres of Up Waltham parish not more than 500 are cultivated.[5] It was probably at this period that scrub invaded the greensward to remain until the well-publicised clearances of 1979 (p.207). Steyning in the mid-19th century was still overwhelmingly rural with 12 resident farmers and 132 agricultural labourers. Servicing farmers in 1841 were a bank manager (but not yet a solicitor), an auctioneer, an insurance man, a surgeon, a surveyor, three millers, a wheelwright, a millwright, a harness marker, a horse dealer, 10 blacksmiths, a lime burner and five saddlers. Shops included only one bakery, as most families still baked their own bread. Industry which was derivative of the cloth trade active in the 16th and 17th centuries still lingered fragmentarily. The traditional craft of fulling cloth before dyeing at a mill was represented by a single individual in 1851, but there were seven fell-mongers and seven parchment makers, the latter amongst the few persons born outside Sussex.

## The Labouring Man

The downsman went to work on a good breakfast of broth (made of coarse ends of meat, oatmeal, butter and flour) or boiled milk and bread and cheese.[6] His hours of work were long, determined by the length of daylight: at harvest a 16-hour day was worked, and the common rule was that one should not stop reaping until a star was seen. Wives assisted husbands at harvest by binding the corn into sheaves. When the sheaves were taken away the wheat ground was left to gleaners, usually women and boys. The latter were employed from eight years of age to scare rooks from seeded fields and to help their father with threshing. By the age of 10, boys were flint-picking and leading the oxen at ploughing. To plough an acre, the normal day's stint, they would walk more than eight miles a day, 'notwithstanding their natural genius for indolence and mischief'.[7] There was plenty of work for everyone on a big downland farm for chalkland was ploughed traditionally three times, harrowed repeatedly to get a fine tilth and rolled twice. The turnips and green crops were also labour-demanding.[8] In the years of acute poverty and distress amongst labourers during the period from 1815 to the 1840s the Downs offered advantages over the Weald of Sussex. In general, the wealthier tenant farmers kept labourers at work all the year round because the lighter tillage land on the chalk was more easily managed and was cheaper to cultivate.[9] Moreover, downland farmers kept more sheep than formerly, wool prices holding up better than for corn. John Ellman of Glynde was able to demonstrate to a Royal Commission that wage rates in the village had actually increased over the period 1791-1821, whereas the reverse was complained of in the Weald.[10] It was similarly reported in the 1820s that the Downs towards Winchester were still cultivated intensively and were well-stocked.[11] In contrast, Wealden soils were less friendly and fertile. Much stiff, wet, cold land of round-frocked farmers was thrown out of cultivation after the peace of 1815 which led to huge falls in agricultural prices, because it was expensive to work on account of the tenacity and low natural fertility of the clay. Wealden parishes became heavily burdened with paupers and farmers suffered from the resulting high Poor Rates which were not nevertheless sufficiently high to help indigent labourers who became discontented and demoralised. On the whole, labourers in 'closed' villages on the Downs did better than did those in 'open' parishes in the Weald. At Glynde, for example, the Trevors made improvements to cottages, and allotments for the cultivation of vegetables were provided. The Earl of Chichester did likewise at Stanmer and Falmer, and wage rates were consistently high and poor rates low. Ringmer parish, an 'open' one, could hardly have been more different in the matter of agricultural unemployment and unrest than the neighbouring 'closed' one of Glynde. When labourers' living conditions reached their nadir in the 1830s and '40s, the era of the Captain Swing riots, Ringmer was the scene of localised acts of protest. The parish became notorious for the bad management of the poor and discontent amongst them. A petition was presented on Ringmer Green to Lord Gage in November 1830. It read:

> We, the labourers of Ringmer and surrounding villages, having for a long period suffered the greatest privations and endured the most despairing situation with the greatest restraint and forbearance in the hope that time and circumstances would bring about some relief, now find our hopes deprived and disappointed in our fond expectation. We have taken this method of meeting in a body for making known our plight in a peaceful manner and in order to ask for redress. We ask whether 1s. a day is sufficient for a working man to keep up his strength necessary for the exertion of his labour. We also ask if 9s. is sufficient for a married man with a family to provide for. We go to work with only potatoes in our satchels, the only beverage being the cold spring, and on returning to our cottages to be welcomed by the meagre and half-famished offspring of our toil-worn bodies. We ask our wages to be advanced to such a degree that will enable us to provide for ourselves and our families without being driven to the overseer.

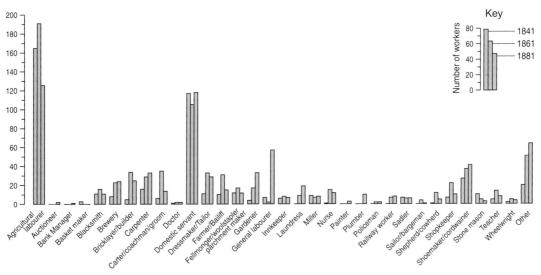

**94**   Occupations: Steyning, 1841-81. Based on Census Returns.

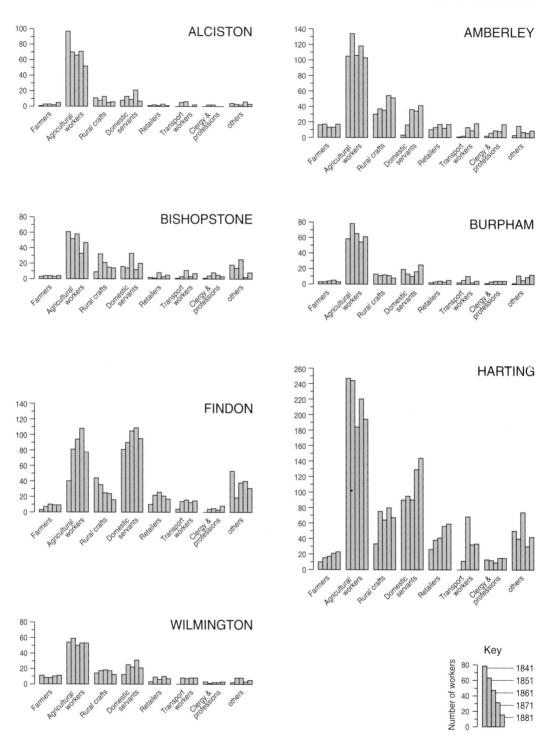

**95** Occupations: downland parishes. Dates based on Census Returns.

**96** 'Thistle-dodging' at Bigenor Farm, 1920s.

On reading the petition, Lord Gage went into the church vestry with local gentry and farmers to discuss it, the crowd of 150 men waiting quietly outside. When Lord Gage returned he conceded the wages demanded and approved the discharge of the Overseer of the Poor and the Governor of the Poor which fear of disturbance, especially of arson attacks targeted on barns and ricks, had made it imprudent to resist. Amongst the numerous hard-up labourers were abandoned characters who frequented beer shops which became brothels and receiving places of stolen goods. The best labourers, inclined to keep off parish relief except as a last resort, were amongst those who were driven to emigrate.[12]

## Crime and Disorder

During the intense and prolonged agricultural depression after the Napoleonic Wars there was a good deal of unrest and steeply rising crime in England and the downland village was the scene of considerable crime and disorder. It is a theme which has until recently been neglected by social historians but Roger Wells[13] and others are now focusing on specific communities and highlighting how notorious were bad characters amongst their inhabitants and how devastating were their effects. Alfriston was a small downland market town which declined from the Middle Ages and peaked in population in 1831 (694 persons) and began to decline after prosperous trading activity with the decline in agriculture, the flight to towns and the establishment of markets in new centres with the coming of the railways. Thomas Geering, writing in old age in the 1880s, recalled Alfriston of his childhood with a tannery, a brewery, a butcher who 'did a large business and made money', tallow makers, candlemakers, soapboilers and 'shoemakers by

**97** The restoration of this cottage at St Anne's in Lewes reveals the use of successive layers of building materials over several hundred years.

the dozen'. There were also builders and carpenters, tailors, grocers, smiths and wheelwrights, glovemakers, saddlers, carriers and carters, for to Alfriston came villagers from Arlington, Litlington, Lullington, West Dean, Berwick and Alciston to buy and sell goods. In the main, the numerous small tradesmen and agricultural labourers supported the 400-seat Congregational chapel built in 1801 whilst gentry, farmers and larger traders worshipped at the parish church. Two prominent individuals emerge in the early 19th century, Stanton Collins and Charles Brooker. The former was the leader of an extensive criminal gang who was doubtless an inveterate smuggler and who rustled sheep and dealt in stolen corn. His father was a butcher by trade (his premises are now the *Smugglers' Inn*, a building 'riddled with doorways and passages' (21 rooms, 47 doors and six staircases as well as cellars and a special hiding place in the roof space). Before he was sentenced to seven years' transportation in 1831 for stealing corn he had repeatedly clashed with Brooker whose family were farmers with a tannery and grocery business, and who was the principal trustee of the chapel and held various parish offices, including that of Overseer of the Poor. Brooker suffered personal abuse, arson attacks, vandalism, shoplifting and boycott at the hands of disgruntled and resentful villagers in the difficult period of the Reform Bill and the New Poor Law which created deep divides amongst communities. During the Swing riots, although Alfriston was not a major centre of violence, Samuel Thorncraft was executed for arson and two other local persons were transported. An arson attack on the farm of a New Poor Law Guardian led to the flight of a culprit to America and, despite Collins' downfall and vigilante patrols, inveterate thieving and disaffection hardly abated at Alfriston until after the repeal of the Corn Laws.

Nor was this downland village exceptional. Smuggling also played a major part in the everyday life of the downland village for generations, especially between 1740 and 1840. East Dean, Jevington, Alfriston and Rottingdean, for example, were heavily implicated. Jevington smugglers used Birling Gap and Smugglers' Bottom at Crowlink and James Pettit ('Jevington Jigg') was the leader of a local gang whilst he kept the inn there. At East Dean smuggling was so profitable that fine houses were built out of the black economy. It was said of Cuckmere Haven in the 1780s that 200-300 men would be seen taking goods from the beach, despite opposition from the Excise, and that as many as a dozen smuggling vessels might lie offshore in broad daylight. A Blockade Watch House and Coastguard cottages were later built to guard this stretch of coast. Around Brighton, Patcham and Stanmer were very implicated with smuggling and it was so much a part of life at Rottingdean that the Rev. Thomas Hooker is said to have acted as a look-out for the local gang. As at East Dean, several substantial village houses are thought to have been built from the profits of smuggling and to be linked by tunnels to the beach. Near Shoreham, West Blatchington, Lancing, Sompting and West Tarring were notorious smuggling communities, much contraband finding a temporary hideaway in buildings which still exist at the *Sussex Pad Inn*.[14]

## 'The Hungry Forties'

The prolonged calamity for the agricultural labourer was extended into the 1840s, 'The Hungry Forties'. Whilst the landed gentry and tenant farmers had 'never been healthier, or happier, or more engrossed in the life of their lesser country houses', the labourer suffered hardship from low wages and the rising cost of bread. A daughter of Richard Cobden published in 1904 people's recollections of life at Heyshott before the repeal of the Corn Laws.[15] Widow Sanders remembered when she and her husband had brought up eight children on 9s. a week with bread at 1s. 2d. a loaf. 'Many's the night I've gone to bed hungry so the children might git me bit o' bread between 'em.'[16] The old method of threshing wheat by the flail in the barn reminded her of her dread that on account of her husband's near-starvation diet she would hear his strokes suddenly stop and that she would know that he ' 'ad dropped from the 'ard work and the empty belly'.[17] Charles Robinson of Heyshott had been better off because he had worked as a woodman in the winter when there was less farm work on the Downs but his diet was very frugal: 'Butcher's meat we never 'eard of, never saw it except in the shops. Salt was 21s. a bushel and when we killed a pig we 'ad to sell 'alf of it to buy the salt to salt down what was left'. He and his family largely lived on 'taters' and puddings made of 'crammings', the residue of the flour after the most nourishing ingredients had been removed. Tea was too expensive so his wife made it last by mixing black crusts with it.[18]

Another Heyshott labourer, David Miles, remarked: 'It worn't no manner o' good a tryin' to raise yerself, 'ee wor just a slave, and that's the truth'. He added, 'Folks used to put up a little 'ill of 'taters' for the winter, not two rods from their winders, but people'd come by night and steal 'em … When a man 'ad a large fa'am'ly they were pretty near starvin' mostly. I got a job once, six and an 'alf mile away, and that seemed a fair step, I can tell'ee, when I come 'ome tired of an evenin' but I used to pass a 'ooman on the way what 'ad to dig up turmuts wid white frost on 'em, and I wouldn't 'a 'ad 'er job, bless 'ee, for a pound a week, that I wouldn't.'[19] Thomas Wapson of Heyshott was so hungry that he stole turnips and ate them for supper with a little bread. His first job as a boy was carrying pails of water up the hill for a penny a day and he walked to Singleton and back (a round journey of eight miles) to fetch medicines from the nearest parish doctor for a penny or two. 'Then there wor the leasin's [gleanings]. We daren't go in the field afore they blew the horn, and then we got what we could. It 'twor only a little, we rubbed it out and threshed it our selfs as well as may be, an' put it in a pot with a pennorth o' milk and a slice or two of turmutt and boiled it up …'.[20] George Pollard, who was born at Graffham but could not ''zactly reklect what year 't was', used to go cow- or bird-minding at threepence a day and dug stones on Heyshott Hill when on parish relief. Grass-mowing with a scythe would take him as far as Wimbledon and Wandsworth. His wife weeded and picked stones from the fields for tenpence a day. Harvest time would find him trudging along the lanes with his children on his back, carrying them as far as Pagham where he worked seasonally as a casual reaper, the family sleeping together in barns at night. Mr. and Mrs. Jenner of Heyshott had a little cart drawn by two dogs.[21]

By the 1860s the condition of the labourer had improved, as also had the condition of their tied cottages. At Singleton cottages were let at low rents and those newly erected had three bedrooms. Others had improved sleeping accommodation, but 16 cottages in the village during Goodwood race-week had their lower apartments turned into accommodation for race-goers. Yet labourers generally were still required to carry four-bushel sacks weighing 2½ cwt. of beans, 2¼ cwt. of wheat, 2 cwt. of barley and 1½ cwt. of oats.

## The Shepherd

On downland farms the shepherd's job was the most skilful. It was he who advised his master in the 18th century what sowings were needed to provide the 'bite' for the sheep in rotation at exactly the right time.

The 19th-century shepherds were generally of families associated with the Downs for centuries for although they moved from farm to farm for work 'they rarely foresook their great habitat—the South Downs—'like certain plants, they only thrive when upon this chalk soil', wrote M.A. Lower. He cited the names of Tupper, Duly, Dudeney, Carter, Thomas, Pettit and Hussey amongst others who traditionally held the shepherd's crook, and he added 'The same could be said for the shepherds' masters, the southdown farmers. For two, three, four even five centuries they had adhered to the soil of the Downs of which they could almost claim to be "earth-born" sons, the Farncombes, Beards, Ridges, Ades, Scrases, Lambes, Saxbys, Dukes, Penfolds and Bottings. The last were so numerous that when one of their number was appointed High Sheriff he selected the whole of his bodyguard from members of his own family'.[22]

Yet Lower expressed dismay at the changes that had come over the shepherds' lifestyle and condition since his youth at the beginning of the 19th century. The old shepherd had been no mere hireling that could be turned off by an ill-tempered or imperious master at a week's notice. In addition to his wages he had kept 30 or 40 ewes of the farmer's for his own for which he paid money when he took his position. The ewes ran with the rest of the flock and, when sold, the shepherd had some of the profit. He thus had a kind of partnership with his master: he was not simply a day labourer. In those days the farmer had little to do with the flock for he left everything to his shepherd. With the improvement of the Southdown breed came a change. The sheep breeder took oversight himself and the shepherd was in reality a kind of under-shepherd. As an old shepherd remarked: 'It made great odds to a shepherd's trying his best when he knew that every pound he earned for his master put sixpence in his pocket … there was always an understanding between master and man'.[23]

Another old custom dying out by the mid-19th century was the institution of 'shepherds' acres'. These were traditional in downland villages and were granted by the tenantry to their shepherd of the common flock whilst holding his position of common shepherd. As the shepherd was usually one of the village landholders he customarily lost his own little holding to his master because his work as shepherd prevented him running his own farm.[24]

The great change influencing the social milieu of the shepherd also affected his life by the mid-19th century. A shepherd's hut was then becoming a rare sight, though formerly every shepherd had one. Sometimes it had been a kind of cave dug into a bank (a 'link' in the shepherd's dialect from the Saxon *hlinc*, meaning bank). Large stones inside were the furnishings. A made hut was built of sods of earth, or bark, boughs of hawth or straw. In rough weather the shepherd sheltered safe and dry, looking out perpetually to see that his sheep did not stray. This type of hut was gradually replaced by the mobile shed in which the shepherd

**98**    Shepherd at lambing, 1920s.

kept all his tools and medicine, some food for the sheep, his own clothing and a bed used at lambing time. The unfenced Downs were the habitats of birds now rarely seen or extinct. An overturned ewe would be the prey of carrion crows and ravens who would put out her eyes before she was dead. One old shepherd of the 1850s recalled the eagle and the bustard (wild turkey). With great cunning and skill shepherds trapped bustards in thorn bushes with a kind of miniature man-trap which held the bird by the legs. A shepherd's boy found a bustard's nest in the gorse (called *hawth* in Sussex dialect) on Norton Top at Bishopstone and by putting a long piece of string with a running knot in it he was able to pull the bird down and catch it by the legs as she sat on the nest. M.A. Lower's own grandfather joined in the killing of the bustards with dogs and bludgeons.[25]

The trapping of the wheatear was highly profitable to the shepherd, the most successful earning more from it between July and September than for shepherding for an entire year. Gourmets so rapturously dwelt upon them 'with such an air rolling a fat delicious morsel in the mouth, and smacking the lips after delutition, and stroking a well-satisfied stomach, that one is led to think that the happiness of the great, the wise and the good of that age, was centred on their bellies, and that they looked upon the eating of wheatears as the highest pleasure man could know …'. The shepherd learned of the birds' habit of seeking holes for shelter when rain threatened, so he made traps called 'coops' which were short tunnels cut into the turf. Entering the opening the bird was caught in a noose of horse-hair at the other end. The noose did not as a rule strangle the bird and tender-hearted parson-poet James Hurdis freed the birds, leaving 'pence of ransom' for the shepherd.[26]

The old shepherds also recalled smuggling. There was a great deal done over the Downs at the turn of the 18th and 19th centuries. Luggers loaded with silk, tea, spirits and tobacco used to come ashore at the Gaps, openings in the cliffs such as Birling, Crowlink or Ovingdean and the gangs met shepherds and others to 'work' the goods. 'Time and often I have seen as many as a hundred men a-horseback with led horses, all loaded with tubs of spirits and bags of tobacco.' Very often they kept contraband among the hawth on Norton Top or dug great pits to hide it. The shepherds were terrified of informing against smugglers for fear of being hurt or killed. 'Many a fearful fray and desperate encounter have these hills witnessed between the "Free-traders" in hollands and tobacco and the Revenue men.'

One of the most remarkable of South Downs shepherds was John Dudeney (1792-1852), a Rottingdean man, descended from several generations of South Downs shepherds, who took up the vocation at the age of eight. When about seventeen he became the under-shepherd of the tenantry flock at Kingston-by-Lewes. His wages were £6 a year but from his allowance of sheep whose lamb and wool brought him about 15s. a year and by trapping and selling wheatears (the 'English ortolan' which were much more abundant in his day than now), he was able to buy books. He taught himself Greek and Hebrew whilst tending his flock on Newmarket Hill and studied geometry and mathematics, depositing his books and slate in a hole dug on the Downs. When he relinquished his shepherd's job he took a job in the printing firm of Mr. Baxter's at Lewes and eventually became a schoolmaster.[27]

One of the last of the shepherds was Harry Coppard, who died in 1963. For more than fifty years he watched his flocks on a patch of downland about three miles square between Patcham and Ditchling Beacon, as his father and grandfather had done before him. He recalled

**99**  Prize Southdown ram, 1920s.

how between the two world wars the sheepflocks in neighbouring deans declined one by one and he remembered the downland sward growing coarse and tussocky and that scrub began to flourish as thick belts of hawthorn and gorse. Brighton came flooding over the downland in the 1920s and '30s and almost reached the open country where Coppard's sheep grazed. His dress was a felt hat, knotted choker, canvas leggings overlapping his boots and a black coat in cold weather. He preferred the crook made by the blacksmith at Falmer to the more famous Pyecombe one, being better balanced and lighter to his way of thinking. Asked whether crops would grow on the sheepwalk, he had a ready reply: 'Would crops grow! Fancy not knowing! There's been hundreds of thousands of sheep for hundreds and hundreds of years all over these hills, putting on more'n ever they took out. Corn couldn't help but grow.' Coppard's prediction was right. Crop yields on the reclaimed grassland were twice as high as the United Kingdom average in the 1950s and '60s when corn was grown as part of the rotation of crops including temporary grasses (leys) which supplied nitrogen to the soil and provided fodder for sheep and cattle.[28]

## Rodmell

Social conditions and change in a South Downs village in the last half of the 19th century can also be reconstructed from a diary kept by two successive rectors of Rodmell, Pierre de Putron and Robin Rossiter.[29] De Putron restored the small Norman church in 1851-62 which villagers fondly called 'The cathedral of the Brookside', notable for lovely stained-glass windows. He rebuilt and extended the rectory, adding a pretty medievalised façade to the old brick-built building still seen at the rear. He also opened the village school in 1859 and encouraged villagers to invest in a penny bank and to use a new lending library. Another sign of better living conditions in the village was the sale in 1859 of the four poor houses to Lord Abergavenny, who owned almost the entire village at that time (these still exist at the bottom of the village though attractively modernised).

Bad farming weather is noted, for example, the severe drought of spring 1859, when water was scarce for many weeks, and the bad season of 1860 which had such a backward harvest that the flower show had to be cancelled and potato blight caused hardship. Social customs included the Christmas party in the rectory for all the children, tithe suppers, the dinner at the New Year for elderly residents and the annual meeting of the friendly society in the public house which was so bibulous that de Putron rather dreaded it. Songs at the harvest supper concluded with a thrice-shouted wild huzza from the labourers called the 'nic' which meant that they had broken the 'neck' of the harvest. Not until 1893 was a Working Men's Club founded with an alternative room to the local pub, when a reading room was also provided. A village hall was not provided until Leonard Woolf thought it essential after the Second World War.

The recollections of old villagers help us to reconstruct life and landscape at this period. Smuggling in earlier times was much discussed and it was said that contraband landed at Saltdean and Chine Gap was stored in the church roof between the chancel and the nave. The repeated flooding of the brookland was kept vividly alive in villagers' memories. The sea came up to the bottom of the village in winter floods and people kept boats to go about the brooks at that season. In summer grass would be rank high and there were tall reeds, although a reported length of 'three rods long' is perhaps an exaggeration. These memories were of the brooks before the river Ouse was canalised and embanked, largely at the instigation of John Ellman the sheep breeder. The cottages, called Navigation Cottages, at the bottom of the village, were built so that employees could maintain the banks and sluices.

**100**   Steyning market, 1895.

There were six farms and some smallholdings in Rodmell at the beginning of the 19th century. At each farm three or four young men were boarded in lieu of wages. When the farmer went to market a horse was taken from the plough team for the purpose. His wife generally mounted on a pillion with him and they jogged along the narrow, ill-kept roads to Lewes. No light spring carts were to be had in those days. Knee breeches and smock-frocks were traditionally worn right up to the end of the 19th century. At harvest time casual labourers were employed for a month as reapers, hence their name of 'Month's men'. Before starting work in the morning every man had his pint of home-brewed ale and bread and cheese 'as large as he chose to cut it'. Wives or children would bring milk into the fields for the labourers' breakfast and at lunchtime a hot meal of either meat pudding or pork and lard pudding would also be brought to workers by their families. By the end of the 19th century Rodmell, like all country villages in Sussex, had experienced a drop of population of something like one third and it was no longer a thriving little rural community as once it had been. The six farms were one by one sold off and merged into a single Rodmell farm and by 1901 there was no resident farmer, Northease Farm being owned by Mr. Brown of Landport and Rodmell Farm by Mr. Stacey of Kingston. The landlord, the Marquis of Abergavenny, of Eridge Castle, who owned 94 per cent of Rodmell, was also an absentee. This, it was said, had a deteriorating affect on the agricultural labourers. In 1895 Richard Hudson died, the last labourer to wear a smock-frock regularly. He was regarded as a fine specimen of the old Sussex labouring man fast dying out.

Not only agriculture was affected by change. Machinery ended the once-thriving bootmaking business in the village. The general decline in village morale was most evident in the deteriorating state of the cottages before the First World War. In the 1860s the cottages were apparently acceptable and neatness and productivity of cottage gardens was encouraged by an annual Cottage Garden Competition, in which all the villagers participated. The first prize in 1863 was awarded for the garden which 'embraced everything which lends charm to the cottage garden', namely beehives, well trained fruit trees and a good collection of flowers. By 1891 concern was being expressed at the fabric of the cottages. The influenza epidemic of that year drew attention to the additional suffering of villagers caused by crumbling and broken-down walls and leaky roofs. 'There is hardly one really good sound comfortable cottage in the village,' was the rector's verdict. This assessment would have been widely echoed throughout the Downs.

## Dialect

Education and the coming of the cinema, radio and television have almost totally obliterated the local dialect of the Downs. M.A. Lower, who was a keen and accurate listener, was the first to try to preserve words and phrases going out of use from the mid-19th century.[30] He noted that the majority of places in the Downs were so pronounced by agricultural labourers as to make it difficult for a stranger to identify them: Selmeston was pronounced Simpson, Folkington Fowington, Alciston Ahson, Alfriston Ahso-town, Henfield Envul, Falmer Farmer, Chalvington Charnton. The numerous terminations of place-names in -ing were changed by local people to *un*, and thus Goring was Gorun, Tarring Tarrun. Stanmer was Stammer, Midhurst Medhas, Petworth Pettuth and Chichester Chiddister.

101 The base of the Free Trade obelisk near Dunford. Cobden wrote: 'After seeing so much of the world's scenery, I think there is nothing in nature so beautiful as the *wooded* parts of the South Downs in this neighbourhood'. To him the escarpment was 'the Hogarthian line of beauty on the grandest scale'. He was born at Dunford, a hamlet of Heyshott near Midhurst, in 1804 and repossessed the family property in 1847. He is buried in West Lavington churchyard.

He also recounts an amusing instance of downland dialect:

A story is told of a Southdown man who did not know either his own name or that of the village in which he resided, and who was obliged to be "axed agin" before the requisite answer could be elicited. A person who had been deputed to enquire for "Mr Pocock of Alciston" and meeting a labourer near the place in question, he asked him if he could point out the residence of the individual. "Noa", was the reply—"never heerd an him and don' know no sich place". It afterwards turned out that the *questionee* was none other than the desiderated "Mr Pocock" himself! "Why" said he, when the true nature of the enquiry dawned upon him—"you should ha' axed for Master Palk of Ahson".[31]

So keen was he to preserve some old dialect and provincialisms of Sussex that the Rev. W.D. Parish of Selmeston compiled in 1875 a dictionary which was augmented in 1957 by Helena Hall, drawing also on her brother, Henry Hall's work in the field.

The great interest of his pages will be evident from the following quotations:

Abouten (Abutan, Anglo-Saxon, Abutan), just on the point of having done anything.
Adone, leave off. The Rev. Parish remarks 'I am told on good authority that when a Sussex damsel says "Oh! do adone", she means you to go on; but when she says "Adone-do!", you must leave off immediately'.
Agen (Agen, Anglo-Saxon, near to), as in 'He lived up'gin the church and died about forty years agoo'.
Aig, egg. 'A'be agwain t'ave a biled aig for me brakfus dracly'.
Allow, to give an opinion. 'I allus allowed she were 'ees darter'.
Arg, to argue. 'Thee chapelfolk always wants to arg'.[32]

Miles Costello, a writer at Steyning, remembers hearing 'paigs' for pegs and children told 'you maunt do that' and that the old cowman driving his cows daily along Steyning High Street would call 'coup, coup, coom along'. R.W. Blencowe was a pioneer collector of folksongs, a field in which Bob Copper and his family have excelled in recent years.

In the 1950s the dialect speech of persons residing at East Harting, Sutton near Petworth and at Firle was recorded, that of the East Sussex speaker being rather different from that of the two others. Probably there are still people in the Downs who talk of being 'leer' when they mean 'hungry' or of 'spaddling' when leaving muddy footprints on a clean floor.

*Chapter Ten*

# NATURE, MAN AND BEAST

Every change in farming methods directly alters the conditions of plants and animals. This inter-relationship between nature and man as farmer is discussed in this chapter. Although the eminent botanist John Ray singled out old chalk grassland as the chief glory of the South Downs as early as 1691,[1] it is only comparatively recently that its origin has been understood. The naturalist Harold Peake, for example, still adhered in 1931 to the old view that turf was natural to chalkland and that the first farmers had taken into cultivation grassland and scrub, not differing much from the vegetation then widespread.[2] Research by Sir Edward Salisbury[3] and the famous ecological studies carried out in the Western Downs by Sir Arthur Tansley led to the acceptance that chalk grassland was the product of human forest clearance,[4] although Tansley did not discount the possibility that some grassy patches might have persisted throughout the forest period, a view held at the present time by Dr. Francis Rose.[5]

Since the last War great strides have been made in the young science of environmental archaeology and related techniques. These have confirmed that the Downs were formerly well wooded. Martin Bell's work at Bishopstone, near Newhaven, revealed a local downland environment progressively becoming more open. In lower levels of sediment, dated to *c*.3000 B.C., fossil snails were found to be mainly woodland or shrub species, whereas in upper layers snails from *c*.1000 B.C. were ones adapted to open short-grazed grassland.[6] Another major source of the evidence of early vegetation on the Downs has been the analysis of pollen grains and spores preserved in peat and other waterlogged deposits where the lack of oxygen has prevented their decay. The peat in the Amberley Wild Brooks contains pollen layers from woodland-clearing impact of the first farmers, now recognised as a very significant event in the environmental history of the Downs. A site in the Vale of Brooks near Lewes has yielded information over a shorter period; and recently, Midhurst Bog has been examined to find out what tree and plant pollen were blowing in the wind between *c*.5000-1000 B.C. It now appears from this and other evidence that chalk grassland is the result of ecological responses to environmental change initiated by man over several thousand years. It is likely that the primeval forest on downland was adapted to the prehistoric soils, with a mixed oak-hazel forest where deep loamy soil existed on flatter and gentler slopes, while steep slopes, including the northern escarpment, with shallower, chalky soil, were probably covered with elm and lime. Beech and yew, so characteristic of semi-natural woodland on the Downs today, do not appear to have been common.

As the clearance of the downland forest proceeded, sun-loving plants so common on chalk grassland were able to expand in numbers and territory. It is difficult to ascertain where these plants came from. Dr. Rose suggests that chalk-loving plants could have been able to

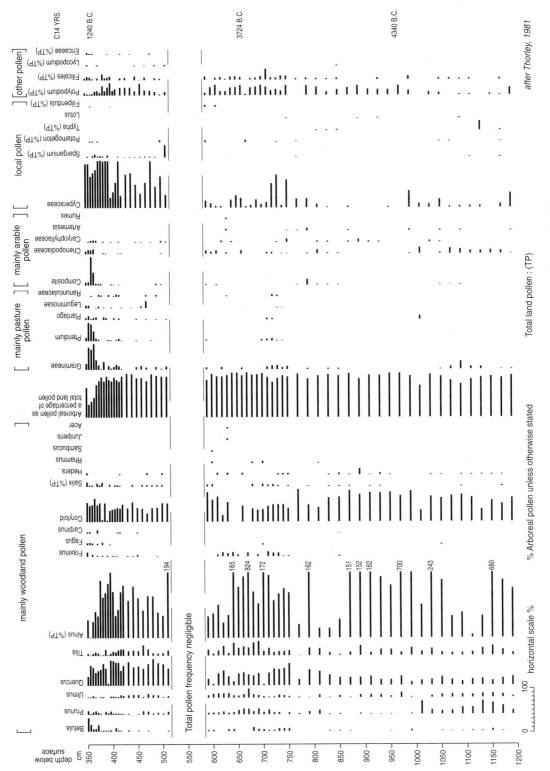

**102** Pollen diagrams from peat lying in the alluvial infill of the Ouse valley, south of Lewes.

survive as relict species despite the advance of the forest in the Warm Atlantic period of climate after the last Ice Age. He believes that the edges of chalk cliffs would have been the most likely places to have acted as 'refugia' and he has identified certain sites within the Downs such as river- and sea-cliffs of the Cuckmere Valley and Beachy Head where this survival of plants may have occurred. Moreover, it is likely that some natural, though possibly transient, clearings would always have existed because of the activity of large grazing animals, such as bison and wild horses.[7] In general, however, chalk grassland cannot claim independence from the ubiquitous influence of man and his grazing animals.

The stages in the clearance of the downland forest are now known with some certainty. In outline, it was begun in Neolithic times (from about 4000 B.C.) and continued progressively over the long span of time through the Bronze and Iron Ages before being virtually complete in the Eastern Downs during the Roman occupation (A.D. 43-410). It thus marks a major achievement of farmers before the coming of the Saxons. We can picture considerable woodland and scrub persisting at times earlier than *c*.A.D. 100.[8] Barry Cunliffe has suggested that in the Iron Age so much woodland and scrub might have persisted that hillforts like Danebury in Hampshire might have stood out like 'a pimple on a hairy chin'.[9] On the Western Downs there was probably a denser tree cover because of the appreciable depths of non-calcareous (non-chalky) soil, and the process of woodland clearance appears to have been slower. It was also less complete. Dr. Rose has identified certain woodlands which may never have been cleared. The evidence comes from his studies of their lichen epiphyte and from floras of woodlands which are outstandingly rich in ancient woodland vascular plants and 'old woodland' lichens. Another approach has been adopted by Dr. Margaret Collins who found deep non-calcareous soils under some woods. This she correlated with lack of forest clearance by man, and hence absence of soil erosion, while elsewhere shallow soils which bespeak of long-continued cultivation.[10] Examples of these apparently ancient, uncleared woods are East Dean Park Wood (a former medieval deer park with a ruinous hunting lodge); Pads Wood near Uppark; Tegleaze Wood; and West Dean Woods.[11] 'Uncleared' does not mean 'undisturbed': such woods were used for timber and for the production of hurdles, firewood and charcoal by coppicing and pollarding.

On the Eastern Downs, where woodland clearance was more ruthless, possible comparable woodlands are rare or non-existent. One may be part of the very unusual habitat at Ashcombe, north-west of Lewes, where the whole succession of vegetation from old chalk grassland through scrub and secondary woodland to what may be uncleared woodland can be seen. The woodland is on a sticky patch of acid soil above the chalk and comprises old coppice once intensively worked by the Coombe Estate as a source of sheep hurdles, and Oak-Hawthorn growing at what may be the 'lost' *Bocholt* where Simon de Montfort's troops lay hidden before the Battle of Lewes in 1264. From late Saxon times (*c*.A.D. 800) onwards cultivation appears to have ceased on the high Downs and the thin, stony and rather sterile soil on the upper slopes and crest were turned over into vast sheep walk. Land-hungry medieval peasants nibbled away, bit by bit, into it for arable extensions for their common-fields, as revealed by long narrow lynchetted fields on Newtimber Hill and at Upper Beeding. Both examples reverted to grassland again with population decline in the later Middle Ages. From the late 17th century farmers broke up 'maiden' down for the sowing of clover, sainfoin and other rotational grasses used as fodder for sheep. More still was ploughed up in the famine years of the Napoleonic Wars and subsequently, though much of this reverted back again later to grass when corn prices fell. Thus the traditional chalk turf, which largely disappeared from the Downs during the last war and the 1950s

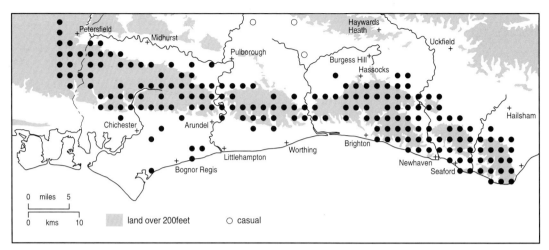

**103** Distribution of *Scabiosa columbaria* (Small Scabious) in Sussex (after Streeter). A striking example of chalk-dominated plant distribution.

has had a dynamic history of retreat and advance over centuries.[12] It is clear, however, that the core of the sheepwalk, the crest and north escarpment, remained virtually inviolate until 1939.

It is estimated that chalk grassland occupied 40-50 per cent of the area of the Downs in the late 19th century; it now occupies about 3-5 per cent. A more detailed picture of the changing acreage of grassland is indicated on p.111.

The centuries-old nibbling and trampling by sheep on the chalk greensward produced a fine short turf dominated by fescue grasses, *Festuca ovina* on the driest and shallowest soils and *Festuca rubra* on somewhat deeper, moister soils. Uniquely it also harboured more species of wild plants than any other land surface in Britain. According to English Nature there are up to forty different species of wild plants in one square yard, including a wide range of miniature clovers, flowers and creeping herbs, some exceedingly small, including the aromatic Thyme and Marjoram, Rock Rose and Horseshoe Vetch, the food source of the now rare Chalkhill Blue butterfly, and the even rarer and more beautiful Adonis Blue. These plants often send down deep roots to collect moisture and some develop a hairy or waxy skin to avoid desiccation. The dense interwoven fibrous roots form a thick layer which gives old turf its springiness and make it so delightful to ride or walk upon. This fragrant ancient chalk turf is now confined to the north-facing escarpment of the Downs and other hillsides too steep to plough. Such fragments now constitute one of the rarest habitats in western Europe and are home to distinctive populations of birds and of butterflies. The fact that they are now a haven for species of insects, fauna and flora declining elsewhere makes them even more important.[13]

Where this chalk greensward still exists it is so smooth as to give the impression of having been mown and tended regularly like a garden lawn. The scaling down of plants which ordinarily would have grown taller is accounted for by the wind, the shallow unfertile soil, very dry conditions and the close and selective grazing of sheep and rabbits, in contrast to the lighter and more uniform grazing by cattle which has meant that they have had to hug the ground tenaciously. The grazing regime over the last 4,000 years gradually brought about the suppression or stunting of all but the coarse grasses, weeds, heathers and sedges, while the close treading led to the compaction of the soil. This common loss of aeration and absorptive capacity also inhibits the growth of species. With too little grazing the short turf develops into one of the longer types of chalk grassland, e.g. tor grass, that now predominates in the Downs.

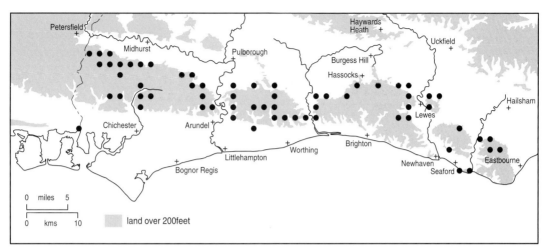

**104** Distribution of the stripe-winged grasshopper *Stenobothrus Lineatus* (orthoptera-Acrididae) in Sussex (after Streeter).

Excessively hard grazing results in more species per square yard but most of the plants are eaten before flowering. Thus this species-rich grassland is a grazing-adapted ecosystem developed over the thin, basically infertile, chalk soil, which had been created by sheep grazing over more than 5,000 years and by rabbits for several hundred years or so, 'living lawnmowers', as H.J. Massingham called both of them. The diversity of plant species in the chalk sward may seem surprising. In general plant diversity reflects poor soils. There is an inverse relationship between productivity of grassland and species diversity. It is common experience that the application of fertilisers will significantly increase the productivity of chalk grassland and that this is accompanied by a decline in the number of species in the sward. On poor chalk soil which was not treated in this way plants had a precarious existence and the constant nibbling by sheep and rabbits prevented any single plant becoming dominant. This plant community remained only as long as grazing was maintained when a multitude of different plants grew together and in turn supported an equally varied insect population.

The form and composition of the chalk sward thus depends not only on the local conditions of soil moisture, shelter and aspect, but perhaps to an even greater extent on land use both past and present. It is these circumstances, which tend to be local, that make chalk vegetation interesting and varied, the flora often changing in the space of a few yards.

Collectively, the miniature flowers and herbs growing in the short dense turf have always been responsible for much of the beauty and fascination of the Downs. The richness of species varies greatly; north-facing slopes, for example, are not generally as species-rich as sunny, south-facing ones. Hence the escarpment of the South Downs is poorer floristically than the corresponding feature on the North Downs which is south-facing. Old chalk pits are especially rich in species.

The high density of flowering plants and herbs make the greensward very coloured and scented, its colour varying from season to season. Early in the year it has a predominantly yellow appearance if cowslips are present (April) or Horseshoe Vetch (May) but changes to a mosaic of purples and mauves in late spring to high summer, when the springy turf smells sweetly of Thyme, Basil and Marjoram. In late March the Hairy Violets are very attractive and in May slopes are bright with the flowers of the Milkworts, two of which are plentiful on the chalk. Salad Burnet, another early flowering plant, is devoured eagerly by sheep. The typical downland orchids appear in May, the Common Spotted is the commonest and the Man, Fragrant, Bee and Pyramidal less common. In June arrives the Rock Rose and three members of the Luminosa family (Pea), the Kidney Vetch, Common Birds-foot trefoil and the attractive pink flowers of the Squinancywort. Two of the most beautiful wild flowers in late summer are Marjoram and Bloody Cranesbill. Also locally common is the wild flower most representative of all the flowers on the Downs, the Round-Headed Rampion, which is more plentiful on the Sussex Downs than anywhere else, and is known as the 'Pride of Sussex'. Chalk grassland supports many species of butterfly as well as the Chalkhill Blue and Adonis Blue already mentioned and it is also rich in grasshoppers, crickets, and diminuitive snails. One species of rare cricket, known as the wart-biter from its supposed habit of biting warts off people's hands, has its British stronghold in the Downs east of Brighton.

## Scrub

On land that had not been brought under the plough for centuries chalk scrub flourished. A chalky soil supports more shrubs than any other, including Box, Dogwood, Elder, Gorse, Hawthorn, Juniper, Privet, Purging Buckthorn, Spindle, Wild Clematis (also known as Traveller's Joy and Old Man's Beard), Wayfaring Tree and Whitebeam. Up until the 18th century every parish deliberately maintained patches of gorse and other shrubs for fuel. In places such scrubby patches still exist despite the ploughing-up of the Downs since the last war, as on the 600 acres in Shoreham Gap owned by the National Trust, which includes Southwick Hill and steep hillsides in adjoining coombes, and in the coombe above West Firle church kept as a fox covert until recently which was one of the few wooded parts of the Eastern Downs. During the past fifty years much scrub has encroached upon the former chalk turf of the Downs' escarpment, as at Black Cap near Lewes. A photograph taken in 1874 shows it kept clean-shaven by heavy sheep grazing but it is now interspersed by scrub which is tending to encroach still further. Similarly, until recently the lower slopes of Chanctonbury Ring were completely free of scrub which now grows thickly at the base of the Ring and does not set it off so dramatically. On the escarpment below Ditchling Beacon scrub has also taken hold on land which has been formerly 'so noble and so bare'. Another example of scrub encroachment on the escarpment is above Poynings village. This much-photographed site was also free of scrub early in this century. Now a dense mass of scrub has completely altered the appearance of the Downs. Readers who have access to old photographs or paintings will be able to multiply these instances of modern scrub encroachment.

The National Trust at Newtimber Hill were amongst the first to attempt to control the scrub invasion.[14] The Trust took the extreme step of ploughing-up the scrub in 1959 when earlier use of a cutting machine to tear down young thorn, bramble and gorse, followed by spraying with a selective weed killer, proved ineffective. This plan was drastic but justified. By means of a leaflet the Trust explained that parts of the northern side of the hill were covered with impenetrable scrub which was impeding access and views. Once ploughed, the whole property (given to the Trust for its preservation as an open space for public enjoyment by Countess Buxton in 1936 in memory of her husband, Earl Buxton, a former Governor-General of South Africa) was leased to a tenant farmer for rough grazing which was stocked hard to keep new scrub growth in check. In addition 46 acres were ploughed by a tenant who took three crops off the land before re-seeding to permanent grassland. Part of this area needed similar treatment in 1976. Meanwhile, other parts of the hill were cut repeatedly with a cutting machine with the help of conservation volunteers. This valiant activity on the part of the Trust was only partially successful because scrub can apparently only be prevented from growing by the hard grazing which traditionally took place on the hills. As light scrub is valuable for some birds and butterflies a strong case for its partial retention has been made by the Sussex Wildlife Trust.

Hawthorn, a mass of white blossom in May, is ubiquitous in this scrub. Some ancient, gnarled specimens are to be found in old grazings where they have sheltered generations of livestock as in several Nature Reserves. Juniper is a conifer able to resist wind and provides shelter for other species of young plants and scrub but it is less common than it once was, partly because of the intense grazing of rabbits which has prevented regeneration. It is now confined to the Downs west of the river Adur. The Common Buckthorn and various roses and brambles make progress through chalk scrub difficult. Scattered amongst the many shrubs are usually a few young trees of Beech, Yew, the Whitebeam (one of the loveliest trees on downland), Ash, Sycamore and occasional White Birch. Traveller's Joy is an important element of the chalk scrub, its rope-like stems, resembling those of tropical lianas, festoon hedgerows and individual shrubs.

Traditional chalk grassland is now of only limited and fragmentary extent. The largest area

**105** Vegetation changes above Poynings village, north of Brighton. *Top*: a photograph of 1934 showing sheepwalk when the escarpment was still grazed; *bottom*: the present change following cessation of grazing.

in the Western Downs is on Harting Down, where sheep grazing re-introduced by the National Trust and the Sussex Downs Conservation Board is gradually restoring a fine area of Juniper-studded downland. The Sussex Wildlife Trust Reserve at Levin Down, leased from the Goodwood Estate, has south-facing slopes rich in chalk grassland species. The richest south-aspect chalk grassland are, however, east of Brighton, the finest being Castle Hill near Falmer. Mount Caburn, Malling Down, the east side of the lower Cuckmere valley and Bullock Down near Beachy Head are also important. On the East Hampshire Downs traditional chalk downland exists on an ancient field system on Catherington Down and in the superb Old Winchester Hill National Nature Reserve where it forms a rich mosaic with scrub and woodland. On the escarpment are also rich sites of chalk grassland, as at Heyshott Down, Didling Down, Sutton Down, Kithurst Hill, Fulking Escarpment, Ditchling Beacon Nature Reserve and Beeding Hill.

Numerous traditional habitats of exceptional interest still exist on the Downs apart from those previously mentioned. Of special importance are some 18 ancient woods where the large-leaved Lime occurs, notably at the base of the escarpment of the Western Downs, the best example being Rook Clift near Treyford. Generally this species of Lime grows in Elm-Sycamore-Hazel woodland which was probably the typical downland tree cover before man began farming.

Several beechwoods and lichen-rich grasslands on the escarpment of the Western Downs have been assessed of European importance. Other interesting woodlands include North Marden Down where 'graveyards' of dead Juniper bushes can be seen beneath yews which originally sheltered them but which have since shaded them out. At the Kingley Vale Yew Forest yews have also encroached on former Juniper-studded grassland.[15]

Chalk Heath is an unusual type of habitat which has developed where acid soils from the last glacial period thinly overlie chalk. It contains a normal mixture of downland species but also characteristic acid soil species. It has been suggested that probably the whole of the Western Downs were once covered with acid clay soils but were mainly ploughed out by the Roman period to end up in the valley bottoms. Patches of heather, bell heather and tormentil can be discovered amongst the characteristic lime-loving plants, however, on the scarps of lynchet banks where, through the downward movement of soil resulting from former ploughing, acidity and alkalinity are presumably approximately neutral. Patches of chalk heath also exist on Bow Hill. The largest area of chalk heath remaining in southern England is at the Lullington Heath National Nature Reserve. The instability of the vegetation here is a classic illustration of the changing relationship between nature and man. It is thought that chalk heath began to develop on the scarps of cultivation lynchets covering the Reserve which were finally abandoned when corn-growing ended in the late medieval period. For centuries close cropped downland turf and heath existed with sheep and rabbit grazing but this was transformed from the 1950s within 15 years with the cessation of sheep grazing and the almost total elimination of rabbits by

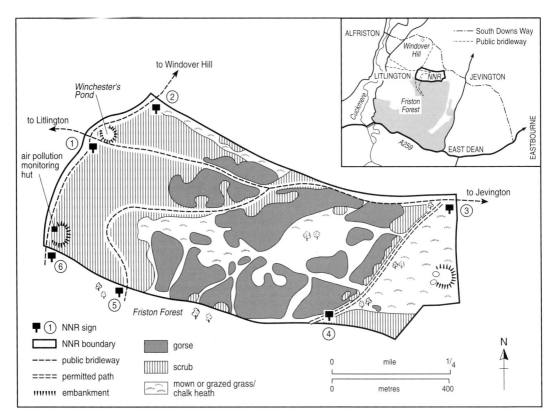

**106**   The vegetation on Lullington Heath (after English Nature).

myxomatosis in 1954. Unchecked by grazing, tor-grass and other coarse grasses, such as upright brome, smothered the finer grasses and short herbs and seedlings of hawthorn, gorse and the wayfaring tree found ideal conditions for establishing themselves, so that much of the Reserve is now covered by scrub. This has had a pronounced affect on birds, those of open downland being succeeded by heathland species and in turn by scrub-loving ones. Mowing and grazing by New Forest ponies has restored some heath and recently sheep have been re-introduced for the same purpose.[16]

## Man's Food, Medicine and Magic

Many of the shrubs, wildflowers and other plants of the chalk and shingle at the base of the cliffs have had such long associations with downsmen as to have written themselves into folk-lore and the imagination. This is because they played a large part in the practice of magic and entered daily lives as food, cosmetics, colourings and medicine as well as in ceremonies. Amongst the chief rural remedies was cobwebs for staunching the flow of blood and healing open wounds. A syrup from elecampane, grown in cottage gardens, eased asthma and coughs and was regarded as an excellent preventative of plague. The burning of the Common Fleabane filled rooms with flea-killing fumes. The use of Hedge Woundwort for dressing wounds was recommended by agricultural writer Leonard Mascall of Plumpton Place in the Tudor period and by William Borrer, botanist of Henfield in 1810. A Mandrake, widely grown in cottage gardens in the Tudor period, gave relief from pain and insomnia and was reputedly an infallible aphrodisiac. According to Dr. Andrew Allen a bryony mandrake was for sale at a chemist's shop in Ditchling as late as *c.*1920.[17]

Indeed, the medicinal plants from the chalk are legion.[18] They include the Squinancywort for quinsy, sore throat and as an astringent gargle; Tansy, which has a warm, refreshing, spicy aroma, was used to stay miscarriages. Viper's Bugloss was recommended for snake bite. Wild Marjoram, something of a cure-all, was made into Marjoram Tea to cure indigestion, earache, coughing, dropsy and bladder trouble, etc. Wild Thyme was a uterine herb. Horehound was supposed to cure the habit of hard drinking, which may account for its rarity now around Arundel whose name is derived from *Har Hun*, the Saxon name for the plant! The orchids, which are now many visitors' chief interest, were a prime source of aphrodisiac and medicine. Of plants connected with love and magic, Knapweed was placed by girls into the house and looked at again shortly afterwards in the hope that it had flowered, this being a sign of imminent love. Birds-foot Trefoil was not picked because it was associated with the fingers of Tom Thumb. Juniper berries were swallowed to procure abortion (oil of Juniper is still sold as a carminative). It was regarded as an apotropaic against devils, elves and witches. The Hawthorn was the lover's tree in poetry and for everyone it symbolises the change from spring to summer and the chief of plants to collect when 'The May' was brought into villages on May Day. The Spindle shrub was used for spindles, skewers, pegs and also for viola bows, keys for the virginal and toothpicks. Blackthorn was used as a purgative. Gorse was of great value as fuel for bakers, lime-burners and, when crushed, made a valuable food for stock in winter. Old Man's Beard was called 'Boys' Bacca' on the Downs because boys, shepherds and gypsies smoked cigarlengths of its dry stems.

Amongst valuable foods for human use was Salad Burnet, good for salads as it tastes like cucumber. The Sea Cabbage, growing mainly on cliffs near Beachy Head, is the ancestor of garden cabbage. Sea Kale was formerly collected from shingle and sold in local markets. Geoffrey

**107**   Medieval rabbit warren; women catching rabbits with ferrets.

Grigson has noted that it has 'Not conquered the world … but served like asparagus with hollandaise sauce or drawn butter, and not doused with Mrs Beeton's white sauce, the shoots are incomparably delicious'. Fat Hen, an invasive weed of muck heaps, was regarded as a succulent food plant as far back as the Bronze Age.[18]

## The Rabbit

No history of downland habitats would be complete without mention of the rabbit because, of all wild mammals, the rabbit has had closest connection with man and in the feral state they have been important agents in modifying chalk grassland. Their destructive effects on vegetation were first investigated by Tansley and Adamson in 1925.[19] They noted of the Downs on the Sussex-Hampshire border that as rabbits reduced vegetation to a height under four feet existing shrubs were 'topiared' into neat, compact bushes. Apparently a rare animal on the Downs during the Middle Ages and much sought after for its meat and fur, the King himself donated 100 rabbits to the bishop of Chichester in 1235. Unlike the hare, it was not indigenous to the British Isles and appears to have been introduced by the Normans. It may have taken about 100 years before rabbits were turned from tender weaklings into healthy, strong, survivors. Then rabbiting began in warrens known as coney-garths (coney being the original name for an adult rabbit), especially fenced off in an attempt to prevent their escape into fields. Gorse, Juniper, bramble and other prickly shrubs were planted or managed to provide food. Chalkland proved ideal well-drained soils for burrowing and grazing. Breeding was also encouraged by the erection of massive mounds of earth known as 'pillow mounds'. The largest of these mounds on the Downs are over 100 ft. long and are 15 ft. wide at the base and more than 4 ft. high, as on Graffham Down. The interior of these mounds was sometimes honeycombed with nesting places built of wood or flint and with deadfalls to contain rabbits for selective culling. A warrener looked after the site from a nearby hut. Wild colonies of rabbits were gradually formed by escapees. By the mid-14th century these had become the bane of peasant farmers.[20] (p.71)

Created warrens appear to have multiplied during the later Middle Ages with the collapse of the wool market and falling demand for grain (pp.71-5). Warrens then developed as an alternative source of income on the Downs. In the 16th and 17th centuries the rabbit was regarded as an important cash crop. Warrens were particularly noteworthy on poorer parts of the Western Downs as at Chilgrove, West Dean, East Dean, Cocking, Goodwood, Graffham, Salvington, Patching (Michelgrove) and Findon. Between Brighton and Eastbourne there were warrens at Wolstonbury Hill, Rottingdean, Telscombe, Piddinghoe, Jevington and Eastbourne, amongst other places.[21] The escaped rabbits survived in a feral state and eventually became destructive, prolific and of little value. Consequently, from the late 18th century warrens tended to be replaced with sheep grazing, reclaimed arable land or tree plantations. One or two new warrens were established with the fall of mutton and corn prices after the 1870s. One example was that at Freshcombe Lodge on Truleigh Hill set up by Colvill Bridger, the land owner, in association with the novelist George Moore.[22] In the farming depression between the two World Wars one drove miles over downs which appeared to be stocked almost solely with rabbits (giving rise to the belief that the South Downs was the rabbit's spiritual home).[23]

To the chagrin of farmers and golf course greenkeepers, rabbits are now re-occupying parts of the Downs after the ravages of myxomatosis in the 1950s. The survivors have developed a degree of immunity to the disease which is passed from one generation to the next and have become a particularly tenacious pest again in many places. The chalk shows white where rabbits have excavated burrows and, unless kept down, they can do tremendous damage to growing crops and to tree and plant species. The relationship between Man and the rabbit is thus due for a change.

Roy Strong has observed that rabbit was part of Man's diet for centuries. The wild rabbit from the Downs was especially gamey and flavoursome because it munched aromatic herbs in the short turf. William Verrall, who was trained in the kitchens of the Duke of Newcastle at Claremont and whose *White Hart* inn at Lewes was famous for its cuisine in the late 18th century, provided elegant recipes for rabbit, one being of tiny escalopes beaten wafer-thin and served with a brown sauce laced with champagne.

The rabbit's relative the hare was formerly fairly common but numbers have fallen dramatically since about 1960 because of the loss of summer forage, the increase in foxes, and poaching.

*Chapter Eleven*

# THE MAKING OF AN ICON

The South Downs have been perceived in different ways at different periods. The earliest recorded writers did not think of them as either romantic or picturesque but wrote with homespun affection of the sport they provided, as when Nicolas and John Deringe of Glynde recalled them as 'fayre hills' *c.*1520 and the many times they had gone up to the highest parts amongst their father's sheep and 'Walked much abroad both for the hunting of the hare and for hawking'.[1] Yet long before the fells of Lakeland, the Devonshire moors or the Norfolk Broads, the South Downs passed into the ranks of the 'Observables' of England, famed for turf as smooth as a bowling green, good for sheep as well as delightful to the eye and also pleasant to the traveller enjoying their wide open skies and limitless views. This is what the pre-eminent botanist John Ray had in mind when he wrote in 1691 of 'That ravishing prospect of the sea on the one hand and the country far and wide on the other which those so keenly enjoy who for the first time visit the Downs of Sussex'.[2] The professional early 18th-century traveller Daniel Defoe was in agreement, declaring both the almost treeless Downs near Lewes and their wooded counterparts beyond Arundel to be 'the pleasantest and most delightful of their kind in the nation'.[3] One of the great virtues of the springy turf was its unrivalled suitability in the world of cricket. The 2nd Duke of Richmond's Elevens were famed in the early 18th century. Hambledon's Cricket Club (flourishing *c.*1772-96) is world famous as the accepted authority and governing body of the game before the formation of the M.C.C.

**108** Commemorating the Hambledon Cricket Club, Hambledon.

The first known celebrant of the exquisitely smooth configuration of the Sussex chalkland was William Hay in 1730 who lived at Glyndebourne, where his descendant, Sir George Christie, is the present host of the famous international opera festival. Hay declared his preference for the smoothness of the South Downs as against more rugged landscapes:

> Thrice happy mountains! Which no outward storm
> Or foul eruptions from within, deform.
> No rocks like rages in poverty they wear
> But a rich verdant mantle throughout the year ...[4]

This love of softly rolling outlines is echoed by numerous later writers, as in Gilbert White's letter to Daines Barrington, dated 1773 and published in his *Natural History*.[5] Wilfrid Scawen Blunt reiterates this in his sonnet *Chanclebury Ring* (*c.*1870):

> Say what you will, there is not in the world
> A nobler sight than from the upper Down.
> No rugged landscape here, no beauty hurled
> From its Creator's hand as with a frown.[6]

and Maude Robinson remarked about the same time that the smoothness of the Downs gave such particular charm to her at Saddlescombe Farm, north of Brighton, that when she first saw rocky hills they gave her the impression of a starved animal, with its bones protruding through its skin.[7]

Another significant early observation on the Downs is Robert Bloomfield's late 18th-century poem. This reveals that their fame was already legendary and that they had become an agent of liberty and the good life, giving benefit to the nation in the public mind, freedom of access being the primary way in which that benefit could be realised.

> Are these the famed, the brave South Downs
> That like a chain of pearls appear ... freedom, thought and peace, how dear!
> To freedom, for no fence is seen:
> To peace, for o'er the boundless green
> unnumbered flocks and shepherds stray ... (*The South Downs*)[8]

## Cobbett's Assessment

The most important of the early observations on the South Downs are those of William Cobbett in *Rural Rides* and in his *Political Register*. These are especially interesting because they are almost entirely agricultural and made before the townsman, the Sussex poets and the Victorian naturalists, who had a different voice, had their say. Much of Cobbett's wild dispersion of energy was expended in riding on the Downs and he devoted some of his best and most vigorous writing in the English language to them. As a keen horseman, he made instinctively for the velvety turf and had a passionate love of bold heaves of upstanding chalkland which were to him the epitome of the agricultural England where he had been brought up. He had such a depth of feeling for the South Downs that he seems actually to get inside them. His piercing eye took in everything from the saddle. The sight of several hundred sheep nibbling their way down on the way to the fold on the arable land for the night, as seen from the window of his inn at sundown near Winchester, moved him almost to tears with the recollection that as a boy he had worn a smock-frock and carried a wooden bottle for drink and food like any other shepherd's boy.[9] He returns again and again to this image: 'I like to look at the windy side of a great down, with two or three immense flocks of sheep on it, belonging to different farms, and to see, lower down, the folds in the fields ready to receive them at night ... the sheep principally manure the land. This is done by folding and to fold, you must have a flock. Every farm has its proportion of down, arable and meadow.'[10]

**109** West End, Hambledon, a former farmhouse owned by John Goldsmith who hosted Cobbett for several days in 1822 and in 1826 (*Rural Rides*) and probably on other occasions. It lies in a gentle fold in low rolling country which inspired Cobbett to write unusually about the beauty of the landscape.

It was not solely the sheep that enraptured him. Writing from the north of England in 1832 he remarked:

> If any of these sensible men of Newcastle were to see the farming in the South Downs and to see, as I saw in the month of July last, four teams of large oxen, six in a team, all ploughing in the field in preparation for wheat, and several pairs of horses, in the same field, dragging, harrowing and rolling, and had seen on the other side of the road, from five to six quarters of wheat standing upon the acre, and from nine to ten quarters of oats standing alongside of each, each of the fields from fifty to hundred statute acres: if they would see these things they would laugh at the childish work that they see going here under the name of farming.[11]

This remark is very significant because it is rare in any subsequent literature on the South Downs to read that its arable farming was so exceptionally enterprising, productive, and on such a large scale, so strong was the later image of the shepherd and his flock against an ultramarine sky with skylarks, the wind in the grass and the drowsy buzz of insects pollinating wildflowers.

Cobbett had other delightful experiences in the Downs, apart from the sight of 'capital arable fields, generally of large dimensions'.[12] For him the view from Butser Hill across the Western Weald was the finest in the world and riding from Petworth through the valley of the upper Lavant to East Dean and Singleton put him in the happiest of spirits (although soaked to the skin by a 'Judge's Wig') on Duncton Hill. 'No misery to be seen here', he noted amongst the beech plantations, the fine great fields of wheat, barley and turnips and good village houses with gardens, some of the best he had seen in England on the Duke of Richmond's estate, but he observed that agricultural labourers were worse off than in woodland counties as they had nothing but their bare pay and less chance of work in winter.[13] Very few abuses fell on Cobbett's eye in the Downs apart from a tendency to 'scratch-up the peerless turf and leave a wreck behind' (p.109) although the estate of the banker Sir Thomas Baring at Candover aroused his ire and thus the voice of the bluff, tough, prickly and over-bearing old fellow was raised to anger[14] (but note the occasion mentioned on p.103). The crudities of the rotten boroughs went unmentioned as he appears to have avoided Bramber and Steyning. Instead his admiration was extended to Lewes, the market town in the heart of the Downs, which filled him with pleasure as a model of solidity and neatness, with good pavements and clean shops. The people were also well dressed, the girls remarkably pretty and the men also notably good-looking, altogether quite a different view of Lewes taken by William Morris and Philip Webb during the later agricultural depression (p.19).[15] With Cobbett we see before us firmly and squarely the South Downs of the agriculturist and loudly hear the voice of a countryman, and this is a good thing. He was one of the few thorough-going countrymen in English literature, which helped to make him the exceptional person and writer he was. Through him, as it were, spoke a thousand Cobbetts of the South Downs, deep-chested yeomen and weather-stained labourers alike. Yet Cobbett was in some respects not exempt from the extravagance that the later tourists were to express about the Downs. His creation of a mythical lost Eden of an older rural England tended to glorify the agricultural labourer in his hardihood, innocence and deep-rooted sense of the soil (pp.120-34).

## Drear were the Downs

When Cobbett was writing in the 1820s cultural influences had combined to produce a shift in aesthetic taste from bare downland and it became fashionable for elegant visitors to Brighton to express dislike at the smoothness and starkness of its downland setting, so reversing the public judgment of earlier centuries. An influence behind this shift in taste was the then newly-created landscape gardening movement. Its genius, 'Capability' Brown, had held that open country was

to be regarded as but a canvas on which a landscape might be designed, and that the aid of water and trees should be called in for this purpose. This Georgian taste for landscape gardening had a pronounced effect on the Western Downs following the clump of beech planted on Chanctonbury Ring in 1760 and it was under its stimulus that Stanmer Park near Brighton was landscaped by the Pelham family.

Another cause of the change in landscape taste at the end of the 18th century was a new aesthetic introduced by the Picturesque movement headed by William Gilpin, which favoured landscapes which were rugged, broken and abrupt, an influence traceable to Romantics popularising the Lake District and other mountain areas of upland Britain. In his essay on 'Picturesque Beauty' in 1792 Gilpin illustrated two versions of landscape, one smooth and rounded with flowing curves, a perfect specimen of typical chalk scenery, which he pronounced 'ugly' and 'disgusting', and the other broken and varied, accounted admirable to the eye (Fig.110).[16]

**110**   Two versions of landscape, one smooth and rounded with flowing curves, pronounced 'ugly' and 'disgusting' by William Gilpin in his *Essay on Picturesque Beauty* (1792) and the other broken and varied, accounted admirable to the eye.

Swept up in this new aesthetic, it is not surprising that writers on the South Downs at the end of the 18th century speak slightingly of them. As Horace Walpole noted, less was then being heard of the once universally loved ocean-like extents of the chalk country of southern England and more of newly discovered landscape, such as the rich blue prospects of the Weald or the mountainous parts of Britain.[17] William Cobbett, who in almost every aspect was a rebel against the conventions of his age, noted in the 1820s that visitors fled from open downland as naturally as from pestilence.[18]

Those visitors who loved Brighton for itself generally chose to be dissatisfied about its setting. Their eyes and limbs appear to have ached at the sight of the featureless convexity of the chalk perceived as a scene of unrelieved dreariness and ugliness. They thought, and hoped, that there could be no more of it: yet there was nothing but turf and ploughed land everywhere, no trees, no hedge, 'all one monotonous brownish-green waste'. Dr. Johnson thought that although Brighton's setting was so dull a man overcome by its dismalness would not be able to find a tree whereon to hang himself.[19] Many visitors were unused to chalk landscapes. Prince Pückler-Muskau was astonished not to see a single full-grown tree … 'Nothing to be seen but hilly dunes covered with short grass'. The contrast with the rest of England, so rich in trees, startled him, though he owned rather guardedly that the sea and its ships, the great town in the distance, and the constantly changing light[20] 'was not without its charm'. The early Brighton doctors, Relhan, Wigan, Granville and the rest, all extolled the tonic qualities of the Brighton air but acknowledged the 'dreariness' of its Downs, Granville being the most censorious.[21] An 'Excursion Guide' of 1822 described Brighton's neighbourhood as a monotonous, 'peculiarly bare and sterile-looking tract', the Earl of Chichester's plantings in his park at Stanmer, alone relieving the eye of pain.[22]

'Victoire, Count de Soligny' (in fact a pseudonym of Peter Patmore) was particularly devastating:

> For leagues around, one uninterrupted range of brown, barren, chalk hills on which a few lean, dirty-looking sheep tantalize their appetites by nibbling at the dry turf, nature has, to be sure, scattered a tree here and there, to shew that the want of vegetation is not her fault …[23]

By contrast the view from the Devil's Dyke, laid out at one's feet in the Weald, seemed to him a vast garden being divided into a patchwork of fields bounded by thick hedgerows and small copses. His eyes, wearied by the downland, felt 'as if they could rest for ever on the beautiful creation which seems to lay breathing and basking in the sunshine', an opinion echoed by the Comte de la Garde whose sight of 'arid' chalk landscape at Brighton left him unprepared for the lush and varied beauty of the 'picture-book' Wealden landscapes, as though designed by 'Capability' Brown, glimpsed on his coach journey to London.[24] John Evans in his *Excursion to Brighton* (1821) was put out of humour on Brighton's Downs for a different reason: the hard, flinty road to the Devil's Dyke was pitiless from want of protection from the sun and the violent jogging of the carriages aroused female timidity: 'There is no real danger, and such alarms are unnecessary, but we cannot reason with the passion of fear, and left of itself, it dies away'.

Such deprecatory assessments of the Eastern Downs continued into the 1860s, when, for example, Mrs. Merrifield noted the fascination of downland plants but conceded that visually the Downs were uninviting.[25] Thus when M.A. Lower wrote an essay on the South Downs in 1854 which may be considered the beginning of their modern literature, he wrote defensively about them as an amenity. He felt obliged to 'sell' the Downs visually, knowing that he would

**111** Part of the Stanmer Estate. Stanmer Park, declared in the 1820s to be the sole attraction in the Downs around Brighton, was landscaped by Henry Pelham with thick masses of foliage forming a striking contrast to the open Downs surrounding it. The mansion is to be restored by Brighton and Hove Council. The Earls of Chichester re-built the church and created a charming estate village in the early 19th century. Little more than a century later this landed estate had collapsed.

have unappreciative readers still in Gilpin's thrall. His motive in writing was in fact to rebut the charge of dullness and insipidity still so generally brought against the Downs.[26] As late as the 1880s the famous preacher F.W. Robertson of Brighton was struggling to promote Brighton's Downs: 'Nay even round this Brighton of ours, treeless and prosaic as people call it, there are materials enough for poetry, for the heart that is not petrified·in conventional maxims about beauty'.[27]

Augustus Hare, author of a *Guide to Sussex*, must have put off thousands of potential visitors to the Eastern Downs, describing them as 'excessively dreary' as late as 1894.[28] The poet John Davidson, although now regarded as one of the 'first of the moderns', nevertheless found the nakedness of the Downs near Shoreham-by-Sea repelling and compared them to the 'limbs and shoulders of plucked fowls'. He endured the ugliness as the 'prime cost of Southdown mutton' and yearned for all its rolling bareness to be clothed in trees.[29]

## The Downs Resurgent

By the 1860s, however, the aesthetic ideals of the Picturesque were on the wane and from late Victorian times the South Downs regained their very special place in the national psyche. This is evident from remarks on the Downs in the *Quarterly Review* (1862).

> We know not of a more tranquillizing scene for the overwrought brain to rest upon than the prospect from the Downs on a fine summer day, the true Copley Fielding landscape … a feast to look upon … slow-yoked oxen, with their peaceful pace and low bent necks, teaching us in these fevered days of steam and electricity a very lesson in patience.

When Sir Leslie Stephen, father of Virginia Woolf and Vanessa Bell, and editor of *The Cornhill*, the most famous Victorian literary journal, wrote admiringly of open downland in 1878[30] the tide of opinion had definitely returned it to favour. This renewed appreciation of the open downland is doubtless in part to be connected with the frenetic rush of life associated with steam and rapid urbanisation which was putting a psychological strain on those living in London and larger towns. The growth of London and its changes in lifestyle had much to do with a growing fondness for the Downs. Hanoverian London had been relatively compact and coherent, enveloped in its fields and market gardens which could be reached on foot. This is the London fondly praised by essayist Charles Lamb and which inspired Dr. Johnson's aphorism, 'He who is tired of London is tired of life'. Mid-Victorian London was, by contrast, virtually a new city which was 'more excavated, more cut-about, more re-built and more extended than at any time in its previous history'. *Pace* Dr. Johnson, there was not in High Victorian London all that life would provide. For Sir Leslie Stephen the daily experience of London was an endurance test involving long daily journeys through crowded streets which required compensating annual holidays and weekend breaks away from London as a restorative from the dirt and grind of the city.

To such persons, the gentle swelling curves of the Downs were soothing and therapeutic. The feeling that this world seemed to have stood still and the past taken over the whole of its undulating landscape gave visitors a physical shock of excitement and pleasure. Before the ploughing up of the Downs the past was everywhere. It was something physically before one and could be walked into, or one could stretch out and reach it. The Downs struck people as a kind of open-air museum or nature reserve, where one could feel the presence of Old England, a most English England where one could lead a gasless, electric-lightless, waterless, bathroomless existence. George Gissing's letter from Eastbourne in 1887 put it succinctly:[31]

> You come upon old, old hamlets, warm, peaceful, sheltered with old trees. Each has its little Norman church, generally built of flints, and with churchyards that make one always think of Gray's Elegy … never have I seen such quaintness and old-world beauty …

This feeling was reinforced by the age-old appearance of the higher Downs and widespread imprint of prehistoric tumuli, habitations and field systems then etched into the turf. To Helen Thomas, wife of poet Edward Thomas, the thrill of encountering what seemed to be part of the oldest England nourished her almost religious sense of belonging to its very soil and being part of its continuity:

> I realised how much the bare downs meant to me; they thrilled me with a patriotism deep and passionate. They had been home to the earliest human beings in England and

**XIV** Wild plants of the Chalk. Clockwise from top left: Common Vetch, Lady's Bedstraw and insect, Viper's Bugloss, Birdsfoot trefoil, Scabious, Round-headed Rampion.

**XV**  A little masterpiece of outdoors literature between the wars was *Hills of the Sea*, written for the Southern Railway by S.P.B. Mais and superbly illustrated by Audrey Weber. South Stoke is depicted here.

**XVI**  Beachy Head, 1935 (by *Punch*).

with their relation to the sea they were mysterious, intimate, tender, wild and sheltering; still almost untouched in time to that rural England where Shakespeare's rustics and Chaucer's yeoman tilled the soil. I felt I was in the heart of England's being. My spirit was filled with content as my feet trod these ancient ways and my heart lifted to know that this rich country belonged to me and I to it with all its history and tradition.[32]

To Edward Thomas the Downs' escarpment was also greatly valued. The 'sixty miles in a single glance' he saw of the Downs on the skyline from his studio on the top of an East Hampshire hanger at Steep, near Petersfield, were hills such as hills ought to be, he felt, 'such as he would himself make, if he could, to show someone who had never seen any'.[33]

Although miles of turf empty of vestiges of mankind, except of ancient forebears linked by a thread unbroken for centuries, added immeasurably to the atmosphere of the Downs, not all found the prehistoric monuments the essence of the Downs. To many this was its Saxon air. Sussex was regarded as *the* home of the 'simple, tenacious Saxon', this character being reflected in the modesty and minuteness of its parish churches, the antique domesticity of its homely working farms and its little villages and hamlets, such as Sullington, Telscombe and Alciston, or of Lewes.

George Moore, writing at Southwick in 1886, admired the flint farmhouses, the great elms, and all the rich fields worked by smock-flocked labourers and said: 'I am by ancestry a South Saxon. The country of my instinctive inspiration would be Sussex, the most Saxon of all. Its very aspect awakens antenatal sympathies in me.'[34] W.H. Hudson, a stranger to Sussex, thought it odd in *Nature in Downland* that poet W.B. Yeats, 'the leader of the Celtic School', should have come to live in Steyning, 'the most Saxon district in England'.[35] Hadrian Allcroft noted that the Downs were strewn everywhere with the bones of Saxons who supplanted the Briton and that the old South Saxon human type—tall, spare, blue eyed and fair haired, 'still meets one at every turn, scarcely modified by the flux of a dozen centuries'.[36] To D.H. Lawrence, finishing off *The*

**112** Few scenes evoked a greater sense of 'Saxondom' than that of strong, slow oxen dragging a wooden plough along the slopes of chalkland just as they had done before the Conquest.

*Rainbow* at Greatham near Pulborough in 1915, it was strange how old England (set in Hampshire for his story but actually a scene at Greatham): 'Lingers in patches, as here, amidst these shaggy gorse commons and marshy, snake infested places near the foot of the South Downs, the spirit of place lingering on primeval, as when the Saxons came, so long ago' (*England, my England*).

This essence of Saxondom was enhanced by farming methods and implements which had changed very little over the past one thousand years. In the Downs strong, slow oxen still plodded with wagons laden with hay or wheat-sheaves, or dragged the wooded plough along the slopes of the chalkland, just as they did before the Conquest. Alfred Noyes conveys this thought in verse inspired by the sight of an ox-drawn waggon at Rottingdean:

> Crimson and black on the sky, a waggon of clover
> Slowly goes rumbling, over the white chalk road:
> And I lie in the golden grass there, wondering why
> So little thing
> As the jingle and ring of the harness
>
> The hot creak of leather
> The peace of the plodding
> Should suddenly, stabbingly make it
> Dreadful to die ...[37]

Bob Copper, also of Rottingdean, has compared a day's work by ploughmen with an extract from a dialogue of Aelfric, Saxon abbot of the 10th century:

'What sayst thou ploughman? How dost thou do thy work?'

'O, my lord, hard do I work. I go out at daybreak, driving the oxen to the field, and I yoke them to the plough. Nor is it ever so hard winter that I dare loiter at home for fear of my lord, but the oxen yoked and the ploughshare and coulter fastened to the plough. Every day must I plough a full acre, or more' ...

and found that 'for over a thousand years man and beast had teamed up in precisely the same manner to wrest a living from these self-same acres of Sussex downland'.[38] Similarly, Maude Robinson observed of Saddlescombe Farm in the 1860s that her father kept 12 oxen for ploughing, the same number as had the Knights Templars who owned the farm in 1225 and that his sheep were enclosed by wattle and hurdles as also were the warrior-priests'.[39] The same general thought overcame John Cowper Powys as his train bringing him to Sussex made its way through the Downs, so much higher, wider, steeper and in every way more formidable than in his native Dorset. There was something about the farm buildings and rural life, the huge barns, mellow cottages and trim, neat, picturesque villages which seemed as though everyone was much more well-to-do than in the West Country and which was profoundly English, 'more English in the narrowest sense of that word than any other country in the kingdom'.[40] The naturalist H.J. Massingham thought the county of Sussex had remained truer to its Saxon foundations than any other in England.[41] Perhaps it is the American naturalist John Burroughs who attains as near as anyone to an appreciation of the subtle and elusive atmosphere of the ageless English landscape specifically evoked by the South Downs:

> The complete humanization of nature has taken place. The soil has been mixed with human thought and substance. These fields have been alternately Celt, British, Roman,

Saxon, Norman; they have moved and walked and talked and loved land, and suffered; hence one feels kindred to them and at home among them. The mother-land indeed. Every foot of its soil has given birth to a human being and grown tender and conscious with time ...[42]

The Englishness of the Downs at the beginning of this century is also conveyed by Lord Avebury in *The Scenery of England* (1902):

... The Chalk Downs occupy the heart of England ... the Downs present a series of beautiful smooth, swelling curves, perhaps the most perfect specimens of graceful contours and are covered with short, sweet, close turf. Turf is peculiarly English and no turf is more delightful than that of our Downs—delightful to ride on, to sit on, or to walk on ...[43]

**113**   William Pannett, hoop-shaving, 1934

## The Naturalists' View

The growing popularity of the Downs is also connected with the growing interest in natural history. The first writer to strike this modern note, writing primarily for an urban readership, was Richard Jefferies (1848-87), who lived in sight of the Downs at Crowborough, Hove and Worthing in the last years of his life. His joy in nature on the South Downs was a passion never quenched even by ill health. His freshness and enthusiasm for footpaths, wildflowers, thyme-scented grass, and the sea, is infectiously conveyed in his essays, such as those on Ditchling Beacon and Beachy Head, and his notes on daily walks at all seasons up the then white and flinty Dyke Road are a model of minute observations and love of locality.

Jefferies is distinguished from most nature writers by his knowledge and interest in farming which underlay the whole downland scene and his preference is for nature interwoven with man's agricultural activities. His sense of the past was quickened by the tumuli and ancient field systems then imprinted all over the highest parts of the Downs and he is the earliest writer to perceive the history of this visible ancient land as a continuous process of evolution, in such forms as the shape of the fields, the lines of trackways, the traditional crafts, the old implements such as ploughs and wagons, and the names of villages, thus anticipating the modern interpretation of the English landscape as a palimpsest of human decisions by W.G. Hoskins in the 20th century.

W.H. Hudson wrote of the Downs (to which he was first introduced at Shoreham[44]) from a rather different perspective. It is instructive to compare Cobbett's observations on the Downs with the very different ones of Hudson seventy years later. One's first impression is to doubt whether the two writers could have been describing the same range of hills, so utterly suffused is Hudson's little masterpiece *Nature in Downland* (1900) with the then new eyes of the town-living naturalist. One also reflects on how transformed in character are the high Downs from Hudson's day, a change so total, sudden and insensitive, that one doubts the possibility of making a meaningful communication with them, except through the medium of Hudson's book.

Hudson's first chapter opens as a kind of overture to some grand symphony, which in a sense the book is, transporting the reader to Kingston Hill near Lewes in the hot summer of 1898, not to look at the view, enthralling though it is, but to witness thousands upon thousands of balls of thistle-down flecking the elastic greensward with silvery white before springing up as the heat opens them and the wind bears them away into the blue sky. Hudson's description of this incident is a brilliant evocation of aerial space and of light, heat, windswept slopes and hollows of the Downs. The cloud of thistle-down of the common purple dwarf thistle sprang from the wide expanse of untilled, unenclosed down which had existed for centuries. This 'wilderness' was Hudson's stage. He had an aversion for the tame and domesticated and avoided contact with human life as instinctively as the wheatear and stonechat, both once common birds on the South Downs. In *Hampshire Days*, one of several books following *Nature in Downland*, he writes of his melancholy yearning for 'wilderness' which he loved best with only wild creatures for visitors and company. H.J. Massingham (who was strongly influenced by Hudson but whose field of observation was wider) has remarked that Hudson always stopped short of the cultivated patch: 'He represented the corncrake and the rabbit in the corn, not the ear and reaper'. In his book on the South Downs, which is both a model of natural history and a distinguished contribution to English literature in the field of rural writing, Hudson says almost nothing about downland farming or villages, market towns and human life. He wrote: 'I seldom care to loiter long in their cultivated parts. It seems better to get away, even from the sight of labouring men and oxen, and of golden corn and laughing birdweed, to walk on the turf'. His Downs are accordingly emptied of people.

Hudson's element was the wildlife habitats of the Downs; the old chalk grassland; the grassland resulting from a re-colonisation of ploughed-up downland; hawthorn and juniper scrub; gorse thickets; chalk heath and beechwoods and yew woods. He gives only incidental references to the sea cliffs and omits entirely the water meadows in the downland valleys. Hudson's success with his book was with people, who, with growing industrialisation and urbanisation in the years since Cobbett wrote, were consciously searching out quiet peaceful places in the Downs where they could sit and 'commune with nature' amidst just turf, trees, insects, bees, butterflies and birdsong as did Hudson on Kingston Hill. Sadly, their interest and understanding of farming, and of rural life, correspondingly diminished.

El Chapo
*Chapter Twelve*

# THE DOWNS THAT WERE ENGLAND
# (1900–1939)

## The Dream of the Downs and the Reality

Between the two World Wars no image evoked more strongly the rural English arcadia yearned for by town dwellers than that of the Sussex Downs. For those who failed to overcome an aversion to the giant polypus of London, the Downs had an irresistible allure, and if London made the escape necessary, the Downs made it practicable by their very accessibility. By catching one of the 'Green Electrics', celebrated in verse by John Arlott,[1] which ran between Victoria railway station and Brighton every hour, on the hour, in the hour, the green hills rolling down to the sea became the place where Londoners smelt the tang of sea air mingled with the scents of harvest and the aromatic herbs of unfenced turf. A green arm of the Downs cradling an 'incredibly perfect' thatched village with its little church and cosy pub and a cricket match on the village green was the beautiful and beloved image that symbolised the spirit of the age.[2] Anyone over the age of 60 years asked what is best remembered of the Downs in their childhood invariably recalls nostalgically of long-remembered pleasure and recalls wistfully a prospect paradisal in its emptiness with bees buzzing round the wild flowers; myriads of butterflies and gold finches singing on the tops of thistle. It remains to them a lasting vision of enchantment, before post-war seaside towns engulfed village after village, which had given them an exhilarating sense of freedom which lent wings to the human spirit.[3] They remember their unfillable longing for the old Downs and the heartbreak that followed the separation when a revolution in agriculture so phenomenally and suddenly brought to an end several thousands of years of a farming system and its rural life. Like all romantics they have continued to pine for what was lost or out of reach.

Downland farmers and landowners saw things differently. After the prosperous years of the mid-19th century came a period of acute difficulty with falling prices for corn and wool and lower rents which fell to ludicrous levels in the bottom of the depression in the 1930s. As early as 1867 poor land in the Western Downs was valued little agriculturally. Less than half of Up Waltham parish was then cultivated and in Graffham parish only about one quarter. The greater part of the downland there was 'scarcely of value as sheep walk'. Unsurprisingly, labourers' cottages were poor and badly overcrowded, people lacked work and some were badly off in winter. An unusual visible proof of early decline is the 100-year-old yew woods at Kingley Vale which have encroached on former sheepdown.[4]

When Rider Haggard visited the Western Downs as part of his investigation into the state of English farming in 1901 he found the downland farms in such a sorry condition that they were capable of producing 'but little grass and less corn'. Small owners who had lived on the Downs were for the most part broken and gone, and the new-style owner, enriched by trade,

El Chapo

bought up farms merely for sport producing little but partridges. As regards labour, all the young men were draining from the land. On the Eastern Downs the situation was little better. Although most farmers clung to traditional sheep-and-corn, through inertia, the more profitable enterprises involved dairying and beef cattle.[5] One of the most notable successes was the Brand farm at Glynde[6] (John Ellman's epochral sheep farm), where the change had been pioneered in the 1880s. Such changes meant fencing across formerly unfenced openness, hence reducing public access. An ominous sign of bad times was the large estate with 'very considerable building value' which was coming on to the market. In 1907 the Earl of Chichester let his Home Farm at Stanmer rent free for two years. Another doleful example of the eclipse of downland farming was long gaps between tenancies as at Applesham in the 1890s.

Much derelict land was temporarily improved during the First World War but after the repeal of the Corn Production Acts in 1921 downland agriculture soon swung back into its old state of neglect. Thousands of acres were given over to ragwort, thorn bushes and rabbits, not normally on the best land, but that 30 years earlier had been well-farmed and well-stocked. Between 1928 and 1931 the average price of all farm products fell by one third and land was worth only what it had cost in 1850. Beautiful and impressive as the Downs were, field thistles and ragwort went into the ascendance again, an inevitable outcome of agricultural hard times. By 1939 farm after farm on the Downs was near-derelict, farms which old men remembered in their boyhood had employed dozens of men, kept pedigree prize-winning flocks and produced bountifully wheat, barley and oats of the first quality. Now little was to be seen but an abomination of desolation.

Bad seasons and increased imports had forced the traditional sheep-and-corn system reluctantly into change or decay. The wool clip (which used to pay the rent) became

**114**   Sir William Nicholson's *Rottingdean, c.*1909.

proportionately of much less value and farmers fell into trouble. George Mitchell of Pyecombe, the last of the Sussex crook-makers, was not making crooks for shepherds in 1939, but only for bishops. His smithy in the 1930s looked out on sheepless downs where he remembered a thousand Southdowns grazing. A man, he boasted, could in the old days have walked for nine miles on the Downs between Pyecombe and Lewes on a sward like a 'billiard table'. Now the grass was up to the knees.[7] The enthusiastic pioneers in 'New Farming' could in no way have foreseen that their way of maintaining fertility by sheep would prove impossible to maintain at a profit in a world market in changed external conditions. Fortunately, some demoralised farmers stayed on: without them there would not have been enough men with sufficient knowledge to cope with wartime food needs.

The memories of older leisure-seekers and farmers alike are like tall stories to persons who care about the Downs but who did not know them before the Second World War. Eric Gill, letter-cutter and sculptor at Ditchling between 1909 and 1924, thought of the Downs in retrospective view in terms of a lost innocence that only persons who had shared his experience would understand:

> If you have been a little child brought up in these hills and in those days, you will understand their mortal loveliness. If, in your childhood, you have walked over them and in them and under them … Then you will know what I am talking about, but not otherwise. No one who was not there as a child can know that heaven, no grown-up can capture it.[8]

Gill's remark raises a problem created by the Downs themselves. The essence of the South Downs has always defied analysis. Their rural character is hard to define, so terribly difficult to convey, yet so unmistakeably there. Virginia Woolf came to realise this when returning to Rodmell on a summer's evening. Even with her exceptional powers of description she could not catch and hold all the beauty 'more extravagantly greater than one could expect … I cannot hold this—I cannot express this—I am overcome by it—I am mastered.'[9]

One who best captures in vivid and authentic detail the Downs before the Second World War is Bob Copper who has lived most of his life near Rottingdean where his family farmed for generations. He writes with unaffected realism of the scene, noting that the long valley between Telscombe and Southease was so thickly stocked with sheep that locally it was called 'Mutton Barracks'. Rottingdean Farm alone maintained about 3,000 sheep.

> From the surrounding hill country their plaintive bleating could be heard down in the village from dawn until dusk; the steep hillsides were ribbed with sheep tracks; sheep's wool clung to the hedgerows and wire fences; the smell of sheep was borne on the downland breeze, and there were times when, if your street door was not kept closed, you would have had sheep in your very parlour. When the shepherds were taking their flocks on to new grazing ground, and had to pass through the village to get there, a flood of woolly-backed invaders would come pouring down, threatening the entire village … The High Street would be so solid with sheep that you could have walked on their backs from wall to wall, and cottage and shop doors alike would be hastily slammed. The dogs, in fact, did jump up and run about on the backs of the sheep, urging those in the forward ranks to move along a little faster …[10]

The most memorable of all these inter-war reminiscences are those of (Sir) Dirk Bogarde whose humour and sparkling dialogue brings to life childhood scenes at Lullington where he shared a summer cottage with his family.[11] He recalled Mr. Dick shepherding his sheep from Windover Hill towards Winchester's Pond; the great horses, 'Their ears capped with little woolly cones to keep out flies, the poppies in great scarlet drifts and little clouds of chalk'. This site now straddles the Lullington Heath National Nature Reserve and was called by his father 'the most beautiful place in England' (Bogarde returned to his country of the Long Man of Wilmington after the War and bitterly regretted the changes: he might now warmly praise the recent renewal at the hands of English Nature and the Sussex Downs Conservation Board).

## The Pleasures of the Past

The Downs became thought of as being as necessary as those cells in the human body which are vital for daily well-being and renewal of the whole. When considering the various enjoyments derived from them, the physical sensation of 'feeling good' was the first of the pleasures that came to mind. The elevation of the animal spirits by means of brisk exercise in fresh, salty air had been one of the elements of the health cure at Regency Brighton, and M.A. Lower, the most entertaining of the Sussex historians, wrote in 1854 how easy it was to love the Downs where the special quality of the turf under the feet almost made walking and riding on horse-back as light and easy as flying through the air. He wandered and galloped without obstruction... 'All around seems to say, Go where you like - make yourself at home - glad to see you'.[12]

It was walking or riding over open downland, whether in gentle or rapid movement, which was also amongst the foremost pleasures of the Downs in the first third of this century. R. Thurston Hopkins, the founder of the Society of Sussex Downsmen, tried to convey his delicious sense of release from urban life that the Downs brought to people like him: 'I felt that for many months I have been in a dungeon and that I have suddenly been given my liberty ...

My dominant feeling ... is of a new companionship, a glow of the heart, as though the Downs and hanging woods of the hills had suddenly embraced and succoured me ...'[13] Amongst other forerunners of modern ramblers was Arthur Beckett, President of the Downsmen and founding editor of Sussex County Magazine. His opening chapter in *The Spirit of the Downs* (1909) tells of striding along the crest of the Downs near Eastbourne in seven-league boots, 'lungs labouring like small bellows, eyes smarting with brine in a south-westerly gale, blissful to be alive'. As if the pleasure of walking was not enough Beckett (and naturalist W.H. Hudson) yearned for wings that they might 'skim along the lean sides of the grey-green downs and float over their backs' as the more daring can now do in a hang-glider.[14]

To the invalid, the Downs were a tonic. The Victorian novelist George Gissing, although in poor health, felt capable of walking on and on with an unwearied lightness.[15] To delicate Richard Jefferies, the glory of the Downs was the turf and the breeze: 'Lands of gold have been found and lands of species

SOUTHERN RAILWAY

A MOONLIGHT WALK!

OVER THE SOUTH DOWNS

TO WITNESS

SUNRISE FROM

CHANCTONBURY RING

With Mr. S.P.B. MAIS (of Wireless Fame)

On SATURDAY (NIGHT) 16th JULY

Special Supper and Breakfast Car Train

### TO STEYNING

| FORWARD | Return Fare (3rd Class) | RETURN |
|---------|------------------------|--------|
| Saturday Night. | | Sunday Morning. |

| | Midnt. | s. d. | | a.m. |
|---------|--------|-------|---------|------|
| Victoria dep. | 12 10 | 4   0 | Steyning dep. | 7 20 |

EXPERIENCE THE NOVEL THRILL of watching a summer dawn from the first streaks to the full sunrise.

**115**  S.P.B. Mais's abortive mass excursion from London.

and precious merchandise: but this is the land of health', he wrote of Beachy Head.[16] The health-seeking poet John Davidson responded to the wind. With a wind like this it is impossible not to be happy. There's oxygen in it, ozone, life - it's flung at you, envelopes you, bathes you, pounds and stitches you, rakes you over again'. Exhilarated, he tramped 'with the rush of a charging host' and took Thundersbarrow 'in a single leap'.[17]

The supreme apostle of mass walking was populist S.P.B. Mais, an inspiring, if eccentric, schoolmaster who lived on delightful Southwick Green and led parties of office workers and shop assistants on organised walking excursions for the Southern Railway. He is a symbolic figure of the new 'outdoors movement'. His very name sent a shiver down the backs of those hostile to the idea of the Sussex Downs becoming the Londoners' weekend retreat. His account of an abortive excursion from London to see the sun rise on Chanctonbury Ring and of a party arriving at Hassocks station are gems of walking literature.[18]

**116** *Punch*'s idea of a 'beauty spot', a new phrase coined between the Wars. The popular tea gardens at Wannock, Litlington and Bramber fitted this description.

The South Downs also had a great vogue amongst cyclists. Bernard Bergonzi has remarked in respect of H.G. Wells' picturesque novel *The Wheels of Chance* (1895) that the chalky roads took Mr. Hoopdriver through a landscape that had much in common with that of Tom Jones or Mr. Pickwick. Murray has written of the social changes the invention of the safety cycle wrought in the countryside. 'The only places of refreshment were public houses and the only goods sold were beers and spirits. No nice girl went into a public house. Inns began to sell teas in gardens and tea shops were invented.'[19]

Sussex tea shops were to have a special place in the promotion of leisure. Ashley Courtenay, author of the famous restaurant and hotel guide *Let's Halt Awhile*, was motoring in the Downs in 1933 when he noticed a sign which read 'Real Sussex Teas'. As he waited in the garden of a thatched cottage to be served, it occurred to him that such places should be better known. This gave him the idea of publishing a guide to tea rooms and hotels. 'And what if the owners should pay him for the privilege? Like a star, the idea stood in the sky over Sussex.'[20]

There were other ways of sampling the experience of the Downs. By the 1920s many middle-class people who had become car-owners and wished for the simple life sought sites on or near the Downs where they could weekend on a private country retreat. Hubert Visick, an Eastbourne dental surgeon, bought 20 acres at Graffham on which he built a bungalow. Another was a well-known Brighton department store owner who paid a nominal rent for a stretch of river bank on the river Arun at Quell Farm, Greatham, on which he erected a cabin. Yet another who bought a plot of land on which he erected a wooden cabin was Mr. Geal who had a business in Hove and 'kipped' for the weekend above an old chalk-pit at Steyning, enjoying a lovely view of the Weald.

It was not only the middle classes who were spreading their wings. Another group which became interested in leisure on the Downs was the Camping Club. This was started in 1901 as The Association of Cycle Campers by T.H. Holdin, a master tailor. In early years it comprised many working-class members who often wore a special jacket with huge 'poacher' pockets to carry a little food and personal belongings such as the stub of a candle sufficient for two days, a few matches and a midget piece of soap.[21]

Another person attracted to the Downs at this period was the Back-to-the-Land simple-lifer. One of the several transient and ultimately unsuccessful back-to-the-land communes lasted for ten years from 1922 and was on part of Heath Common, near Washington. This was an experiment of Vera Pragnell, daughter of Sir George Pragnell, a wealthy textile manufacturer, who formed a Christian community where settlers would attempt to carry out the teaching of St Francis of Assisi and devote themselves to rural life and the making of handicrafts. Her vision and achievements are set out in her booklet *The Story of the Sanctuary*, which was published in 1928, but sadly the colony fell short of her ideals. The calvary she set up on Longbury Hill is now in the refectory of Our Lady of England Priory, Storrington. Vera Pragnell also set up a wooden chapel-cum-theatre, a school (temporarily in a disused omnibus) and a general store, and land she purchased from the Sandgate Estate was divided into small plots which were granted free to colonists for building wooden bungalows and shacks. The settlers were left entirely free to live their lives in their own way. Local people described the Sanctuaries as 'Bolshevik, atheist, diet-cranks, contraceptionists and similar scum' but the local poet Victor Neuburg, who was a close friend of Vera Pragnell, saw them as people who might by experiment transform a Europe ravaged by war, poverty and ugliness which had been created by modern cities and the factory system.[22]

## Englishness

It was from about 1900 and until 1939 that the South Downs secured a tenacious hold on the national psyche in a crucial period in the formation of attitudes and ideas which were to dominate English culture up to the end of the Second World War. With the rise of ugly cities and towns during the Industrial Revolution and general concern at conditions of urban life, John Ruskin, William Morris, Leslie Stephen and other prominent writers on the national identity sowed the notion that the 'real' England was the natural beauty of the countryside and its rural life. The view was also expressed that life in the countryside offered a positive alternative to that led in the city. In drawing this conclusion a long literary tradition of an idyllic vision of past rural life was drawn upon which is now recognised as essentially a fiction. Although the quest for innovation and invention had made the nation economically great the values extolled by Ruskinites were tradition, constancy, stability, continuity and harmony, supposedly offered by rural life. After 1918 this countryside ethic was spread well beyond the middle classes and espoused by such rural elegists as prime minister Stanley Baldwin, writer and statesman John Buchan and Sir George Trevelyan, the most famous historian of his generation and leading member of the National Trust.[23] These viewed the countryside as an ark of refuge, a bulwark for troublous times, and a source of the 'spiritual' values which had made Britain a world power and which would outlive the Empire.

The mythologised Downs became prominent in the revolution of thought that occurred as to what constituted the national identity. In the vision of England as a rural and bucolic environment in which new and worldly things were inherently bad, old and ascetic ones good, the Downs seemed to embody the very quintessence of English ideals. Southern English authors had long considered it as the most 'psychologically' English of the nation, a notion held by Jane Austen, for example, who expressed admiration for the concept as 'sweet to eye and mind, English verdure, English culture, English comfort'.[24] This belief that chalkland had a special place in this southern English rural cosmogony was enhanced by its rarity outside England, so making it more English than any other rock, and on account of it being one of the oldest of man's possessions, Lord Avebury appears to have been the first to identify quintessential Englishness with chalk,[25] and his idea was followed up by E.M. Forster who wrote: 'Chalk made the dust white, chalk made the water clear, chalk made the clean rolling outline of the land, favoured the grass and the distant coronal trees. Here is the heart of our island.'[26]

In this vein it was almost inevitable that the South Downs should be identified as having qualities which made it so English as to fill one with a sense of England. We have noted these in chapters one and eleven. The Downs still remained as late as the 1930s largely untouched by incessant noise, speed and the other 'acids of modernity' and as a snug, homely and very livable part of the nation with its unique Saxon heritage, traditional ways of farming, and unhurried lifestyle. With its extraordinary wealth of associations, historical, architectural, literary and artistic arising from human occupation over several thousands of years the Downs could still be thought of as representing England itself.[27] Such a cultural nostrum was even enshrined in local planning policy. The Advisory Planning Scheme for the central Downs recommended in 1932 that 'the best that can happen to the Downs is that they should be kept as they are, a feeding ground for sheep, a great sanctuary for nature lovers, a haven from the fret and hurry of the busy world'. The aim appears to have been to set aside the Downs as a kind of Human Conservancy where rare plants, birds and animals would also have been protected. The future of the Sussex Downs as a National Park seemed assured with the saving of the Downs from indiscriminate development. (Chapter 13)

Some felt alienated by the current idea of 'Englishness' and all it stood for. It grated on Cyril Connolly, one of the most prominent literary figures of the time, an anarchist always

117  A wooden bungalow constructed at Brighton Heights (1934).

**118** The view towards the South Downs from the Shoulder of Mutton Hill at Steep, Hampshire. The sarsen stone commemorating Edward Thomas is shown.

ready to attack the spirit of the age. He had been educated at a preparatory school in East-bourne, lived for many years at Firle, greatly loved the unparadised Downs and is buried in Berwick churchyard. With idiosyncratic melancholy he thought of the Downs in 1929 not so much for their natural beauty but for the 'awfulness' of the people who wrote about it—Kipling's thyme and dew ponds, Belloc's beer, Chesterton's chalk, together with the despised lyricism of the Georgian poets, the Drinkwatermen, the Squires and the Shanks (all connected with Rodmell).[28] He was driven to distraction by the sight of people of the 'county habit has me by the heart' and the 'England, my England' fraternity whom he found spreading over the Downs as if on a fly paper—the ardent cyclists, the pipe-smoking, beer-swilling, young ramblers, the brass rubbers, charabanc trippers and motorists picnicking 'over a space for building lots'. With an aloof and brooding ferocity he wailed of the Downs: 'Why not let the countryside be finished instead of propping it up in this long agony, this imbecile position between life and death'.[29] A similar explosion of wrath later came from Evelyn Waugh.[30]

Nor did the 'Englishness' of the Downs find favour with principal landowners who struggled to come to terms with a mass outdoors movement which was unimaginable a generation earlier. They wished to retain a life of privileged seclusion and enjoy the Downs in traditional ways and to have freedom from ramblers and trippers (although several of their descendants clamour for brown leisure signs). Not the least of the charm of November was that the hiker, caravanner, picnicker, trespasser and other intruders and disturbers of the local rural scene had departed to their winter quarters in towns. Road traffic went down more than half; discordant notes of the gramophone, the wireless set, the motorbike and the motor-horn were no longer heard. A natural, pleasing, quiet reigned once more.[30]

## The Last of 'England'

In actual fact the idyllic view of rural life that was the basis of 'Englishness' never really existed. It was a romantic myth, already a thing of the past, an escape from encroaching urbanisation and technology for those who were unaware of the agricultural decay of the inter-war years. There was no recognition that a day's work in the fields was back-breaking or that it could be lonely, miserable and squalid. Visitors tended to be ignorant about farming and took little interest in it. They took little part in the life of the village. Socially they did not recognise villages' existence, though they might subscribe to village cricket and football clubs. They admired downland views, took frequent excursions by car, but rarely walked over the Downs. Their roots were in London: from London came their friends at weekends; from London came their food and drinks. Joad castigated such people in 1939: 'For such, tennis, golf and bridge players, the trees go into leaf, the corn is gathered, the mists come and the fruit, the smoke of bonfires rises and the golden glory of autumn is diffused about the land, in vain. They do not see such things'. Joad claimed that most were not country people at all, just townsmen 'camping'.[31]

Moreover, it is clear that the Downs could induce disagreeable sensations. As early as 1918 A Hadrian Allcroft drew attention to new fences 'yearly' blocking former access to the Downs.[32] The Congress of the South Eastern Union of Scientific Societies, meeting at Eastbourne in 1920, brought to notice extensive enclosures which had already been made on the Downs, and which threatened to close up many routes familiar to ramblers from time immemorial. Barbed wire fences appear to have been rendered necessary by the great increase in cattle then being maintained on the hills. So great was the concern that it was considered that public rights should be examined. A resolution on this matter was passed unanimously:

> That the Congress, being of the opinion that the preservation of the South Downs in an open condition is a matter of national importance and interest, some of the finest scenery of the Southern Counties, deplores the recent and growing tendency to enclose the Downs, thereby depriving the public of their treasured and immemorial custom of wandering over these beautiful uplands.[33]

Furthermore, the resolution urged that steps should be taken forthwith by the local authorities, the National Trust and various national organisations, as well as inhabitants of the county of Sussex, to acquire and protect for the use of education and public enjoyments, typical stretches of the Downs, including land along the crest which included the most magnificent viewpoints over the Weald. The aspirations of the Congress were to put into practice on an *ad hoc* basis in the late 1920s and the 1930s when local authorities, notably Eastbourne and Brighton Corporations and the National Trust, acquired land to protect the Downs from the

OUR VANDALS ON THE DOWNS.
"GLORIOUS VIEW, ISN'T IT?"
"YES, BUT THE SURFACE IS REALLY DISGRACEFUL."

**119** Arrogant motorists on the Downs, 1927 (by *Punch*). This was not the only problem at this period. The threat of electricity pylons in the village street of Amberley was averted in 1932 by adverse publicity in *The Times* which printed five letters, three photographs and a map of the potential disaster.

threat of building (p.172), but it is only in the last few years that the aim has been conceived of a wider application of these objectives. An instance of the changing character of the Downs is conveyed by Mais' account of his walks from Devil's Dyke to Truleigh Hill in the 1930s, when he found modern intrusions and heavily-barbed wire fences obstructing the way.[34]

The peace and solitude extolled at this period were also being injured substantially, not by farmers or the circumstances of war, but by droves of tourists and resident newcomers when the Downs were being promoted with white-hot heat by arch-publicists Rudyard Kipling and Hilaire Belloc. As the *Manchester Guardian* cynically observed in 1926, 'The beauties of the county [Sussex] seem have been fairly safe till the 'Sussex school' of writers descended on the land and proceeded to elaborate on Mr. Kipling's well-known appreciation'. Kipling himself wrote his verses entitled *Very Many People* (1926)

> … They take our land to delight in,
> But their delight destroys
> They flay the turf from the sheepwalk
> They load the Denes with noise …

It was never the intention of newcomers to kill what they loved of the Downs, but by sheer force of numbers they had begun unwittingly and unwillingly to do so. Few realised that the continuance of a rural culture depended on those inheriting it and at the hands of sophisticated, urbanised people the old downland order simply began to dissolve.

# Chapter Thirteen

# THE CALL TO ARMS

It was not until the advent of the motor car and economic and social changes following the First World War that circumstances threatened to mar the beauty and peace of the Downs. Certainly by 1900 Brighton was brimming over the two chalk valleys north of the Regency watering place and was surging up the slopes of downland, already threatening to engulf whole villages, such as Preston and Patcham. Hove was also at this time invading the Downs themselves, as was also Worthing to a lesser extent. The main loss of downland was at Eastbourne where the seventh Duke of Devonshire was responsible for solidly-built villas springing up behind the sea-front in a sustained burst of town-building which turned the town into the most fashionable seaside resort in England.

Yet nothing suggested that sporadic new settlements were about to spring up. Indeed, trends were operating in the interests of conservation. Brighton kept indiscriminate housing at bay by its purchase of Mile Oak and New Barn Farms in the 1880s and also by the acquisition of Hollingbury Park in 1900 as public open space and the East Brighton estate in 1913, also partly for the purpose of recreation. The town thereafter embarked on an *ad hoc* purchase of downland, within and without its administrative boundaries, to protect its water supplies and the landscape of its hinterland (p.172).

Furthermore, the rescue of an ancient vernacular building before 1900 can justly be regarded as a milestone in conserving the historic environment in England. In 1879 the Bishop of Chichester and the patron of the living authorised the demolition of the Old Clergy House at Alfriston. This was fortunately not carried out, largely because of concern expressed by the Sussex Archaeological Society, and in 1891 the building came to the attention of the Society for the Protection of Ancient Buildings who identified it as a prime example

**120** The Clergy House, Alfriston before and after restoration.

of 14th-century domestic architecture which had not been subsequently altered. In 1896 the Rev. Beynon, who then held the living, contacted the National Trust only ten days after its formal incorporation. Although the building was then in the last stage of dilapidation money was raised by public subscription to bolt the decaying timber to a duplicate frame inside and the saved building became the very first of all National Trust built properties.[1]

The main cause of the lack of speculative development on the Downs before 1900 was not only the shortage of water which then had to be supplied expensively from deep wells, but the inaccessibility of most parts from railheads which made the carriage of building materials difficult and costly. A landowner with much marginal downland on his hands who attempted to wrestle with these problems was Carew Davies Gilbert, owner of about a third of the then new resort of Eastbourne and of the manor of Birling which included Birling Gap on the cliffed coast between Beachy Head and Seaford. Between 1885 and the 1930s Gilbert never lost faith in his dream of a new seaside resort at the Gap. In 1885 his agent proposed to the London, Brighton and South Coast Railway that it should construct a new railway between Eastbourne and Seaford to serve the intended watering place. The railway company rejected this proposal on account of the heavy costs of building over such hilly terrain and an alternative proposal put forward by Gilbert to build a branch line from the Lewes-Eastbourne line at Berwick was also given short shrift by the company.[2] Undaunted, Gilbert revived his town-building plans in 1887-8 on the basis of a proposed Cuckmere Valley light railway. With intended stations at Wannock, Jevington and Birling, this was supported by the Duke of Devonshire, but it encountered opposition from neighbouring landowners, including James Gwynne of Folkington Manor and Lord Gage of West Firle. After a public local inquiry (commendably lasting only four hours instead of the four days, or longer, it would probably have taken today), the Light Railway Commissioners turned down the scheme as potentially damaging to farming interests.[3] Nevertheless, Gilbert continued to persist with his town-building plans and these are of exceptional interest because of the high quality of the proposed design, contrasting markedly with the shoddiness of Peacehaven which was audaciously perpetrated shortly afterwards. In 1898 Gilbert announced that his new town at Birling Gap was to be called 'Southdown Bay' and by 1904 this was taking clearer shape on the drawing board, clearly influenced by the new town near Baldock, Hertfordshire, which was soon to become known as Letchworth Garden City.

Michell Witley, Gilbert's agent, was ambitious for a purpose-built seaside resort unhindered by earlier piecemeal development and which sensitively preserved, as far as possible, the downland setting. Simple private gardens and an unusual amount of public space were to be features of the new town and local building styles were to be adopted sympathetically. Despite his previous abortive negotiations, a site for a new railway station and a site for an electricity works were allocated. The whole of the seafront was reserved for a promenade which was to have lawns similar to the Leas at Folkestone, together with an elegant crescent of detached houses. A pier was considered a future project.[4] Even with the final collapse of his railway scheme, Gilbert's entrepreneurship did not languish for, in 1927, when the motor vehicle had resolved the problem of public access to Birling Gap, he was promoting a 'Motorists' Estate de Luxe' at Crowlink Gap, just west of Birling, which was, however, forestalled by the intervention of Arthur Beckett of the Society of Sussex Downsmen and the National Trust.[5]

Although Gilbert failed to build a single house at Birling Gap other speculators with fewer scruples and with more accessible sites had already created an invasion of townspeople on to the Downs too great to be without damaging effects. As motor transport multiplied and roads were improved so sporadic housing development on open downland had begun to produce

**121** Birling Gap, c.1934. The relentless erosion of the chalk cliffs has already destroyed dwellings and others will shortly fall into the sea. The National Trust has acquired property here and the general character, although ramshackle, is less obnoxious than before the War because all the cliff edge from the second cottage on the left has since fallen into the sea. Originally built on Beachy Head 150 years ago one hundred feet from the cliff edge, the former lighthouse of Belle Tout (now restored and in residential use) was brought to within a few feet of the sea by erosion which was particularly severe in 1893, 1896 and 1998. In 1999 the building was pulled back fifty feet by the use of greased float pads and hydraulic jacks at a cost of £250,000.

even before 1914 an unregulated spatter of buildings, including shacks, bungalows, tea houses, roadhouses, garages and advertisements 'only worthy of some American gold rush'. Early examples were at Woodingdean, east of Brighton,[6] and at 'Brighton Heights', adjacent to the Whitehawk estate near Brighton race course. The most elaborate and potentially destructive proposal was a large plotland at Denton, at the mouth of the Sussex Ouse. This was promoted as 'Newhaven-on-Sea' with 'highly eligible access to main roads'. More than one hundred plots on downland east of the attractive little village of Denton were sold for dwellings, each with a very narrow road frontage. Fortunately, only a small part of this was realised.[7] By the beginning of the 1920s the public awoke to the realisation that given the then rate of destruction, the Sussex Downs could be completely wrecked, 'The one nearly perfect thing left to us in England'. The effects of this crisis were to band people together into associations whose efforts were directed to preserving the amenities and educating the public at large to a better understanding of the Downs. These included the Society of Sussex Downsmen, founded by R. Thurston Hopkins in 1923, which found a valiant President in Arthur Beckett, founder and editor of *Sussex County Magazine*. Other founder members were Captain and Mrs. Irvine Bately,

Lewis Cohen (later Lord Cohen of Brighton) and S.P.B. Mais, the broadcaster. There was also a new national body, the Council for the Preservation (now Protection) of Rural England, created in 1926, which sought to co-ordinate the efforts of the individual societies in a general protection of rural amenities over the whole of England, but whose origin was largely due to the damaging effects on the natural environment on the Eastern Downs. The National Trust, the Ramblers' Association and the Commons and Open Space Society also became actively involved. Such bodies drew repeated attention to the Downs' imminent peril of widespread disfigurement from a scattering of houses. The leading question of the day was how the new urbanised population flooding into the Downs should be housed so that the downland did not suffer a complete change in consequence (Plate XVII).

At the centre of this controversy was Charles Neville (1881-1961) who gained both fame and notoriety by buying large stretches of downland and promoting housing development between the two World Wars along the five-mile stretch of cliffed coast between Rottingdean and Newhaven. Not all Neville's development deserves censure. The Rottingdean houses Neville built in the mock-Tudor style had a bad press and were generally reviled by architectural critics in the 1920s and 1930s, but they were the work of serious architects, builders and craftsmen in the Arts and Crafts mode, and details such as re-used timber from derelict buildings and the elaborate Tudor-style carving have since won praise. Saltdean with its ultra-modern houses also gave offence to many contemporaries but is increasingly being seen as a successful example of a superior kind of middle-class resort. The Lido (1935) is now regarded as one of the finest Art Deco buildings in the country and it is planned to restore it. Peacehaven, the earliest of Neville's creations, has been consistently reviled and derided. Thomas Sharp, a leading planning consultant in the 1930s, summed up the contemporary view of it: 'Peacehaven has been called a rash on the countryside. It is that, and there is no worse in England'.[8] Nikolaus Pevsner in the Sussex volume of *The Buildings of England* scorns the place as the 'reduction ad absurdum of the garden city … which has rightly become a national laughing stock. Garden city enthusiasts disown any connection with the place, and are as willing to jibe at it as anyone else.'[9] Graham Greene in *Brighton Rock* (1938) was so horrified by the ugly desecration of the downland at Peacehaven that he selected it as the destination of the gangster Pinkie's and Rosie's drive into the 'country' as his way of indicating how remote they were 'from any inkling of natural beauty, and how untouched by its benign influence'.[10] When reflecting on the bucolic peace of the Downs before 1914 when writing his autobiography in 1968, stern and unillusioned Leonard Woolf, self-styled 'a socialist of a rather peculiar sort', regarded Peacehaven as a symbol of the civilisation annihilated by the First World War. He contrasted it with the downland and its country life through which he and Virginia Woolf had walked from Asham to the sea on the day war broke out. Recalled were unchanging buildings, great flocks of sheep and the lack of human habitation all the way to the cliffs. Even on the later site of Peacehaven and Telscombe Cliffs were visible only a farmhouse, a Post Office and few houses where a few years later small plots of land were being sold 'and a rash of bungalows, houses, shops, shacks, chicken runs, huts and dog kennels' spread from the cliff edge. Faced with this higgledy piggledy shoddiness, Woolf thought with a truly daunting severity that if one had to choose between sheep, shepherd and sheep dogs, and the occupiers of hideous houses with their TV, football pools and bingo he was not sure that one should not prefer the civilisation of the sheep.[11] (Plate XVIII)

Woolf's opinions were apparently widely shared amongst the middle classes. The unspoilt subject of their fury had been hauntingly portrayed by Sir William Nicholson (plate XVIII) a few years earlier. It was the sheer audacity and scale of Peacehaven which outraged contemporaries, and this was seen as symptomatic of all that was wrong with *laissez-faire* attitude to land then widely shared by government and governed alike. There is a tendency today to be less fiercely judgmental of Neville's Peacehaven, partly because the still uncouth and squalid appearance it bore on the eve of the Second World War has since been rectified by the East Sussex County Council and other local authorities which filled in gaps between bungalows and provided basic amenities which Neville failed to supply. Yet it is difficult to believe that the almost universal adverse verdict of more than seventy years will be anything but irrevocable. The historian of suburbia, Arthur M. Edwards, selected it as 'the worst example of shackland' in Britain.[12]

Charles Neville was only 33 years of age when he began to create the new town that was to become Peacehaven and a varied and adventurous life abroad had included mining and prospecting in New Guinea and real estate business in Australia and Canada. He had tentatively laid out his township on a chessboard or grid-iron pattern on the eve of the First World War but cultivation by the Board of Agriculture destroyed the entire layout of the estate. A new plan of development on the same lines had to be undertaken when the site was re-requisitioned in 1920. The town then became notorious as one of the last occasions in England when private land speculators had a completely free rein and it will always share a place in history for the then novel promotional techniques employed by Neville which included newspaper advertisements and competitions with rash promises which never squared with stark reality. Mr. Justice Younger, summing up at the end of a libel action, described these as 'appealing to the vanity, not to say the stupidity, of the public' and charges made that Neville was a clever fraudster were proved in court.[13]

## The Desperate Battle to Save the Downs

By the late 1920s the activities of speculative building syndicates had greatly multiplied on the Downs east of Worthing. Although Peacehaven remained the paramount scandal, bungalows at Brighton Heights and Woodingdean, north of Rottingdean, and numerous other shanty towns, such as in the Cradle Valley near Alfriston, at Birling Gap and at Crowlink on the site of two of the Seven Sisters, were as unprepossessing. With the publication of her diaries and letters, we can discover Virginia Woolf's thoughts and emotions during these epochral events. Every solitary walk brought up fresh eyesores or threats of development. Wherever and whenever she came across anything new breaking her cherished sweep of the Downs, whether houses, bungalows, shanties or race- or motorcycle tracks, she broke out into explosions of rage or despair according to her mood. The most terrible blow to her was the fate of Asham, her Sussex home until 1919, blotted out of sight by the toxic white dust of a cement factory, 'the hill hollowed out as though it had been a diseased tooth'. Visiting the unspoilt Berkshire Downs reminded her of her 'ruined ones'. In a brighter mood she vowed to see the 'elephant sheds' at the cement works as 'Greek temples' but in her last years her diary and correspondence is scattered with her horror at the persistent erosion of the Downs. In September 1934 she is brought to total despair: 'A road is to be made [at Rodmell] along the Downs path. Is it worth buying the land? Is it worth saving one crumb when all is threatened?' Yet, on leaving this blighted spot she could still be charmed beyond all measure by the old habitual beauty of the unspoilt bits of the Downs, such as Alciston, and return home over-excited, her mind 'glowing like hot iron'.[14]

In these circumstances the National Trust and other organisations and individuals did magnificent work in saving parts of the Downs from adverse development. One of the most celebrated achievements in these early years was the saving of the Crowlink estate from speculative builders, which prevented the strong probability of another Peacehaven on one of the finest cliff walls in England. This comprised part of the famous Seven Sisters Cliffs and land on the east side of the Cuckmere valley. Its 480-acre site was originally sold to the East Dean Building Company for £6,700. In 1926, a Mr. Hayward, acting for a building syndicate, secured an option on the estate for £9,750. When Colonel Mathias and Arthur Beckett of the Sussex Downsmen entered into negotiations to secure the property for the public the price demanded was £16,450. Mathias subsequently put down a deposit and an intensive fund-raising campaign was conducted in newspapers, including *The Times*. As a result of this publicity Mr. & Mrs Hornby-Lewis of Eastbourne contributed the cost of the deposit, but the appeal produced £5,000 less than the sum required. When all seemed lost, William Charles Campbell loaned the balance in addition to his earlier contribution of £2,000, and later forewent the payment of the loan. Hayward thus not only made a handsome profit out of the deal but retained a farmhouse, outbuildings and land estimated to be worth £4,000. Beckett and Mathias were so conscious of the absolute necessity of preserving this splendid area from building (it is now part of the Heritage Coast) that to them it was only a question of paying whatever the developer chose to demand. The lesson of the Seven Sisters 'Ramp' was, however, taken to heart and applied in the case of later negotiations with the Birling Manor Estate which also included part of the Seven Sisters. As Beckett ruefully remarked, the only outlay against the developer's large profits seemed to have been some trifling expenditure for the preparation of an elementary development plan, the cost of a few notice boards, stationery, correspondence and possibly some small building expenses.[15]

In finding a way of protecting the Downs, the East Sussex County Council and other local authorities, and such organisations as the Sussex Downsmen, had also to consider another major problem, resulting in the disfigurement of the Downs. This was the change in Brighton's policies and attitudes. In the late 1920s Brighton's reputation in the sphere of town planning and downland conservation was a very high one. A principal reason for this was Brighton's purchase of downland.

By (Sir) Herbert Carden's energy and foresight parts of the downland were acquired by Brighton, notably Gorham's Estate at Telscombe, which came by deed of gift to the town, 650 acres at Standean which was being threatened with building and extensive areas at Newmarket Hill, Norton and Balsdean. This encirclement of 'green belt', which subsequently included part of the Chichester estate in Stanmer and Falmer still remains mostly undeveloped and has greatly enhanced Brighton's townscape and justly earned Carden the Freedom of Brighton. Carden was also concerned with early town and country planning. As early as 1923 he initiated the Brighton and Hove Regional Advisory Town Planning Committee, which eventually covered the area between Shoreham-by-Sea and Seaford. Although its recommendations were, in default of tougher planning powers, merely permissive, the Committee formulated the first broad planning principles for any sector of the Downs. The 1932 Report defined the area of Down to be protected against building as that above the 300 ft. contour line. Carden also deserves some credit for the design of the Moulsecoomb Estate on the edge of Brighton's downland which Professor O'Reilly, a notable town planner, declared to be the finest example of municipal enterprise of its kind.

From all this, it could be imagined that Brighton's planning of the Downs was universally respected and acknowledged. This was far from the case. There was the contrary opinion, gathering steadily during the 1930s, that it was essentially opportunist and selfish. A profound difference of opinion arose in 1933 as to the future of the downland between Brighton on the

122 The speculative development of the 'Brighton Heights' near Woodingdean in 1934.

one hand and the East Sussex County Council, and other rural authorities and voluntary bodies concerned with the amenity of the Downs, such as the Sussex Downsmen.

It was at this time that the Downs were first recognised as of national importance. When the Duke of York (later King George VI) came to Brighton in 1928 to dedicate Brighton's Devil's Dyke estate to the use and enjoyment of the public for ever, he remarked that 'the Downs are not merely a local but are a national possession' and when in the following year he joined in the celebrations of the purchase of Beachy Head and 4,000 acres of downland by Eastbourne Corporation he praised Eastbourne for doing a national service and added that 'it would be a sad day for England if the Downs' amenities were to be ever lost'. In the ensuing uproar that broke out at a proposal to construct a motor racing track at Portslade *The Times* referred to the Downs as a 'national treasure', seeing how much the remainder of England had lost its powers to offer the same enjoyment. The newspaper underlined the national significance of the issue and the strength of the growing commitment to the Downs by publishing over two months from Lord Buxton's opening salvo in November 1933 a deluge of correspondence, largely critical of the proposal, two leading articles in support of objectors, a photograph of the threatened area, from the Art Editor, Ulric van den Bogaerde, the father of Dirk Bogarde, and verse. Other national journals took up the fray including *Punch*, the *Spectator* and *Country Life*, indeed almost all the national press was abuzz over the future of the Downs. *The Times* warned that the 'sordid horrors' of Peacehaven could be repeated and that the episode was likely to prove eventful in the history of the Downs and in the cause of town and country planning in England.[16] This prediction was amply fulfilled.

The *cause célèbre* arose from Brighton's ambition to construct the motor racing track on the Downs, close to the Devil's Dyke and Mile Oak Farm in Portslade, on land outside its jurisdiction but purchased to safeguard its water supplies. An initial proposal in 1927 did not come to fruition because certain financial guarantees from the promoters were not then forthcoming but it was revived in 1933, as a 'super' racing track some four and a half miles long, with 450 acres enclosed by a perimeter fence to accommodate up to 500,000 spectators and to be served

**123**  Peacehaven in 1934.

by a new road across the downland to the north. Brighton defended its scheme on the ground that the town had a reputation to maintain as the health and residential resort which had become 'The Queen of Watering Places'. As England had no national motor racing course a course at Brighton was conceived to be as invaluable. The motor racing track was only one planning issue with which Brighton was concerned which worried conservationists of the Downs.

In connection with the jubilee of King George V, Sir Herbert Carden had presented his vision of Brighton as 'The City Beautiful' which painted a glowing picture of a vast and noble Brighton stretching between the Adur and the Ouse by 1960. He envisaged Brighton as the finest residential city in the world with slum clearances from Brighton's central areas, and nondescript buildings swept away in Shoreham, Southwick and Newhaven together with an improved Peacehaven, fine hotels, imposing houses, a university—'indeed a city worthy of the finest site in the Empire'. Clearly his ambitious plans had serious implications for downland.[17]

Many of Carden's visions were praiseworthy but discussions between Brighton and her neighbours made clear a fundamental difference of view as to the concept of downland preservation. There appeared to be two quite different ideals, that of a 'National Park', or a 'Maritime Playground' of the Hampstead Heath variety. It was the aim of the East Sussex County Council and of organisations such as the Society of Sussex Downsmen and the C.P.R.E. to facilitate the preservation of the Downs in their existing state so as to benefit the walker, rider and others seeking quiet, informal enjoyment, and to resist the encroachment of uncontrolled housing development. George Strauss, a government minister, adopted this view by stating that it was as culpable to destroy the Downs by unworthy building as it was to go into the National Gallery and hack away at all the old masterpieces: 'If you took the latter you went into a lunatic asylum, if you took the former you made a fortune'. Arthur Beckett pointed out how particularly important it was to prevent the smooth rounded lines of the Downs from being intruded upon by building. 'Break one of these lines by an artificial erection and the scale is lost, the harmony destroyed.' Conservationists regarded Brighton's attitude as that of a speculative builder rather than that of an enlightened authority seeking to preserve the Downs. Brighton insisted that land purchased as downland would be kept unbuilt on for ever, but it was clear that special provision was to be made for aerodromes, gliding grounds with essential buildings, roads, hotels, sanatoria, hostels, hospitals, golf courses, tennis courts, sunbathing and pools, etc., Brighton argued that 'it must have the power to move as the times move ... the time may come when new amusements and desires on the part of the public and others will demand that portions of the land shall be used entirely for amusement and amenity purposes.' This was the central point at issue. The evolution of the South Downs had reached a climax and their future was in the balance.[18]

To provide long-term protection for the Sussex Downs in the light of these many difficulties the East Sussex County Council promoted the abortive South Downs Preservation Bill in 1934. Its broad strategic aim was to prevent housing development on the coastal margins spreading over the Downs in their entirety.

This attracted wide support and publicity. The Society of Sussex Downsmen in giving support stressed that as early as 1926 it had urged the need to plan the Downs on general principles over their entirety, Arthur Beckett and Sir Arthur Chubb of the Ramblers' Association both considered that better co-ordination in the planning of the whole Downs by a statutory authority would facilitate their eventual preservation on National Park lines. Even *Punch* entered

**124**   The Cradle valley near Alfriston, 1934.

**125** A light-hearted impression of Sir Herbert Carden's achievement in securing a 'green-belt' and out-of-town residential estates for Brighton.

the fray with verses commenting on the fact that the Wilmington Giant was to have his name enshrined in an Act of Parliament, a reference to a clause which prohibited the cutting of letters or emblems in the chalk turf. This light-hearted sally drew attention to clauses in the Bill which were of a novel and unexpectedly drastic character, including some restrictions affecting the design and siting of farm buildings which to this day are not in planning legislation. For these reasons, and because of restrictions to be imposed on building on the Downs, a number of landowners objected to the Bill as an unreasonable and unnecessary encroachment upon the ordinary rights of owners and tenants of land.[19]

A principal opponent of the Bill was D.N. Pritt, later to become a famous QC and MP, who argued before a Select Committee of the House of Lords on behalf of Brighton that the preservation of amenities in the South Downs could effectively be secured by the existing means of Section 34 agreements under the 1932 Planning Act between local authorities and landowners. He also argued that the Bill was too rigid and did not provide for the kind of Downs' user that Brighton had to consider. The Select Committee accepted virtually none of these arguments. Although Lord Zetland, moving the second reading of the Bill in the House of Lords, let Peacehaven have it hot and strong and the East Sussex County Council had spared no effort and expenses to show by aerial photographs and close-ups how uneconomic and unimaginative Neville's design was and what little use he had made of the fine natural sea cliffs, the Bill was rejected. The County Council considered that the protection of the Downs could hardly be left where it stood because it grew daily more urgent. Consequently, the struggle for the preservation of the Downs entered on a new phase.[20]

## A Hard-Won Victory

Whilst East Sussex County Council were engaged in the abortive passage of the South Downs Preservation Bill, West Sussex County Council had entered upon a highly successful strategy for downland protection of its own. The idea of the Bill had originated with West Sussex and it was intended to cover the whole range of the Downs from Beachy Head to the Hampshire border, but, owing to the different character of the Downs in the two counties, both East and West Sussex County Councils

**126** The Downs at risk. *Punch*'s impression of Lord Howe, the famed racing-driver, being expelled from Brighton Downs by conservationists led by Earl Buxton of Newtimber Place.

**127** A photograph taken for *The Times*, 3 December 1936, when Lewes Town Council were negotiating for land from the Marquis of Abergavenny for the erection of council houses on part of Landport Farm near Lewes.

**128** Black Cap near Lewes. A photograph published in *The Times*, 27 April 1938, when the newspaper reported the saving from the builder of 26,779 acres of downland between Eastbourne and Brighton.

found difficulty in drafting the Bill and West Sussex was unable to accept some of the drastic measures East Sussex included in the Bill. With hindsight, West Sussex was proved correct in this . Under provisions in the 1932 Town and Country Planning Act, the District Councils in West Sussex delegated their planning powers with respect to the Downs to the County Council (Worthing Borough and Southwick excepted, which had made considerable progress on their own).

The County's South Downs Scheme involved voluntary agreements with more than 100 landowners who co-operated so wholeheartedly in the preservation of the Downs that some 125 square miles of downland above the 200 ft. contour were saved from building. This Scheme was put into place in the nick of time. With electrification of the Southern Railway from London developers, one after another, put up proposals for large-scale residential development which threatened huge tracts on the southern slopes of the Downs. The whole county became alive to the disastrous consequences and with commendable speed the Scheme was prepared and ratified by the Minister of Health at a time when many people had given up hope of saving the Downs.[21]

East Sussex County Council's approach after the demise of the South Downs Preservation Bill had a similar objective but was on a different basis. The District Councils remained the

**129**   The downland backdrop to this recent photograph of the heavily urbanised coastal belt at Shoreham-by-Sea has survived unspoiled on account of an agreement reached by local authorities in West Sussex to restrict housing development to below the 200-ft. contour. In East Sussex, as at Portslade, a similar agreement was reached but because of pressure around Brighton, the 300-ft. contour was adopted.

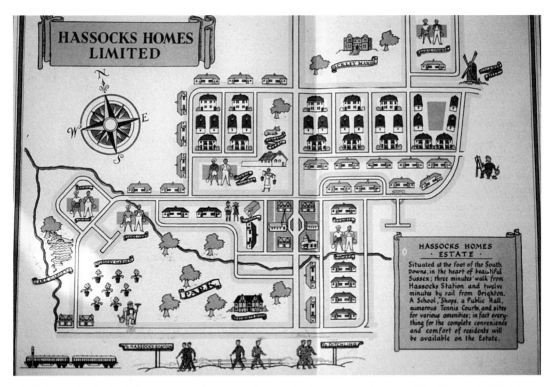

**130** Hassocks Garden Village was one of numerous housing developments on the edge of the Downs which failed to match the developer's brochure-speak.

executive planning authorities, the County assuming a co-ordinating role and accepting the obligation to pay an excess of compensation to landowners (a requirement of the 1932 Act) over the amount a local authority could be expected to bear itself. To avoid expensive compensation the preservation of downland aimed at was above the 300 ft. contour. The differing height selected to control development is evident near the boundary between the two county councils, pre-war housing at Portslade, in East Sussex, visibly extends higher up the Downs than in neighbouring Southwick, part of West Sussex.[22]

The negotiations between local authorities and individual landowners were as successful as in West Sussex. Led by Mr. Illiffe, the clerk to the County Council, and assisted by W. Comyns of the legal department and W.C. Humphery, the County Planning Officer, more than 85 per cent of the downland covered by the abortive Bill became protected by voluntary agreements. Viscount Gage did a great deal single-handedly to restrict building development on the Eastern Downs as Chairman of the County Planning Committee.[23] Professor Abercrombie, the Honorary Secretary of the C.P.R.E., pronounced the regional planning schemes of the two counties as the best in England.[24]

The County Councils' strong stand against development did not entirely stop potentially damaging proposals. In September 1939 Ditchling village became the focus of national attention when a 'Ditchling Garden Village' was proposed on land below the Downs and the village of Keymer, which had already been developed on similar lines. *The Times* took up the issue and the C.P.R.E., with the aid of Frank Pick, the corporatist art patron of the London Passenger Transport Board and a member of the C.P.R.E. executive made a promotional film entitled

'England' depicting the bucolic peace of the South Downs and the 'threats to the very places where peace and recreation can be found'. The proposed development fell a victim to the War but was again revived unsuccessfully in 1964.[25]

In West Sussex one of the areas of greatest concern was the Findon valley on the outskirts of Worthing, where considerable bungalow building was approved by Thakeham Rural District Council. This threatened the integrity of the hill-fort of Cissbury Ring which was purchased by the National Trust, with the help of Worthing residents, to save it from spoliation in 1925. Fresh controversy arose when a developer created a gigantic advertisement by cutting letters 45 ft. high in an inscription over 500 ft. long on the turf below the Ring. The nearby High Salvington Down was preserved from house-building by the actress Nancy Price who was helped by *The Times* to raise money by public subscription, which enabled Worthing Borough Council to purchase the land as a public open space.[26]

Considering the very limited planning powers of local authorities before 1947, the tangible achievements of initiatives taken before 1939 to protect the Downs from overwhelming development were substantial, and

131  A memorial erected by the Society of Sussex Downsmen to those who helped to rescue the Seven Sisters Cliffs from housing development.

were crucial to efforts building upon, and inspired by, the pioneer efforts after the Second World War. An immense debt of gratitude is owed by lovers of the Downs to all those who fought so strenuously with limited powers and resources to save them for posterity. In the voluntary sector, no person was more assiduous in cultivating the Downs' image or so concerned for their future than Arthur Beckett, the President of the Society of Sussex Downsmen. Another who vigorously held out for the protection of the Downs was A.H. Anderson, the chairman of the Downsmen's Planning Committee. Another who deserves special recognition is the 6th Viscount Gage (d.1982) whose fight to protect the Downs on behalf of East Sussex County Council was unsurpassed. One way of assessing the success of early efforts to protect the Downs is to visit the Crowlink memorial erected on Flagstaff Point by Beckett's Society to commemorate its purchase of the threatened cliff-tops near Birling Gap. Yet so extensive was the downland saved that invariably today's beautiful places were the scene of victories scored by planners, conservationists, and others; the Falmer-Lewes corridor on the outskirts of Brighton, the stunning views from Black Cap, near Lewes, virtually all the Cuckmere Valley, the Cradle valley near Alfriston, the high downs above Southwick and Shoreham-by-Sea, the unravished southern slopes of the Western Downs between Ferring and Arundel, and so on.

*Chapter Fourteen*

# AFTER EDEN

## A Land at War

Immediately after the declaration of war the East and West Sussex War Agricultural Executive Committees began the reclamation of derelict land abandoned in the 1930s and reported how ideal the Downs were for producing low cost corn with their ample supplies of lime, the absence of hedges and ditches and 'virgin' soil which needed little by way of artificial fertiliser. By the spring of 1942 the East Sussex Committee had reclaimed 8,000 acres of former turf-covered downland for wheat with the aid of Fordson tractors and Land Girls, and yields were outstandingly high. It was estimated that this land, and further downland scheduled for reclamation in the Eastern Downs, would produce annually enough wheat bread for 240,000 persons, 2,400 gallons of milk together with fresh vegetables for the coastal towns and sugar ration for 125,000 people. Similar immense reclamations were completed in West Sussex. The agricultural output would have been still greater but for the requisition by military authorities of land near Ditchling,

**132**   Land Army girls celebrating their first wartime harvest at Mary Farm, Falmer.

Falmer and West Firle. Thus, under the stress of war, the chalkland had changed in just two seasons from a depressed agricultural district living off its past to a positive cornucopia of food with a future. This reclamation of the Downs was given widespread publicity by the wartime Ministry of Information in the form of news reels and special feature films.[1]

The year 1942 was, however, to be a great setback agriculturally. Some 22,000 acres of downland lying between Littlehampton and Eastbourne were requisitioned by the War Department as a military training ground, despite strenuous arguments put up by the East Sussex War Agricultural Committee that an immense amount of food would be lost from land that included almost all of the largest and most efficient farms in the county and much of the best and most economically cultivated soil. It was originally intended to leave islands of cultivation but this was eventually considered impracticable. By May 1942 virtually all the previously reclaimed area under arable cultivation had to be abandoned. A large body of troops moved into the area where livestock were removed, several hundred persons living on high farms were evacuated and roads were blocked. Farmsteads such as Lee Farm in Angmering, Toy Farm at Black Cap, Pangdean, Standean, Ashcombe, America and Mary Farms were used for target practice and large camps and installations were built.[2]

The Downs became a vast camp and training ground for thousands of soldiers and airmen who came to train for their own special part in the Normandy landings. Burton Park, Lavington House (which later became schools), Wiston and Danny became headquarters of military units and the whole of the Downs was cut off from the rest of England as a part of what General Eisenhower called 'a great human spring, coiled for the moment when its energy should be released and it would vault the English Channel in the greatest amphibious assault ever attempted'. Earlier, the Air Ministry had requisitioned farmland on which to build an airfield on the present site of Goodwood civil aerodrome. As R.A.F. Westhampnett it became a satellite of Tangmere and played a crucial part in the Battle of Britain. In 1944 Typhoons made rocket attacks from the airfield on enemy tanks in Normandy and Douglas Bader flew his last mission from it.[3]

Most of the once 'slumberous' farms in the military area were so badly damaged that they had to be rebuilt at the end of the War. Of the villages, Stanmer suffered worst. Fondly imagined to be snugly folded in its hollow, it was chosen by the War Department for street fighting with live ammunition after the D-Day invasion of Normandy. Although the whole village had been evacuated since more than two years earlier, the damage to buildings had so far been inconsiderable. Faced with the prospect of an almost total obliteration of the village, the East Sussex County Council made a strong case for its survival as an excellent example of unspoilt Sussex. These representations secured the promise that live ammunition would not be used in battle practice. This did not save Stanmer from being left gutted and in ruin after its use for training troops in hand-to-hand fighting. The village had to be rebuilt by Brighton Borough Council in the years after the War together with most of the surrounding farmsteads and dwellings on the Council's estate. Owing much to the care and forethought of the Council at that time, the village today retains its old-world charm 'complete with cows walking up the main street and muck and slurry, which is loved by the visitors but not by the inhabitants'.[4]

The occupation of the Downs by the military had a permanent effect. Several specially made metalled roads were left, notably roads from Steyning to Sompting, Rodmell to Telscombe and roads up to the crest of the Downs at Bo Peep, near Alciston, Firle Beacon and Beddingham Hill. These were opened to riders, walkers and motorists after the War but they no longer had the character of a traditional bridleway with its border of wildflowers, as captured by Eric

**133**   Mary Farm, Falmer, was part of the downland vulnerable to sporadic housing in 1934, owing to the collapse of the Chichester Estate. For much of the Second World War it was part of the military training ground for D-Day. It is now one of the biggest arable farms in Sussex. *Above*, photographed in 1946; *below*, in 1948.

**134** The end of the sheepwalk, Falmer, 1941; Fordson tractors reclaimed semi-derelict turf for low-cost corn.

Ravilious' watercolour of the chalky track going up to the crest of the Downs near Firle Beacon (plate XX). The Society of Sussex Downsmen objected to the retention of most of the military roads because of the new access which would be gained to the Downs by motorists. The County Councils in the early post-war years tried to discourage their use for this purpose. More serious was the final collapse of the old farming economy in which farms on the 'bottom' land had used the hill land for sheep and store cattle. The military occupation had severed these traditional links between the lower and higher parts of downland farms and they were not renewed. Wealden farms also lost permanently their age-old links with the Downs, notably the over-wintering of sheep from downland farms and their use of its straw.[5]

By October 1945 areas of the Downs which had been banned to the public during the War were gradually being de-requisitioned and horse-riders and walkers began again to enjoy their beauty, but as late as 1947 large parts of the Downs were still in the hands of military authorities. Clearing operations were criticised and unwanted articles were collected into un-sightly dumps and slit trenches remained unfilled. Rehabilitation was made slow by the great volume of unexploded missiles at wartime bases, including Friston Airfield.[6] The chalk turf which had survived the earlier wartime ploughing was irretrievably damaged by the movement of tanks. Moreover, scrub had engulfed many places. In reality, the military occupation contin-ued on the Downs much longer than had been expected. Indeed there was public concern that some of the most beautiful and ecologically valuable parts of them might have to be perma-nently surrendered to the requirements of military training. Chichester Rural District Council opposed a War Office proposal in November 1945 for the acquisition of a training ground at Kingley Vale and Bow Hill. When it was drawn to the attention of the military that among 20 sites of special scientific importance (out of an initial total of 200) selected at the request of the Ministry of Agriculture as far back as 1914, Kingley Vale had been number one on this list, the proposal was withdrawn. Sir Arthur Tansley's long-held ambition to bring Kingley Vale into being as a National Nature Reserve had narrowly averted disaster. He finally achieved his object in 1952.

It was not until the spring of 1947 that the military finally de-requisitioned the Downs and even then the Air Ministry had not reached a decision about Friston Airfield, which was eventually

**XVII**  Woodingdean, 1928, showing the earliest bungalows.

**XVIII**  Sir William Nicholson's *Judd's Farm* (1909). This existed on the cliffs near the present site of the post-1914 settlement of Telscombe Cliffs. Sir William recalled that the site was near the Brighton outfall sewer.

**XIX**  Charles Knight's *Ditchling Beacon* (1935) is one of the most tranquil images of the Downs of this period.

**XX**  Eric Ravilious's *Firle Beacon* (1934).

released.[7] The War Agricultural Committees then resumed their management of the military zone. The first stage was to graze the ravaged land with store cattle. Tenants on the Brighton Council's extensive estate remember their parents battling with long lank grass, entrenchments and concrete foundations and Charles Granshaw faced similar problems when he began to turn former well-defended downland into a farm at Slonk Hill, Shoreham-by-Sea (including 'wild' land that had been beloved by archaeologist Cecil Curwen before the War (p.34).[8]

By the summer of 1947 another army had moved onto the Downs, a great body of farm-workers, including women from the Land Army, and the first post-war crops of corn were being harvested, though on most of the downland the first possible harvest was in the following year. After the handing-back of land by the War Agricultural Committees, landowners re-organised farm tenancies on the basis of arable farming and the traditional downland farming with its interlocking compartments of corn, hill-land and brookland was not revived. The newly-cultivated land was fenced and largely closed to the public. Landowners and tenants had formerly given the public leave to roam across the chalk grassland, or had acquiesced in this. Except on legal rights of way, this facility to roam had been a 'permissive' right, granted or withheld at the owner's discretion. The difference between a legal and a 'permissive' right had hitherto been theoretical. Now in many instances 'private' signs began to be erected and the public were prohibited in spaces to which they had formerly been given access.

Most importantly for the future of the South Downs, the great success of arable cultivation on the high downland at the beginning of the War led to demands that it should continue. It was even suggested that on much land on the Downs corn could be grown at an expenditure of labour and machinery so low that it would compete with the large corn-producing countries of the New World. This attitude was to prevail, but no one could have foreseen just how dramatically and in so short a time.

## The Post-War Agricultural Revolution

The immediate aftermath of a bloody conflict was to prove a watershed in the history of the Downs. Much of their legendary beauty was extinguished as indiscriminately and as finally as were the lives of so many men and women who went to war to defend them. These were exceptionally difficult times, marked throughout by austerity and privation. The need to grow the largest possible acreage of wheat in Britain was as great in the immediate post-war period as during hostilities because after a great and debilitating war the crippled British economy lurched rapidly towards ruin. The shortage of coal, smaller rations, and a travel embargo were only the tip of the iceberg of war weariness. In the worst financial crisis in British history a period of retrenchment inevitably ensued and a world food shortage also clouded the peace. The 'million-hearted' British people forwent wheat imports in 1946 to feed war-torn European and Far Eastern countries. Bread rationing, which had not been required during the War, was introduced in peacetime and existing rations of other foodstuffs were reduced to below wartime levels. Economising in bread consumption continued for some years and other foodstuffs continued to be rationed until the early 1950s. The government moved speedily to ensure that wheat that could be grown in England should be encouraged by reinstating acreage payments and gave preference for the sowing of winter wheat, rather than the more 'chancy' spring crop, a change that was to bring its own special problems to the Downs (p.209).[9]

It was not only foodstuffs that were scarce in the austere aftermath of war. The severe winter of 1947 brought on a shortage of fuel which led to the curtailment of BBC programmes

**135** Danny Park, Hassocks. Originally built by George Goring, 1582-93, a south-facing front was added by George Campion in 1728. The War Cabinet met at the house in the First World War and in the Second World War the country house was one of many others requisitioned by military authorities.

and the reduction of the paper ration for magazines. In such grim conditions wider considerations, such as the place of the Downs in English culture, were not seriously raised. Indeed the government had to give such absolute priority to getting food and warmth to people that writer Cyril Connolly wondered whether 'the government had gone from neglecting culture to plotting an outright assault on it'.[10] In these gloomy and tumultuous years there was little chance of stirring and forming public opinion environmentally. Yet much as home-grown food was urgently needed, there were persons who considered the change taking place on the Downs had bolted and got out of hand. In vain they turned to public opinion, which Arthur Beckett had suggested before the War was 'the greatest force in the preservation of public amenities' but the public in the late 1940s were still shell-shocked and in disarray on account of the gloom-laden overall situation. In any case the public were out of touch with reality. The general view, except that of farmers, was that the Southdown sheep were the natural inhabitants of the Downs and that the breeding of large flocks should and would continue. This sentimental view was even held by the Duke of Norfolk who, reviewing Barclay Wills' book on the old shepherds, thought that memories of them would keep them green in people's minds 'against their return'. Unsurprisingly, the shepherds did not return and it is surprising that so many then thought they would.[11] Somehow Sussex people assumed that, although the corrosion of English downland was inevitable, the South Downs would prove to be the one saving exception. Had sheep been profitable under the traditional system of management practised for centuries little of the downland would have been touched by the plough. As we have noted, sheep grazing on unimproved pasture had been dying out from the 1880s, was greatly reduced by 1939, and ended completely with the War.

From the late 1940s intensive arable farming on the Downs was promoted by successive governments to provide a greater sufficiency of home-produced food, especially cereals, and by means of grants and subsidies farmers were encouraged to plough up old grassland, scrub and similar unproductive land. The introduction of artificial fertiliser such as potash made corn growing independent of sheep dung and with the coming of the tractor in the 1930s and that of the combine-harvester and other new equipment, such as the deep subsoil disc harrow and the bulldozer, the onerous task of reclaiming turf and scrub was greatly eased. So the permanent possibility occurred of raising heavy crops of corn where none had been grown for over one thousand years. This success was completed by crop breeding which produced crops that resisted pests and yielded more. In a more favourable epoch a master-plan for the Downs might have provided for a more diversified farming economy consistent with the various soils and degree of slope. Variety is, after all, not the spice of life, but life itself.[12]

Quite forgotten in the austerity of the immediate post-war years were the doughty defenders of the ancient downland turf as an amenity and an ecological and archaeological treasure. With great prescience, as far back as 1931, Dr. Cecil Curwen, the doyen of Sussex archaeology, Professor (Sir) Arthur Tansley, the foremost ecologist of his day and O.G.S. Crawford, the pioneer of aerial photography and editor of *Antiquity*, had warned that the destruction of the mantle of turf covering the higher parts of the Downs could be 'equivalent to the destruction of a priceless and unique manuscript'.[13] These timely words went unheeded.

Moreover, the scheduling of ancient monuments was very inadequate at this time and farmers lacked precise knowledge as to where many archaeological remains were sited and had little understanding of their cultural value. This helps to explain why in the immediate post-war years tractors and bulldozers shattered indiscriminately most vestiges of the past, cutting through Bronze-Age barrows, Celtic lynchets and Saxon burial sites as if a few extra tons of corn were the only thing in life that mattered. In 1934 L.V. Grinsell estimated that one per cent of barrows on the Downs had been scheduled. Very slow progress was made in the years up to the War and, when the Chief Inspector of Ancient Monuments of the Ministry of Works responded in 1954 to increasing public concern at damage done to archaeological sites, he made it clear that owing to the lack of national funds and qualified staff less than half both historic and scientifically significant sites were then scheduled, and not necessarily the most important. This practical problem of conserving heritage was also frustrated by arrangements by the Ministry of Agriculture for ploughing-up. A farmer was not obliged to notify the authorities before he began to plough. All that was required of him was to give written notice of ploughing within 21 days of the ploughing being completed. There seems no doubt that important heritage sites suffered unnecessarily in the widespread destruction.[14]

It was not until 1954 that the increasing amount of arable land on the Downs became an issue reported in the national press. People who knew the Downs well were then shocked to see the extent of old chalk grassland which had survived the War but was then being ploughed up continuously on the upper slopes and crest for sixty miles between Beachy Head and Harting Down. Walkers who had come up in the spring of that year to roam over Cocking Down, as they had for the past thirty years, reported to *The Times* that they had found 'there were no downs'.[15] It was in this same year that conservation organisations began to register their concern at the extensive ploughing-up of downland and so the Downs entered into the international arena again. The C.P.R.E. convened a national conference in 1954, with the situation of the South Downs uppermost in mind, and one in the following year to obtain the views of naturalists and amenity societies as well as those in government, forestry and farming about the future of land use in the Downs. It was the view of C.P.R.E. that farmers should pay heed to some of the other interests concerned when bringing marginal land under the plough, such as ancient monuments, nature conservation and rights of way, for example. It emerged that concern about damage done to archaeological sites and those in which the Nature Conservancy was interested, together with the curtailment of public access, had aroused more public concern than in any other area of English chalkland.

The inadequacies of the Nature Conservancy also came under fire. Planning officers were critical of its role in protecting sites which had been given 'Section 23' status as sites of scientific

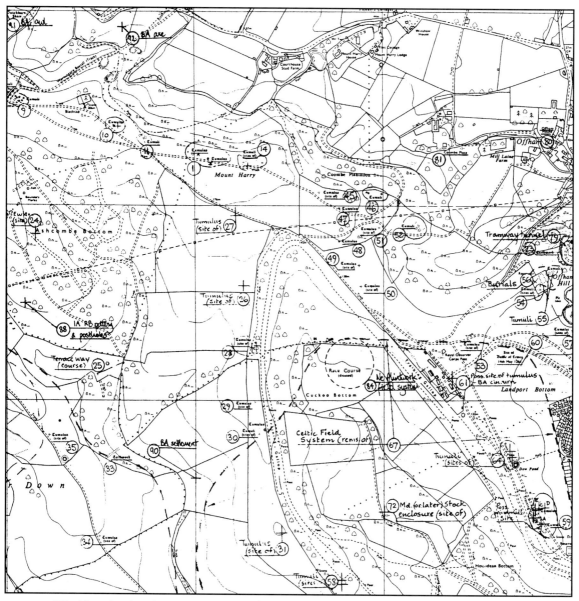

**136**  The archaeological heritage near Lewes. (East Sussex County Council Archaeological Sites and Monuments Record.) (Scale six inches to one mile.)

importance but without sufficient 'clout' to ensure their preservation. By 1954 numerous Section 23 sites had already been ploughed up. The Conservancy explained that with only one regional officer in the whole of South-East England it could not give sites proper protection without making them into National Nature Reserves which took a long time to do. Getting the co-operation of landowners had also been a long and difficult business. It proposed not to save all the Section 23 sites in the circumstances but would try to save the very best pieces of them and would have to take each case as it came to its notice. Meanwhile, grants for ploughing up by the Ministry of Agriculture were being made without any regard at all as to whether the areas had been scheduled under Section 23. Planning powers of local authorities were largely inoperative over such sites. The fact that it was not possible to plough downland turf without irretrievable damage, although it might be possible to save an archaeological monument by ploughing lightly, made the fate of old chalk grassland especially serious. Little wonder that pessimism about the future of the Downs settled like a cloud in conservation circles.[16]

Not all scientists took such an extreme view of the situation. G.P. Burstow of the Sussex Archaeological Society, who had dug with the Curwens before the War, drew attention to some bad examples of damage but he felt one had to keep a sense of proportion in an area which was so very rich in antiquities. 'Most of the hills of Sussex have some remains of ancient man and it would be impossible to preserve everything. The people of 1954 have got to live …'. Again it was the inability of government or other organisation to provide a measure of overall co-ordination that was at the heart of the crisis.[17]

Public access had become again another contentious issue. Farmers generally were not giving the required notice to plough a public footpath and restore it after the agricultural operation. The point was made that public access largely depended upon the land not being used for arable. The farmer ploughed downland because sheep did not pay and if it had not been ploughed, public access would soon become limited, if not impossible, by reason of the encroachment of scrub. Many people thought that it was important to make a positive effort to find ways or means of making sheep, or cattle, more productive, that it was better for the government to subsidise sheep than ploughing, but this proved unrealistic.[18]

One of the most controversial issues affecting public access was the decision of East-bourne Corporation and the National Trust to turn into arable, downland at Crowlink that had been acquired as an amenity for the public. The Society of Sussex Downsmen was concerned at both developments and particularly that on National Trust land because this had been purchased as a result of a public appeal by the Society and conveyed to the National Trust in 1931 ' as an open space for the benefit of the public for ever'. The National Trust believed that in war time and also at the then critical state of food supply, the needs of food production, at Crowlink, as elsewhere, should have priority over amenities, but that this would be a temporary measure. The Downsmen reluctantly acceded to this view, which was also adopted by Brighton Corporation and other local authorities, with respect to downland they had acquired in the inter-war years.[19]

Other substantial areas of former open downland were also in the early 1950s being enclosed by wire fence, in most cases to protect growing crops. This brought out into the open the fact that the Downs were privately

**137** Eastbourne Council has recently restored much of the downland to grass and installed electric fences to permit sheep grazing. More access for the public has also been provided.

owned and that rights to walkers and riders over them were limited legally to the footpaths and bridleways along which, by long usage, a public right of way had become established. No-one had power to prevent owner or tenant farmer from erecting fences on his own land wherever he wished, as long as in doing so he kept open the ways along which the public were entitled to pass.[20]

## No National Park

The matter of the ploughing up of the South Downs in the 1950s aroused added concern from the fact that the Downs were a prospective National Park. John Dower's 1945 White Paper *National Parks in England and Wales* and Sir Arthur Hobhouse's 1947 *Report of the National Parks Committee* identified the South Downs amongst areas which in their view met the requirements for designation as National Parks, defined as being 'An extensive area of beautiful and wild country' which afforded opportunities for public open-air enjoyment. The South Downs were the only candidate in South-East England which both John Dower and Sir Arthur Hobhouse considered appropriate for designation.

Sir Arthur's description of the South Downs now reads like a kind of fairy tale and was even then hopelessly out of touch with what was actually happening to their character as he wrote: 'Here the town dweller can enjoy, often in surprising solitude, the sweeping views of the chalk uplands, the springy turf under his feet, lark song and the crooning of turtle doves, and the scent of wild thyme and hawthorn...' As they read these lyrical words in his 1947 report local residents were mourning acres of ancient, flower-spangled downland and scrub ploughed up for intensive arable production and watched with dismay the tentacles of development spreading from all sides as a result of the insatiable demands of the South Coast towns. By the early 1950s the C.P.R.E. was joined by the Commons and Open Spaces Society and other 'open air' organisations in the belief that further ploughing up of chalk turf would compromise the candidacy of the South Downs as a prospective National Park.[21] Already in 1953 John G. Jefferson, the West Sussex County Planning Officer, had expressed the view that National Park status for the South Downs was then threatened by the intensification of farming.[22]

With these considerations in mind, the matter of ploughing-up the South Downs was raised with renewed urgency in the Houses of Parliament.[23] One of the strongest critics of ploughing-up was the Marquess of Willingdon. In the House of Lords debate on the Ploughing Grants Scheme in May 1955, he urged the exemption of downland from the provisions of the scheme, especially that of the South Downs, which was then still being considered for designation under the National Parks Act. The government responded by actually increasing the rates of grant: the standard rate for land that had been continuously under grass for at least three years was raised and a higher rate was added for bringing into cultivation difficult pre-war grassland where the cost of doing so was abnormally high. Farmers attached a great deal of importance to these grants. Without them, they maintained, it would not be possible to sustain arable production in the country at the then high level. Lord Willingdon predicted, correctly as it turned out, that ploughing the South Downs right up to the crest would cause soil erosion. He also considered that by ploughing too much there would be insufficient space for bridle paths for horses or turf footpaths for walkers. He observed that once farmers had brought their heavy machinery for ploughing and clearing upon the hills they would be irresistibly tempted to plough all the turf in sight, suitable or unsuitable. He envisaged trees and bushes uprooted by bulldozers, footpaths fenced in or entirely obliterated by the plough. He urged that certain parts of the downland should come under special categories of protection. He was supported by Lord Farringdon who remarked that to attract the lower rate of subsidy no permission or inspection by anyone was required as to whether the land was in fact suitable for ploughing. Earl St Aldwyn, the government spokesman, argued that the responsibility of safeguarding downland and land in National Parks rested with local planning authorities (which it did not) and refused to accept that the extension of arable farming should necessarily be regarded as detracting from the amenities of the South Downs.[24]

In November 1957 the matter of ploughing-up the South Downs was raised in the House of Commons. Captain Pilkington, MP asked what steps the Ministry of Housing and Local Government was taking to preserve the turf which had been such a distinctive feature of the South Downs and argued that too much had already been destroyed and that the surviving areas should be preserved in the national interest. The government reply was to the effect that what Captain Pilkington had in mind was very desirable but that ploughing was not subject to planning control and that the government had no powers, and would not seek any to control ploughing on privately owned land. This reply was at least more accurate than the earlier government statement.[25]

By then, many echoed Garth Christian's comment that it would be sad, indeed little short of folly, to try to grow corn on the remaining thin belts of turf where the harebells and bee orchids still lingered. 'If we act wisely, with a thought for the future', he wrote, 'the walker on the South Downs of tomorrow may still know the feel of the great garment of downland turf beneath his feet and watch splendid new beech woods growing out of the protecting shield of scrub on the steeply-sloping hangers. And Sussex will be Sussex on account of the South Downs.' But the damage was already irretrievable and was still increasing.[26]

Meanwhile, Lord Gage, chairman of the Planning Committee of East Sussex County Council, had put the case for local control versus a National Park administration for the South Downs. Writing to *The Times* newspaper in 1948 he observed that the whole area of the Downs was now farmed 'more intensively than at any time in living memory' and that to safeguard their beauty the East Sussex County Council had spent large sums of money. He considered a national park administration could upset local government control which had only just been overhauled as a result of the Town and Country Planning Act of 1947 and which had drawn no complaints from any organisation, national or local, as to loss of amenity, bad planning, lack of access, obstruction or anything else.[27] In the event, the National Parks Commission, the body then responsible for designating National Parks, did not deal with the status of the South Downs until 1957. It then stated that since the Hobhouse Committee's recommendation concerning National Parks, the recreational value of the South Downs as a potential National Park had been considerably reduced by extensive cultivation and that the designation as a National Park was no longer appropriate. The Commission was left with little choice. Year by year the plough had been turning in the ancient turf and the disappearance of sheep was causing the growth of scrub.[28]

## The Area of Outstanding Natural Beauty

The outstanding event of the 1960s was the designation of the Sussex Downs as part of an Area of Outstanding Natural Beauty (AONB). The East Hampshire Downs were so designated in 1962. Although one of the loveliest and most vulnerable areas of England, it took nine years from 1957 to 1966 to achieve the same protection for the Sussex Downs, years during which time the Society of Sussex Downsmen and other amenity bodies had well-justified fears that a heritage of beauty might be lost entirely. The National Parks Commission's initial boundaries of the AONB did not include the river valleys breaking through the chalkland, nor the line of villages below the northern escarpment in West Sussex.[29] A second attempt at negotiations with landowners ensued and the Commission made a designation order in December 1961. The Minister of Housing and Local Government, Sir Keith Joseph, declined to approve it on the grounds that the public should have the opportunity of raising objections to the substantial amendments from the original proposal. In effect a fresh start had to be made and when [at last] news broke that the Downs were to be given a new deal, relief was tempered with the knowledge that the delay in designation had been detrimental to the Downs.[30] Extensive quarrying had occurred, beauty spots were marred and unacceptable development had taken place which might well have been prevented with stronger protection earlier. The Downsmen wrote just before designation: 'Earnestly we hope that the designation will be signed (by the Minister responsible). Meanwhile the beauty of the Downs is being eroded and it is no exaggeration to say in 1966, or after, that it will not be as great as it was in 1956'.[31] A correspondent to *The Times* in 1964 noted that 'wunt be druv' was the county motto, 'But at the present rate towards designation Belloc's boy that sings on Duncton Hill will be an ancient of days weeping into his beard as he gazes eastward to the bungalows on Chanctonbury Ring'. These fears were fortunately exaggerated but there were many who had felt that the Downs were going under with remorseless exploitation for commercial ends and worse was to come.

A disappointment to all lovers of the Downs at this time was that the menace of overhead high tension electricity power lines became realised in 1966 when the government made a ruthless decision to run a 400kv trunk line of pylons across some of the most beautiful parts of the

**138**  Electricity pylons crashing through the valley at Coombes. They soon 'skylight' on an adjacent ridge.

Sussex Downs in the face of vigorous opposition, and against the recommendation of the Minister's own Public Inquiry Inspector.[32]

The battle for rights of way on public footways and bridleways also continued unabated up to 1966 and bodies such as the Ramblers' Association and the Downsmen did stout work for posterity with their hearty vigilance. A celebrated instance of this occurred in November 1966. A party of ramblers from the Society of Sussex Downsmen walked along the bridleway between Kingston Buci, near Shoreham-By-Sea, and the crest of the Downs above the village of Upper Beeding. It was no ordinary excursion. The walkers had responded to a call from their society that a public right of way was in grave danger of being lost because of ploughing-up and fencing. At the start of their walk was a notice stating: 'Private, Please Keep Out'. The party, which included three barristers, ignored it. After about a mile they were brought to a halt by barbed wire and a ploughed field which excluded them from the hilltop. Wire cutters were brought into operation and they went across the field. Two similar fences were cut after maps had been consulted showing the line of the public path. Then at Mossy Bottom the old track-way began again and there were no more obstructions. A few days after this incident was reported in *The Times*, the newspaper published a letter from a person who had lately farmed on the Downs, remarking on the frequency by which he himself had suffered from the 'Activities of those who spend their weekend cutting wire without considering the cost to the unfortunate farmer who had to repair the damage on Monday morning'. This overlooked the fact that in some instances the public were being wrongly locked out of paths they had formerly enjoyed, as the Society of Sussex Downsmen were determined to prove.[33]

These set-backs were compensated to some extent by a notable milestone in the recent history of the South Downs, the designation in 1963 of the South Downs Way, the ridgeway

**139**   In places the South Downs Way is narrowly confined within barbed wire fences and the pre-war sense of freedom is lost, as here, above Plumpton.

track along the crest over some 70 miles of the Sussex Downs. This was extended to Winchester in 1981. This was the first long-distance trail to be created in Britain and this was due to the deep commitment taken in the Downs by both local and national groups alike. This was particularly valued by riders and ramblers because in places the recent ploughing of the Downs had led to fencing which forced visitors from the escarpment, so losing the sweeping panorama of the Weald, hundreds of feet below. Members of the Society of Sussex Downsmen have walked the South Downs Way every Easter, by way of commemoration. The newly designated Way, however, was a narrow track enclosed in fences for much of its length, whereas before 1939 it had been possible to walk from Beachy Head into Hampshire over pathless buoyant turf.[34]

This chapter marks a landmark in the history of the Downs. It would appear that, until the 20th century, changes in the rural life and landscape had been *in general* gradual enough not to destroy the image of the Downs in the minds of those who loved them. This was change in continuity. The outbreaks of war in 1914 and 1939 were catalysts which accelerated the pace and scale of change thereafter. This was change which utterly broke with the past, creating discontinuity, and so changing the character of the Downs that they would never be the same again. The vision of the Downs as 'England' wilted from the consequences of the First World War and died from the effects of the Second and its immediate aftermath. In 1946 H.J. Massingham could still write of the Sussex Downs as 'the very core of human life on earth, the pillar of human stability … Home and place and reality in a world of nightmares …'. Little did he know that he was writing an elegy for the part of England which to many was the epitome of England itself.[35]

*Chapter Fifteen*

# PLACES AND IDEAS:
# THE DOWNS IN LITERATURE AND PAINTING

'The danger of English landscape as a poetic ingredient is that its gentleness can tempt those who love it into writing genteely'                                              W.H. Auden

Like any other Eden the Downs have been over-described, over-written, over-painted (and consequently) over-visited. Writers and artists, mostly hacks working for an urban public, have given the Downs vast publicity, whether of verse, 'country writing', breezy landscape painting,

or the giddy superlatives of brochure-speak. The smooth maternal lines of the Downs became one of the most familiar and mimicked images of English countryside. They were evoked as the essence of the English summer scene by the sea, whether by the books or voice of broadcaster S.P.B. Mais, who lived at the foot of the Downs near Brighton; half-page photographs in *The Times* on Saturdays (thanks to its art editor Ulric van den Bogaerde, who helped thereby to save some of the loveliest parts of the Downs from irrevocable damage); or as advertisements in L.M.S. and Southern Railway carriages or in the saloons of ocean liners and airships. Such public declarations of love in innocuous prose and verse or its equivalent in chocolate-box landscape painting invariably has the soul of a picture postcard and a chronometer set at about 1900. Such an avalanche turned the Downs between the two World Wars into a literary cliché, almost a familiar joke.

Between the wars there was hardly a village in or below the Sussex Downs that did not resound with the click of a typewriter or the cultivated voices of putty-faced 'Georgian' poets and novelists, literary critics, journalists, artists and handicraftsmen; in several, the

140    *The Week-End Book* published by the Nonesuch Press by Francis Meynell and edited by his sister Viola of Greatham.

London Expatriates rivalled in number the local farming population (p.165). The response of such writers was generally that of an exile, a habitual weekender, oscillating between departure and return. His city, as T.S. Eliot remarked, was 'that of the man who would flee to the country, his country being that of the man who must tomorrow return to town'. It is no coincidence that the line from Harold Monro's *Week-End*, 'The train! The twelve o'clock for paradise'[1] became the motto for *The Week-End Book* (successive editions from 1925), edited by Viola Meynell as 'country writing' for the urban reader on holiday and published by her brother Francis, who themselves had country cottages at Greatham, near Pulborough (p.204). Such writers inevitably bred sentimentality for the countryside amongst townsmen. With a deep sense of estrangement from natural life in London they had heightened perceptions of the Downs, making cockney visions of them fantastically romantic. For them every bush was a burning bush, and their writing about the Downs tends to be wholly external, a thing to feel, observe and measure and to act and react upon but, because it was merely a fleeting experience, rarely one in which to be absorbed. These writers lived in literary England, not in agriculture, so it is not surprising that, despite this huge harvest of 'country writing' and verse, a feel for the soil as a factor in production, or a knowledge of farming as a way of making a living, was so utterly lost under a welter of sentiment for 'country life'.

Thus although the Downs emphatically became part of writers' and artists' England, they tended to figure in the imagination as a snug retreat which put people out of sight and mind of the business lunch, the social scramble and the 'electric light' type of existence. They thus became a kind of 'never never' Kate Greenaway land of shepherds, tinkling sheep bells, country pubs and cricket on the village green an England just out of reach which everyone longed to recapture but which they knew never existed in reality. There is little sense of history, nor hardly any of the realism of Hardy's novels of the Wessex chalkland, and no writer to match the stature of Crabbe's or Wordsworth's vision of the Suffolk coast or the Lake District. Instead the Downs' literature and painting is generally expressive of an easy-going contentment, a kind of light-opera among friendly hills.

Nevertheless, there are accomplished and distinguished visions of the Downs which have gained a permanent place in English literature and art. They make a very substantial corpus which preserves our knowledge of past downland landscapes and testifies to the powerful inspiration exerted by the Downs on thought and the imagination over more than two centuries. Some of this has exerted a great influence on contemporaries such as Copley Fielding's landscape painting or Eric Gill's handicrafts: others, important individual works of a particular genre such as Kipling's and Belloc's verses and Eric Ravilious's landscapes.

W.H. Hudson was wrong to suppose that the Downs did not figure greatly in artistic and literary imagination before the avalanche from the 1890s which has been described as a 'minor Romantic Movement'.[2] On the contrary, the Downs have the considerable place in the long English tradition of topographical verse of so many other distinctive districts in England. Proud landowners and country clergy wrote downland verses from the early 18th century and this comprises more than 350 pages in the first anthology of Sussex verse edited by James Taylor in 1851.[3] Much of this minor 'hill' poetry is dull and insipid to modern taste and thus now unread, but it is of interest as an indication of a growth of admiration for the Downs and a gradual realisation of their fuller delights. We have already drawn attention to the readable verse of William Hay of Glyndebourne and of Robert Bloomfield (p.147). Another early versifier who can still be enjoyed is Gideon Mantell, the Sussex geologist, who surprises with whimsical touches and sharp observations of nature. There is a tradition that it was the Downs viewed by

William Blake when he was at Felpham (1800-03) that inspired his celebrated lines about 'England's mountains green' in *Jerusalem*.

A representative poem is that by the Rev James Hurdis (1763-1801) entitled *The Favourite Village* which is in the style of his friend Cowper's *The Task*.[4] He combines his love of his native place of Bishopstone near Seaford with a celebration of God's divine creation of the Ouse valley. To John Betjeman it is the most observant, melodious and entertaining of all the English topographical poems, with some of the best descriptions of winter ever written. Also rewarding to some ears are the verses of the lady who signed herself 'Charlotte Smith, of Bignor Park, in Sussex', who may be thought a more accomplished poet than Hurdis. Born in 1749, she lived her entire existence with dashed expectations, honing her verse to feed her eight children after separation from a feckless and adulterous husband. Although she would have preferred to have written in a 'more lively cast of mind' her success was immediate and for long after her death in 1806 she was accounted one of the best, as well as the first, of English romantic poets.[5] Another neglected poet is Wilfrid Scawen Blunt (1840-1922) who thanked God he was born in Sussex (Kipling and Belloc were incomers). He is certainly the most distinguished Sussex-born poet and in virile, youthful sonnets, recalling the flavour of the 16th-century verse of Sir Thomas Wyatt and Sir Philip Sidney, he combines his passion for Downs and Weald with that of his lover of the moment:

> To-day all day, I rode upon the Down,
> With hounds and horsemen, a brave company.
> On this side in its glory lay the sea,
> On that the Sussex Weald, a sea of brown.
> The wind was light, and brightly the sun shone,
> And still we galloped on from gorse to gorse.
> And once, when checked, a thrush sang, and my horse
> Pricked up his quick ears as to a sound unknown.
> I knew the Spring was come. I knew it even
> Better than all by this, that through my chase
> In bush and stone and hill and sea and heaven
> I seemed to see and follow still your face.
> Your face my quarry was. For it I rode,
> My horse a thing of wings, myself a god.
>
> *St Valentine's Day*

For all his espousal of progressive causes, he was at heart a wistful traditionalist who revelled in rural seclusion. His Garden of Eden, which he hoped would last at least for his lifetime, and which has held out longer (but how much longer?) is commemorated by his sonnet *Chanclebury Ring*.[6]

Soon after Blunt's verses were written in the 1860s the appreciation of the Downs developed as a popular taste. This was connected with the growing interest in natural history. After Richard Jefferies, major works in this field appeared, notably, W.H. Hudson's *Nature in Downland* (1900), to which we have previously referred (pp.155-6), and that of Tickner Edwardes of Burpham, a distinguished naturalist who was also a novelist of Sussex life. They were also forerunners of a spate of similar books which satisfied a new readership such as Arthur Beckett's *The Spirit of the Downs*, which went through repeated editions from 1909 and his close colleague, R. Thurston Hopkins, who was an entertaining writer on the Downs for those who wanted light reading on holiday.

In landscape painting the first to master the Downs was Copley Fielding (1787-1855). When he executed his well known pictures between about 1829 and his death at Hove he imposed a personal vision on the Downs and helped change taste in landscape for his genera- tion by extending landscape painting to a conformation of surface which had hitherto been neglected by artists on account of Gilpin's Picturesque theories. With astonishing skill, ex- pressed in flowing lines, washes of lovely colour and an immaculate eye for atmosphere, he was a true innovator achieving a totally fresh natural vision of downland. His work reveals the influence of the pioneer watercolourist, John Varley, and also that of Turner. Like Turner, Fielding developed a facility for evoking a likeness of immense space and the effects of mist and shimmering haze which concealed detail with broad shows and tender light and conveyed a sense of mystery.[7] Fielding was followed by Herbert Hine, whose paintings of luminously misty Downs around Lewes are hung in Lewes Town Hall; Edward Stott, strongly influenced by the French artist Millet, who experimented with the effects of moonlight at Amberley; and La Thangue, trained in London and Paris, who painted several scenes of farm workers in farm- yards and orchards at Graffham.

Around 1900-1910 the splendour of the Downs' light and purity of atmosphere was at its peak of popularity in its appeal to the landscape painter. In 1910 the *Sussex Daily News* reported that no fewer than 36 artists resident in Sussex had exhibited their work at the Royal Academy summer exhibition. By this time numerous writers and other creative artists had also expressed a strong preference to work in Sussex above that of any other county. Several downland villages became home to an extraordinary concentration of writers and artists as at South Harting and Steep, both within the sphere of Bedales.

Ditchling is the most remarkable of these. It was the first downland village to be estab- lished nationally and internationally as a refuge for those at odds with the world of the machine. Its air was of a rural backwater but accessibility by railway at Hassocks station made it specially attractive to those who wished to retain some links with London. It was at Ditchling Beacon that Jefferies' first encounter with the Downs began *c.*1882 and by then a number of artists had already come to reside in, or near, Ditchling, including Ruth Dollman, who illustrated Jefferies' *Nature near London* and *The Open Air*.

The forerunner of Ditchling artists in this century and a focal figure in the whole move- ment to the Downs was Eric Gill, the artist-craftsman renowned as letter cutter, sculptor, wood engraver, typographer and social reformer who lived in the village between 1909-13 before moving out to Ditchling Common where he resided until 1924 when he trailed his family, cats, goats, ducks and geese to Capel-y-ffyn in the Black Mountains. At Gill's instigation, Edward Johnston, the foremost modern calligraphic designer and Douglas (Hilary) Pepler, hand printer and publisher, both of whom were colleagues of Gill at Hammersmith, arrived in 1915.[8]

Gill's move to Hopkins Crank on the Common was the beginning of a unique religious experiment in British artistic life, an attempt to create a religious fraternity as a communal way of life in the countryside for those who used their hands creatively. The chief architect of this religious community was Father Vincent McNabb, a Dominican who propounded the teaching of St Thomas Aquinas with galvanic energy. These doctrines, together with Belloc's and Chesterton's idealistic land-sharing proposals on the basis of small-scale agriculture, confirmed Gill and Pepler in their attack on the modern industrial and political system. The Guild of St Joseph and St Dominic was founded at Ditchling in 1920 and not wound up until 1989. Its founder members, including Gill and Pepler, were lay brethren of the Dominican order. They built a chapel and workshops on the Common and set up a calvary above them. A community developed, living as far as possible off the land. As Winefride Pruden observed, 'None who had any knowledge of rural conditions would have chosen to settle on Sussex clay. It was excellent for making bricks and tiles but hopeless for producing potatoes bigger than cherries or leeks thicker than pencils'.[9] The community did, nevertheless, brew their own beer, bake bread, cure their own hams and wove at least part of their clothes. 'The free-standing outside privies, when overgrown with ivy or half-hidden by honeysuckle and wild roses, acquired quite a romantic look, like carefully cultivated ruins on an eighteenth-century nobleman's estate.' Joining this 'holy tradition of working' though engaged in different media, were Joseph Cribb, Gill's first apprentice, George Maxwell, Valentine Kilbride, David Jones, Denis Tegetmeier, Philip Hagreen, Dunstan Pruden and numerous others.[10]

In 1918 Sir Frank Brangwyn R.A. also moved from Hammersmith to the house called 'The Jointure' which he greatly enlarged in the Arts and Crafts tradition. He had started as an assistant to William Morris and became a distinguished painter-etcher, lithographer and muralist. Through friendship with Pepler, the Mairets arrived in 1917. Ethel was a renowned handloom weaver who used the warm tones of vegetable-dyed, hand-spun wool. She and

141 Eric Gill was a visionary and innovative artist whose sculptures and uncluttered typefaces broke new ground with their economy and simple sweeping lines, qualities shared with his downland home from 1909-24. Since the publication of Fiona MacCarthy's biography (1989), the question has arisen whether his works intended to inspire veneration and spirituality can be disassociated from revulsion at his lifestyle.

her husband Philip, a writer, designed their own home and workshops in Beacon Road, the chief feature of which was the large barn-like room with tall windows used for weaving. Bernard Leach, the famed potter who also lived in Ditchling for a period, recalled the Mairets' home pervaded by 'Warm smells of dyed hanks of wool'.[11] Amy Sawyer, the dramatist, Esther Meynell, author of several books on Sussex, and Eleanor Farjeon, author of children's books and a friend of Edward Thomas, also lived at Ditchling in the inter-war period. Edgar Holloway the etcher and Charles Knight were also drawn to Ditchling. Knight was attracted by the special quality of light behind the Downs and became famous for distinguished watercolours of landscape between Eastbourne and Brighton for the 'Recording of the changing face of Britain' project, sponsored by the Pilgrim Trust at the start of the Second World War when an enemy invasion was feared would cause widespread destruction. His *Ditchling Beacon* (1935), which finely captures the magic of the steep and flared velvety escarpment in the stillness of evening, was a tranquil image that became instantly popular and is the most arresting vision of the Downs in this century.[12]

In recent years the stature of several of the Ditchling artists has grown. David Jones is now seen as the most important mystical painter in Britain since Blake. Gill's and Johnston's

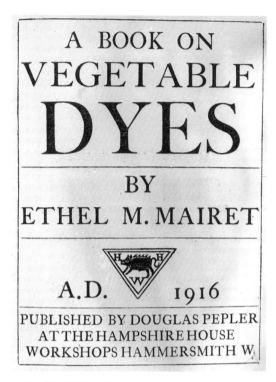

A BOOK ON
VEGETABLE
DYES

BY
ETHEL M. MAIRET

A.D. 1916

PUBLISHED BY DOUGLAS PEPLER
AT THE HAMPSHIRE HOUSE
WORKSHOPS HAMMERSMITH W.

**142**   Ethel Mairet's book on natural dyes, published just before Douglas Pepler's move from Hammersmith to Ditchling.

lettering design and typography lies behind the revival of calligraphy in Germany and the USA. In Japan Shoji Hamada set up a guild of potters based largely on what he had seen and heard of the Ditchling model. Thus the role of Ditchling as a major contributor to 20th-century art, design and thought is very significant. The full story is waiting to be told.[13]

Rottingdean was first made famous by artist Burne-Jones who had a holiday home there before 1882. His nephew Rudyard Kipling lived there between 1897 and 1902. The poets William Watson, Alfred Noyes and John Drinkwater also resided there for a time, as did Sir William Nicholson, the artist, and Maurice Baring, novelist and writer. Others with a close connection with Rottingdean include William Black the popular Victorian novelist and writers Angela Thirkell (a grand-daughter of Burne-Jones) and Enid Bagnold. The former remoteness of the village has been captured by Thirkell and Kipling himself evokes the old village atmosphere in his autobiography *Something of Myself*:

In 1882 there had been but one daily bus from Brighton, which took forty minutes, and when a stranger appeared on the village green the native young would stick out their tongues at him. The Downs poured almost directly into the one village street and lay eastward unbroken to Russian Hill above Newhaven. It was little altered in '96'[14]

The Downs moved Kipling to write his verses called *Sussex* and Michael Smith has noted that circumstances combined to make the Rottingdean years particularly fruitful for Kipling and some of his finest work, both prose and poetry was created or developed there. In this period he absorbed the true character of the Downs in expressions such as 'our blunt, bow-headed, whale-backed Down', 'We have no waters to delight our road and brook-less vales' and *The Run of the Downs. A Smugglers' Song*, and *The Absent-Minded Beggar* belong to this period, as does the story *The Knife and the Naked Chalk*. Other writings of the Rottingdean period include *Recessional, Just So Stories, Stalky and Co* and poems like *The White Man's Burden*.[15]

In recent years Bob Copper, who was born in the village, has made it the scene of his delightful reminiscences of Sussex and is famed for keeping alive the old singing traditions of the Downs. He has noted that when the English Folk Dance and Song Society was founded in 1898 one of the first acts of its Honorary Secretary, Mrs. Kate Lee, was to record songs sung by two members of his family.[16]

Some of the most memorable downland paintings are by Sir William Nicholson when he lived at the Grange (1904-1909). Beginning as an innovative poster designer inspired by Toulouse Lautrec, and then pioneering coloured woodcuts in Britain which have been acclaimed

**XXI** Lytton Strachey reading his book *Eminent Victorians* in the garden at Charleston Farmhouse. A painting by Duncan Grant.

**XXII** Wall paintings in Berwick Church by Duncan Grant and Vanessa and Quentin Bell.

**XXIII** Adrian Berg, *Seven Sisters*.

**XXIV** Ivon Hitchens, *Waterfall, Terwick Mill* (1945)

**XXV** Stanley Roy Badmin (d.1990), a painter of the gentler sort of idealised downland landscape who could never let himself see electricity pylons or other blemishes. Much of his work was commissioned for Shell's *Guide to Britain* and *The Reader's Digest*. The scene shown is at Greatham, near Selborne, Hampshire.

**XXVI** Monkton House, formerly part of the West Dean estate, a surreal interior devised by Edward James.

**XXVII** Rolling on the Downs at Sompting, September 1992.

**XXVIII** The purchase of Saddlescombe Farm by the National Trust from Brighton Council (1995) together with the Devil's Dyke Estate (*background*) has consolidated and enlarged the downland holdings of the Trust.

**XXIX** Waterhall, Patcham. The most vulnerable open downland near Brighton and Hove. The site lies immediately beyond the Brighton by-pass (A27) and if it were to be developed it would open the door to damaging proposals on the open downs.

internationally, he then became a successful portrait painter. This remarkable sequence of reputations throw light on his Rottingdean landscapes. He frequently walked up to the windmill (which, through him, became the colophon for Heinemann the publishers) to paint the Downs. His work will be remembered for the profound silences conveyed by the simplest means. He also brilliantly extracts sun, shadows and wind by a subtle simplification of line, tone and colour, a perfect technique for the subject of bare downland, especially towards late evening in summer, his preferred time for landscape, when buildings stand out boldly and in depth against the smooth lines of the chalk and the huge sky.[17]

Rottingdean later became the home of writer and wit Maurice Baring and of the Beerbohm Trees and their actress daughter Gladys Cooper. Here, too, Enid Bagnold (Lady Jones), who lived in Burne-Jones' North End House, wrote of a quintessentially English family, The Browns, rooted in the Rottingdean countryside. This was *National Velvet* (1935), the story of a young girl, modelled on a daughter of a local butcher, who won the Grand National. Repeatedly reprinted, filmed, turned into a play, and eventually televised, the book captures the spirit of the South

Downs for a world weary of war. Subsequently, Bagnold brought her delightfully cluttered garden room at Rottingdean on to the stage of New York and London in her ingenious play *The Chalk Garden* (1955-6), which despite having capital punishment as its theme, is a witty comedy in the style of Congreve.

Rodmell in the Ouse valley near Lewes was also home to a remarkable group of writers. The Woolfs' association spanned a period of over 20 years in Virginia's case and Leonard lived there for half a century. Initially Monk's House was merely a refuge from work in London and a place where Virginia could work in peace. It was not until 1928 that she began to think of herself as a member of the Rodmell community. Whereas the Woolfs spent about one-fifth of their time at Rodmell in the 1920s, this increased to about one-third in the next decade and Virginia Woolf spent the last years of her life marooned in the village on account of the war. Walking the Downs usually got her into fine writing trim. She tossed off ideas for a new novel as they arose in her mind and she locked herself back into writing between breakdowns. It was at Rodmell that Virginia Woolf did much of the elaboration of her technique in imaginative fiction which is one of the most influential forms of written art this century. The Sussex scene permeates her Diary and Letters and her last novel, *Between the Acts,* which is set at Alciston.[18] Rodmell was the home of other

**143**  Virginia Woolf's unpretending, ugly, cluttered home of Monks House at Rodmell offered beautiful views from its lovely garden over the brooks in the Ouse valley and to the great sky of the Downs.

literary figures, notably Edward Shanks and Sir John Squire, J.M. Allison, the publisher and news-paper owner, Kingsley Martin, editor of the *New Statesman,* and Beachcomber of the *Daily Express.*

The 18th-century Charleston farmhouse became from 1916 the home of Vanessa Bell's strange *ménage*, which included her husband, the writer and art critic Clive Bell, artist Duncan Grant, art critic Roger Fry, her lover for a while and her life-long admirer, and writer David Garnett. This summer retreat of the Bloomsbury group and her highly disorganised household was periodically augmented by the Woolfs, Maynard Keynes, Strachey and E.M. Forster. The unabashed assaults on the conventional in matters of social mores and dress were extended to the visual and Charleston became the home and refuge of the Post-Impressionist movement in British art when it was at its most experimental and exciting. Victorian and Edwardian aesthetic taste in furniture, ceramics and fabrics were scorned and Roger Fry's household designs from the Omega workshops, which had been founded in 1913, and was influenced by the colour and force of Cézanne, inspired the furnishings and the exciting interiors with an idiosyncratic mix of subtle and exuberant colours streaked and splashed on every surface in sight. The influence of Cézanne also extended to the garden and a Frenchness permeates everywhere. At Charleston, Duncan Grant painted with verve his inventive and original works, still-life, portraits, massively-rounded women, pottery and glass, drawing inspiration from the peace of the place and remaining produc-tive and youthful into his nineties. Vanessa Bell had a highly successful exhibition of her paintings in 1936. She captures the mood of the Downs at its most carefree, comfortable and easeful.

Grant and Bell, with Quentin Bell, painted 'the hot stuff in the sacred art line' in Berwick church. Vanessa Bell died in 1961; Duncan Grant worked at Charleston until his death in 1978; both are buried in the churchyard of Firle. It was in the farmhouse or the carefree garden with its unexpected sculptures that Lytton Strachey read aloud *Eminent Victorians* (1918) prior to publication, Maynard Keynes wrote *The Economic Consequences of the Peace* (1918) and E.M. Forster explained T.S. Eliot's *The Waste Land.*[19]

To Frances Partridge Charleston in its heyday was an enchanted place—'a place of such potent individuality that whenever I stayed there I came away grateful to it, as it were, for giving me so much pleasure, so many rich and various visual sensations, such talk, such a sense that lives were being intensely and purposely led there...' She tended to picture it at noon on a summer's day with the garden normally in the hot summer, 'a rampant jungle of sunflowers and hollyhocks, and the apple trees are bowed down with scarlet apples; pears hang bobbing against one's head', set contrastingly against the majestic height of the Downs and the short grey-green of their flanks.[20]

Another centre of a creative community was an old shepherd's cottage called 'Furlongs' near Beddingham.[21] Peggy Angus created here an interior more curious and beautiful than that by Vanessa Bell and Duncan Grant at Charleston and the house (with two fever wagons from Asham Cement Works which acted as additional accommodation and a studio) became a week-end retreat for London artists including Eric Ravilious and his wife Tirzah, Edmund and Char-lotte Bawden, Helen Binyon and Percy Horton. Angus was a considerable landscape painter and a gifted teacher and pattern designer of tiles and wallpapers. Percy Horton later rented the folly at Firle for painting.

It is Eric Ravilious who has most successfully expressed the essence of the great sculptural folds of the Eastern Downs this century. Born at Eastbourne and taught by Paul Nash, whose own fascination for chalk landscapes influenced him, his rural nostalgia comes through his many wood engravings in the style of Bewick as in the magical presence of the bull about to leap over the figure of the Long Man of Wilmington illuminated by a full moon. But it is his subtle watercolours and a willingness to tackle new themes which won him an even greater reputation. Much of his work has as its subject the Downs near Peggy Angus' cottage. *Tea at Furlongs* (1939) depicts with a touch of surrealism a sunshade over a tea-table set in a tight corner of a garden wall and contrasts with *Downs in Winter* (1934), a stark and dramatic scene representing the bleakness of winter on the Downs. His *Waterwheel* (1934) combines wire fencing and machinery with superb lines of downland. Other paintings of landscapes near Furlongs include the dolly engine, railway track, rusting machinery and dazzling white surfaces at the Asham Cement Works, developed round the first Sussex home of Virginia Woolf and Vanessa Bell. Ravilious expels the hackneyed vision of idyllic downland and evokes a placidly rural impression with an even, radiant light as delicately as that of the 'Chalkhill Blue'. He also captures the pallor of the chalk in winter which few artists have tackled. With meticulous downland lines he depicts in a three-dimensional form, almost sculptural, the massively rounded shoulders of the Firle escarpment and the great spaces of the coombes between. No artist appears to have expressed with such verve and originality a love for the Eastern Downs.[22] (Plate XX)

Moving to the Western Downs, Hilaire Belloc (1870-1953), who with Kipling doubly answered M.A. Lower's plea for some 'heaven-made man of song'[23] to do justice to the Downs, had the outsider's devotion to Sussex and its traditions and harked back to the idyllic rural retreat before changes wrought by the motor car. Patrick Garland has remarked that Belloc's famous poem *The Boy that Sings on Duncton Hill* which closes *The Four Men* should be thought of as the National Anthem of Sussex.[24] Its still wider English influence is evident on Richard Ingrams who made it the epilogue to his anthology *England* (1989). Perhaps Belloc is closest to the idea of the laureate or prophet of the Downs but he was robustly French as well and like all brilliant talkers and facile writers his pen took him into many other different fields. Sadly the muse dried up with the death of his wife in 1913 and his *County of Sussex* (1936) had nothing more to say than what he had written thirty years earlier.

A distinguished landscape painter who worked in sight of the Western Downs was the strange and paradoxical Ivon Hitchens (1893-1979). Quintessentially English, his first contact with the chalky downland was as a pupil at Bedales and from 1939, when he came to live in a caravan on Lavington Common, the landscape backed by the Downs south of Midhurst always remained his particular motif.[25] We have already noted Patrick Heron's description of Hitchens' woods of pine and oak, its towering masses of rhododendron opening out at Heyshott and Graffham to sudden views of the beech-hung rampart of the Downs. (p.18) Yet another writers' colony was at Greatham, below the Downs near Pulborough. In 1909 this became the home of writer and publisher Wilfrid Meynell and his wife Alice, the poetess.

**144** Ivon Hitchens (see Plate XXIV).

They bought old cottages nearby, and had others built for their daughters, one of whom, Viola Meynell, was herself a writer. Her brother, Francis Meynell, director of the Nonesuch Press and a broadcaster, also built a house at Greatham. Visitors included Edward Thomas, Eric Gill, John Drinkwater, whose charming poems *Of Greatham*, *A Picture* and *Morning Thanksgiving* were written in thanks for his visits. Eleanor Farjeon likewise wrote fondly of Greatham. D.H. Lawrence completed *The Rainbow* there in 1915 and in a short story in *England, My England* gives an accurate account of the local landscapes and an inaccurate account of the life of the Meynells.

Stanley Roy Badmin, one of Britain's foremost watercolour painters, settled at Bignor below the Downs in 1939. Earlier, his work had become uniquely familiar and dear to the post-war generation through illustrations in nature and travel books, including *Puffin Picture Books* and *Shell Guides*, and they have figured on innumerable greetings cards and calendars. Badmin began as an etcher of distinction in the pastoral, idyllic tradition of Samuel Palmer. In the seclusion of his beloved Sussex village he expressed contentment in a prolific series of watercolours in a charming 'chocolate-box' image, yet so exquisitely meticulous in fine detail that they will become properly regarded as historical records.[26] (Plate XXV)

In recent times artists have tended to turn their back on landscape but several living painters have continued to be drawn ever and ever again to the towering cliffs of Beachy Head. Adrian Berg has dwelt on them lovingly in a series of sparkling watercolours with an intensity of observation of colours changing week by week (Plate XXIII). No one has made more of the horizontal strips of flint embedded in the chalk cliffs or the compacted layered mass of the chalk itself. Jeffery Camp has a truly personal vision of sheer originality. His paintings can surprise and exhilarate but also soothe to dreamy golden reveries. No previous artist has captured the physical sensation of windiness at Beachy Head so imaginatively. His figures float through the air, blown in the wind. One can imagine peeping recklessly down to the Royal Sovereign lighthouse, or leaping into the wind whipping through the gorse. Adapting to his theme, Camp's canvases are kite-shaped and others elongated, as if being blown away. His former wife, artist Laetitia Yhap, appears in some as a siren. Camp has also developed another untried theme at Beachy Head, the idea of a place precious to English culture and long seen and long loved. This he has accomplished by fossilising into a mental construct a tiered mass of heads on a towering peninsula of cliff, the earliest generations at the bottom.[27]

Amongst other recent works are Norman Clark's affectionate observations of idiosyncratic characters found at Hurstpierpoint; Douglas Gray, who lived in S.P.B. Mais' house on Southwick Green, has painted a fine series of interiors and gardens in the style of the 'plein-air' Impressionists;[28] Carol Weight's strange and haunting interpretations of the West Sussex downland must be seen as one of the major artistic developments of the present time[29] and Edgar Holloway's etchings have established himself as Britain's leading revivalist in this field.

To conclude this chapter, it is worthwhile coding geographically the numerous writers and artists so that by putting them back in their beloved landscapes the locale of their inspiration can be identified. Two sources that lend themselves to this are James Taylor's *Sussex Garland* (1851), the first anthology of Sussex verse and Thurston Hopkins' *Literary Originals* (1936), which although difficult to follow and not fully comprehensive, lists places connected with writers. On this basis it is clear that no Haywards Heath Group or Crawley Road School has yet emerged. It is the Sussex of Hilaire Belloc, that is, the southern and coastal part of Sussex, and the rural rather than the urban that predominates. Of the rural environments that of the South Downs stands out to overwhelm the Weald and the marshes, and it is the Eastern Downs which has attracted most inspiration, the part of the Sussex Downs regarded in the 1930s as 'the fairest and most famous'.

*Chapter Sixteen*

# THE AUSTERE PRESENT

The delayed designation of the Sussex Downs as part of an Area of Outstanding Natural Beauty did not prove to be the turning point in their protection as had been expected. In retrospect, the ostensible protection failed to arrest the seeping tide of development from the coastal towns. The bulldozers remained in full flood. In fact, more damage has been done to the Downs within living memory than at any time in their long history. A sense of reverence due to one of the most beautiful stretches of downland in England has been lacking. Instead, the Downs were seen as material for roads, bungalows and houses, and out-of-town developments. This short-term approach led to the Downs' persistent erosion in the absence of any visionary masterplan which would have prevented it happening.

The location of much new development had a particularly adverse impact. Urban-fringe expansion from the coastal towns brought shopping malls and out-of-town recreational developments on to the edge of the Downs while the inner parts of towns decayed, as at Newhaven, Lewes, Hangleton, Shoreham-by-Sea, Worthing and Chichester, giving rise to something like 'Edge City' in America. Heavy recreational pressures evident around Brighton and Shoreham-by-Sea are resulting in inappropriate planning applications for sports stadia and other recreational facilities which would destroy the fauna, the flora and the very character of the Downs. In the same peripheral zone new industrial parks are proposed on greenfield sites whilst those established in the 1960s in the now urbanised area are left to decay.[1]

The effects of dense motor traffic also began to cause concern. Ground levels of ozone, monitored in Arun district since 1995, have exceeded recommended limits on hot summer days, sometimes by a large margin. Widespread road improvement, particularly along the A23, A24 and A27 roads, can be seen for long distances and has had a major impact on landscape, noise and light pollution. People have felt less tranquil and secure as a result. Amongst the major environmental issues in the 1980s which exposed the vulnerability of the Downs to new forms of development was the construction of the Brighton by-pass as eight miles of dual carriageway on big embankments and deep cuttings through beautiful downland north of the Brighton conurbation, cutting National Trust land at Stanmer and at Southwick, damage at the latter location being mitigated by a tunnel. This clearly exposed the contrast between the protection ostensibly afforded by the AONB status of the Downs and the ruthless support of national and local government for trunk road construction across them. The initial proposals by the Department of Transport for the improvement of the A27 between Lewes and Polegate were insensitive and although recent ones mitigate potential damage the proposed split-level roundabout with a through route for a much enlarged A27 at Polegate would seriously degrade the scarpfoot landscape from Folkington eastwards. An urgently needed by-pass for Worthing, Sompting and Lancing presents special problems. After the longest, most fraught and expensive

Local Public Inquiry in Sussex the Inspector recommended a partly on-line route through ur-banised north Worthing and a new downland section eastwards along the boundary of the AONB. An alternative route across the Downs near Cissbury Ring supported by Worthing Borough Council and Worthing's Member for Parliament, Sir Terence Higgins, would have been even more damaging. The controversy this aroused, and the high cost of the project, has led the government to put it into abeyance.

## Sparks Fly Upwards

Another grave issue was the appeal of British Telecom against the refusal of planning permis-sion by Chichester District Council for a microwave radar station to be sited on the Trundle. An eyesore previously existed of obsolete wartime radar masts. An even more elaborate structure was required in order to improve TV reception and other purposes. Although a strong case was put up that the Trundle was scheduled as an Ancient Monument of national significance, as well as offering superb views and facilities for recreation, the Secretary of State for the Envi-ronment awarded permission (against the advice of her Inspector after a Public Inquiry).

A new wide-ranging threat to the Downs arose from oil exploration at Singleton, Graffham, Ditchling Beacon and other places. Great concern was expressed in Parliament in 1983 at the potential threat to the Downs and both East and West Sussex County Councils drafted new policies in their Structure Plans with which exploration companies had to comply. The bare, open Downs were included in 'no-go' areas. Professor Marion Bowley stated, 'We are sacrificing the landscape of which we have too little to get more oil, of which we have more than we need: this is not what is usually considered sound economics'.[3] Fortunately for the Downs, no oil was found at Ditchling. The Graffham well proved commercially unviable. The only commercially worked oil well in Singleton is unobtrusively hidden by woodland.

On the open downs the loss of elm trees to Dutch elm disease has reduced the charm of downland villages and farms and reduced shelter in winter. Moreover, as economic pressures on downland farmers to increase efficiency became more insistent so the conflict between modern industrial agribusiness and conservation intensified. The first great battle between the two inter-est groups was in 1978 over the proposed pump-drainage scheme for the Amberley Wild Brooks. Two government bodies simultaneously pursued contradictory policies towards this wetland.

**145** The saving of the Amberley Wild Brooks as a wetland was a *cause célèbre* of the 1970s.

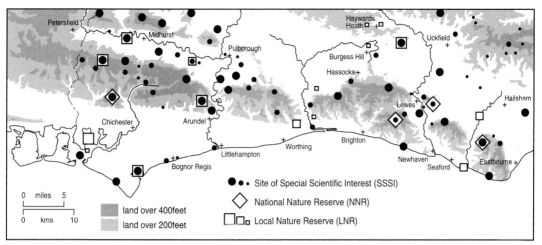

**146**   Sites of Special Scientific Interest and other statutory sites.

The Nature Conservancy (now named English Nature) wanted to conserve them for the nation and was intending to classify them as a Grade I Site of Special Scientific Interest, whereas the Ministry of Agriculture was examining whether it should use public money to help pay for their destruction. It was established in evidence by David Streeter and other objectors that the Amberley Wild Brooks was one of the most important wetland sites in lowland Britain from a conservation point of view and that the proposed improvement scheme was likely to result in the destruction of its unique status. It was convincingly put at the Local Inquiry that the taxpayer was proposed to pay a substantial sum for a negligible agricultural benefit at the cost of a major conservation loss. The Minister of Agriculture decided on the recommendation of his Inspector not to pay grant aid towards the cost of the scheme.

In words which became the *leitmotif* of the coming decades, David Streeter's evidence included the statement, 'If the national interest is to be considered, it is legitimate to argue that we should not be considering whether to spend large amounts of public money on improving the agricultural potential of low-grade farmland but to properly compensate the farmers in order to ensure the actual survival of high-grade conservation land'.[4]

Another *cause célèbre* (and far less happy in its result), which demonstrated the growing risks to the downland was the ploughing-up of Woolavington Down, above Graffham in 1979. This became a national issue with the publication of Marion Shoard's controversial book *The Theft of the Countryside*. Although her description of the site as 'A traditional downland landscape' was disputed, and some selective scrub clearance was desirable to open up views, the ploughing-up destroyed one of the few remaining areas of chalk grassland, damaged scheduled archaeological monuments, obliterated rights of way and virtually cleared scrub, a fine habitat for warblers, at a time when the need to bring any more land into cereal production was being widely questioned. The incident clearly demonstrated the correctness of Shoard's central thesis that some regulation was needed to control the industrialisation of the Downs brought about by new farming technology supported by agricultural policies of the European Community.[5]

Nearly 20 years later the fragility of the Downs landscape was again demonstrated in 1997 by the ploughing of Sites of Special Scientific Interest through a flax subsidy loophole of the European Union. On account of agricultural surpluses, 'Set Aside' schemes have been introduced which have not been favoured by farmers and have limited conservation value. High-

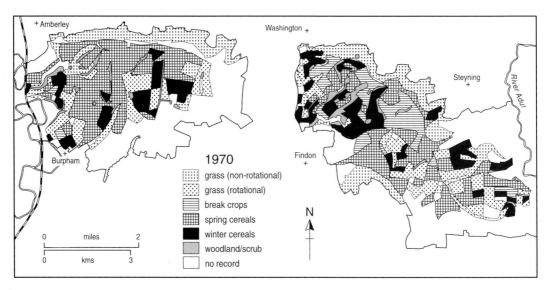

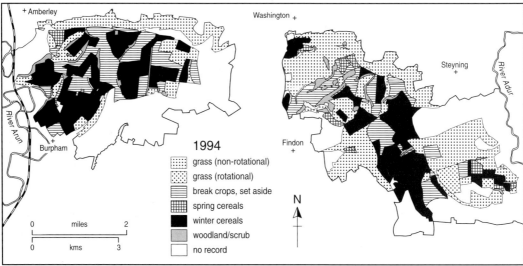

**147**   The changing crop system of the central South Downs, as monitored by the Game Conservancy (after Aebischer and Potts).

input agricultural methods, and also the more intensive use and development of the country-side in other ways, have caused substantial losses of the richest traditional wildlife habitats as well as their increased fragmentation which is a particular problem for the breeding and feed cycles of many species. The West Sussex County Council has recently stated that evidence strongly suggests that the battle is not being won.[6]

The problem to be addressed in downland agriculture is well known. Its farming, as else-where in Britain has, paradoxically, become too successful. It has become industrialised and substantially more productive: a success achieved at considerable social and environmental cost. Chemical companies have developed new pesticides, herbicides and fungicides; crop breeders have developed more productive domestic animals and food plants, big machines have re-shaped the landscape and chemical sprays against every known pest and disease can be applied to huge areas in a matter of hours. Cultivators biting more deeply than those of our ancestors have obliterated thousands of years of history in a single afternoon. This intensive, chemicalised agriculture has led to a dramatic decline in wildlife and extensive damage to the downland landscape. The corn bunting, lapwing, grey partridge, hare, butterfly, bee, together with plants and animals which were also part of the everyday farming scene, are almost absent.[7]

The tract of chalkland between the rivers Adur and Arun provides a clear example of how the now utilitarian landscape of near-monoculture is linked to the loss of wildlife. This section of the Downs has been monitored since 1968 for the Game Conservancy by Dr. Dick Potts as a unique project in Britain.[8] Bio-diversity measured on computer maps has been used not only to throw light on its decline in the Downs but by implication in the English countryside as a whole. Called by the naturalist W.H. Hudson, 'A land of wild nature and wild prospects', the wild prospects remain but there is so little wild nature that Graham Harvey has remarked of such prairies in general that, 'The most stunning feature is the silences. There is no soul in this rolling prairie … no buzzing of bees, no rasping of crickets, no birdsong … the skylarks have gone from the modern cornfield. Here the heavens are as devoid of life as the waving wheat beneath them'.[9]

The Game Conservancy has highlighted the cause of the problem in this central section of the South Downs. Up until the mid-1960s its farmers followed the traditional mixed farming which had effectively created the landscape of the Downs from the late 17th century. They under-sowed clover and temporary grasses with spring cereals, mainly barley. These rotational sowings (called ley) was a means of restoring humus and fertility to the soil. John Goring, of the Wiston estate, wrote to *The Times* in 1956 extolling this system of farming in which spring cereals were the dominant crops and the undersown ley the key element in low-input traditional downland agriculture.[10]

From the early 1970s, however, agricultural subsidies encouraged winter wheat monoculture and farmers raced each other for higher cereal yields. The changing pattern of farming is indicated on p.208. In 1994 the picture was almost completely different from that of 1970. Spring cereals had almost disappeared, while winter wheat was the dominant crop. Most significant of all, rotation grass had all but vanished from the study area, being restricted to a single farm (Applesham).[11] The very considerable increase in non-rotational grass is also notable.

This changed pattern of farming has apparently had an adverse effect on wildlife. The importance of under-sowing leys was in the bio-diversity it created. Temporary grasses containing weed species which attract insects providing food for farmland birds. The single farm continuing the old regime accounts for less than 10 per cent of the area monitored but now accounts for 23 per cent of the grey partridge and 21 per cent of the skylarks and corn buntings, and yet the farm has an excellent overall production of food. The grey partridge is one of the few species of farmland birds on which the effects of insecticides and insecticidal effects of herbicides are known. Apart from the retention of legume-grass leys at Applesham Farm, care is taken not to plough or spray heavily the base of grassy-bottomed hedges and fence lines. This leaves suitable nesting sites in long grass remaining from the previous season's growth. When partridge chicks hatch in mid-to-late June they feed mainly on the caterpillar-like larvae of the sawfly (Doleros gonager) and Lepidoptera (moths and butterflies) which over-winter in leys established under cereals and then migrate to nearby cornfields. Favoured feeding sites for partridges later in the year are the stubbles undersown with clover. The young corn bunting needs the same food for its survival.

Potts argues 'Politicians, scientists, authors and journalists have pleaded for years for new integrated farming systems for a sustainable future. Meanwhile, traditional leys have been staring them in the face'.[12]

Meanwhile, although many villages have barely altered in physical appearance over more than a generation owing to strict planning regulations against development, socially there has been a phenomenal transformation. Gone are most farms from village streets, Ferguson tractors and sheep dogs have disappeared and there has been an exodus of farm workers. Their cottages have been taken by retired persons, holiday-homers, 'tele-cottagers' and commuters. There is no longer any strong sense of vibrant life in the downland village. An eerie silence prevails where once children's voices rang. A number of village schools have closed. These social changes are those facing English rural communites in general, but various factors are responsible for making downland problems more severe. Owing to the small size of most communities in the South Downs, the vital village services such as shops, post offices and banks are in steep decline. Affordable housing is even more scarce than in most parts of southern England because restrictive planning policies have led to high house prices. The industrialised and substantially more productive downland agriculture has been achieved at considerable social cost, the agricultural workforce declining more steeply than in England generally. Urban visitors see the downland village as 'scenery' rather than as a living and working entity and still regard the villages as 'incredibly perfect' motoring to their pubs though they do not yet serve the new Surrey dish of wind-dried Yak meat and Aqua Libra on draught.

A vital resource which has been taken too much for granted on the Downs since the last War is the soil, a finite, non-renewable, resource. This has not been recognised for what it is— an essential natural resource—nor given the protection it deserves for underpinning the natural environment as the starting point for the beauty and diversity of landscape. These remarks are particularly relevant to the South Downs for they are extremely susceptible to soil erosion resulting in land degradation. Prehistoric and Romano-British farmers were responsible for the irreversible loss of the thin chalky soils on steeper slopes through ploughing (p.41) and we have noted other instances of soil erosion at later periods.

Post-war soil erosion is not unique to the South Downs but it appears to have been more serious than in most other parts of Britain. Most damage to property and soil erosion and flooding have been associated with the growing of winter cereals which became pronounced from the 1970s.

In the relatively wet winters of 1982-3, 1987-8 and 1990-1, topsoil was washed down from hillsides during heavy rain at Sompting, Lancing, Bevendean, Falmer, Rottingdean and Lewes, amongst other places. This resulted in considerable costs, which were borne largely by local authorities, individual householders and their insurance companies. The switch to intensive arable cropping is the chief cause of the soil erosion. The problem has been exacerbated by the widespread adoption of higher-yielding autumn-sown cereals in preference to the less productive spring-sown varieties. This has meant that large areas of the South Downs have relatively little crop cover to inhibit water run-off during the rainy months of November to March. The ploughing of hillsides which traditionally have been considered too steep for cultivation and the increase in field sizes have further intensified the problem. The building of the Brighton bypass and the reversion of arable to grassland under the South Downs Environmentally Sensitive Area (E.S.A.) Scheme have reduced this risk of flooding and erosion. Nevertheless the problem has drawn attention to the adverse effect of agricultural incentives which have encouraged farmers to use all available land, much of it less than ideal, for the growth of arable crops, which but for subsidies would be unviable. Boardman has monitored erosion in the Eastern Downs between 1982-1991 and has urged that specific high-risk sites should be targeted. Shall we see Soil Erosion Environmentally Sensitive Area Schemes? The answer may come shortly from the government's promised Soil Protection Strategy.[13]

## An Agenda for the Future

*Turning the Tide*

The old century has not done well for the South Downs. When it is finished and audited, assuredly among notable losses recorded will be the adverse change in the Downs' character. Extreme pressures, greater than the pressures experienced in most of our national parks, have made the Downs a special case amongst Areas of Outstanding Natural Beauty. Squeezed by expanding coastal towns, damaged and further threatened by improved roads and intensive farming, and with the number of car-borne visitors increasing relentlessly, it is hardly surprising that the question raised in many people's minds is 'How can the peace and beauty of the Downs be safeguarded in the face of all this?'. Yet for all the environmental disruption they have suffered, the Downs are still heart-warming in their beauty, and it is hard to find anyone who does not believe that they are important in their lives. Safeguarding the Downs is a national, indeed international, concern. They are still central to our idea of Englishness and thus need to be defended by all kinds of people.

We now need to consider a permanent solution for their protection and enhancement so that we can pass them on to our children as a richer and more satisfying environment, saved for ever as one of the finest examples of England's countryside. The Downs remain one of the most important natural and cultural assets of southern England, but conserving them and bringing them into harmony with the commercial and recreational needs of the 21st century will be especially challenging. There is a need for imaginative new ways to involve people in a more meaningful way in planning their future. As the history of the Downs makes clear, the landscape evolved over millennia from the coming of the prehistoric hunters to today's communities, and elements of it have taken centuries to mature. In drawing up an integrated environmental planning and management strategy for the Downs it is critical to take this into

**148**   New housing at Foredown, Portslade created by the new Brighton by-pass.

account by taking a long view of the landscape in an extended vision that looks beyond even the next 100 years, planning for a time when the apparently impossible may become subsequently possible. The Sussex Downs Conservation Board has made a good beginning.[14] By building on this with greater resources and more determination, and with the willing collaboration of those who have created the landscape of the Downs for centuries—landowners, farmers, farm workers and foresters—the Downs could regain their former admired place in our national culture and become once more internationally acclaimed.

The organisation responsible for the Downs in the future should embrace the combined area of the Sussex and East Hampshire Downs and the goal should be a vibrant, living countryside and not an over-interpreted and signposted museum. Market forces must not be allowed solely to dominate the Downs' development and the object should be not to preserve the most picturesque parts of the Downs but to enhance the whole, so that nowhere in their whole expanse should there be noise, crowds, traffic, prairie and dirt or any development in flat defiance of the very qualities which make the Downs worth conserving as a national treasure. Creating such a new pattern of landscape on the South Downs would be one of the most exciting challenges for the present generation.[15] Downland which has not been aggressively commercialised, such as the West Dean estate of the Edward James Foundation, would furnish much inspiration.

*New Agricultural Landscapes*

The opportunity to alter the way the South Downs look and function will be greatly dependent on new policies of the European Union. Yet much progress in balancing production and conservation could be attained within the present funding system of agriculture by switching an increasing proportion of agricultural subsidies from production-based payments to rewards for environmentally-sensitive farming. For example, the viable system of agriculture at Applesham,

**149**    A view to Mount Caburn and Firle Beacon from Black Cap, a recent acquisition of the National Trust.

previously referred to has at last influenced the Ministry of Agriculture which recently introduced into the South Downs E.S.A. Scheme payments to farmers who retain winter stubbles and under-sown spring cereals. This should be extremely beneficial to birds and a wide variety of wildlife and will help to reverse the declining trend in bio-diversity. It is the type of farming system which is at the core of the Arable Incentive Scheme which has been proposed by English Nature, the Game Conservancy and the Royal Society for the Protection of Birds (R.S.P.B.), which these organisations would like to see implemented by the government as part of an overall extensification and bio-diversity programme for the Downs.

Another environmentally-friendly system of agriculture which has a potentially wide application because not specifically tied to the under-sowing of cereals, is the integrated crop management advocated by the organisation called L.E.A.F. (Linked Environment and Farming). This advocates the best traditional methods with appropriate modern technology, minimises reliance on fertiliser, pesticide and fossil fuel and gives weight to the enhancement of landscape and wildlife.[16]

Yet other ways to reform are available. The South Downs E.S.A., amongst the first of those declared in the UK, has been very successful since 1987 in stopping the conversion of chalk grassland to arable. It has been less successful in the river valleys cutting through the Downs because payments have been too low in relation to arable potential to be an incentive for farmers to switch to grassland. The monitoring of the Game Conservancy has clearly proved, however, that subsidising reversion from arable to grass has actually reduced bio-diversity because much of the grassland replacing the cereals is grazed almost to nothing in drought. The E.S.A. Scheme could also have been improved by targeting areas with the greatest opportunity for environmental gain, e.g. by expanding existing habitats, so establishing better wildlife corridors. Revisions to the Scheme have already increased the sensitivity to wildlife protection, payments from 1997, for example, favouring ground nesting birds as never before, thanks to lobbying by the RSPB, and there is much further scope for improvement. Although successful in restoring some of the old character of the Downs, the Scheme has not added much to the enhancement and re-creation of bio-diversity.

The major contributions to the debate on the future agricultural landscapes of the Downs are two publications of the Sussex Wildlife Trust. *A Vision for the South Downs* (1993) and *A Vision for the Wildlife of Sussex* (1995), both of which are remarkable for their target-oriented approach and the clarity of their objectives. The key habitat on the Downs is the most species-rich of all British habitats, old chalk grassland, an internationally important and threatened environment which now exists only fragmentally. The battle is on to save the last remaining fragments of it but there is no guarantee that they will survive for with the reduction in grazing there is increasing encroachment of scrub and secondary woodland. As the Sussex Wildlife Trust explains, the re-establishment of chalk grassland is not an impossible dream, but it needs a long-term commitment, because even with careful management such a greensward will take 50-100 years to develop into a useful range of plant species and invertebrates. As an example, permanent grass in the E.S.A. scheme which has been unploughed for at least thirty years and not chemically treated during this period on a farm in the Western Downs is now plentifully strewn with Harebells and Lady's Bedstraw but Wild Thyme has only just made a tentative appearance. There is hope that landowning bodies such as the National Trust and local authorities will become committed to this long-term creation of chalk grassland. Eastbourne Borough Council which led the way with the purchase of downland in the 1920s has now prepared a management plan for the 4,200 acres of downland it owns. The Wildlife Trust suggests that about 50 per cent of the scrub which has invaded old chalk grassland should be cleared to restore the grassland chalk habitat, the remainder being allowed to develop into mature woodland and that the re-creation of species-rich grassland would be most valuable adjacent to existing areas, so extending these habitats, and on south-facing slopes. Such changes would require additional incentives for farmers and better downland turf seed mixtures.

A greater understanding of the various management options for chalk grassland is also needed. The National Trust has observed in respect of its Devil's Dyke estate that cattle grazing, rather than that by sheep, would be more beneficial to some parts of the greensward. David Streeter has recently remarked that the creation of the ideal chalk grassland that so many aspire to will need careful consideration of grazing regimes and ecological priorities which are as yet not fully understood by the public. If we advocate a return to sheep grazing we will end up with a short flowerless turf (evidently the myriads of wildflowers and butterflies which is the romantic vision of the Downs was largely due to the reduction of sheep nibbling from the 1880s). Streeter adds '… If the picture in your mind is a tall Rampion-rich grassland, your management prescription would be very different from that if the object of your interest was a large colony of Adonis Blues … If, on the other hand, you want Silver-spotted Skippers the prescription is different again …'[17] A possible overall scenario for the Downs envisaged by the Wildlife Trust is 'With its best wildlife sites well-managed, with flower-rich ancient grassland properly grazed and with woodland replacing the present scrub in some areas, key skylines, viewpoints and arable fields linking now separate remnants of ancient grassland would be progressively reverted to long-term grassland. Much arable would remain, especially on the dip slope, but with wide field margins to increase wildlife interest. In some cases the margins would be put down to grass and left unfenced so that walkers, riders and cyclists could enjoy the freedom of the countryside. In other cases there would be kept uncultivated but unsprayed strips in which attractive wildflowers such as poppies could flourish, together with a diversity of butterflies and other insects. The Downs would still be an economically vigorous area, but with more financial security for farmers in parallel with ecological sustainability.' This broad strategy now has much public support with the increased emphasis being given to sustainability in the broadest sense and to Agenda 21.

The reader is referred to the Sussex Wildlife Trust's 1993 publication for proposals to conserve the remaining fragments of chalk heath and ancient woodland.

## Other Management Issues

One of the most serious problems for the next generation will be managing tourism. Everyone will have more leisure time in the 21st century and the South Downs will become more valuable with each year that passes because they provide an enormous reservoir when more and more people are looking for something worthwhile to do. Furthermore, as urban life becomes more artificial and technically driven, so the value of the Downs as a source of physical challenge and spiritual refreshment will increase. The implications of this for the Downs are profound. For the Downs to retain their integrity, their needs and their special qualities must come before visitor considerations. Tourism poorly managed, or simply left to market demand, could strangle otherwise peaceful communities and damage or even destroy sensitive landscape and wildlife habitats that visitors have come to enjoy. The broad aim should be to provide for tourism and visitors' activity which relates to what is special about the South Downs, is ecologically sustainable and yet contributes to the prosperity of the local community. Tourism should not take out of the Downs more than it puts back. For people to come to the Downs its landscape must be protected at all cost. Commercial pressures are already apparent at Goodwood, Arundel, the Devil's Dyke, Alfriston and Beachy Head. Once-peaceful villages such as Amberley and Alfriston retain less of their pre-war charm at weekends. Good planning for tourism is needed to change ways visitors travel in the Downs, in particular, by improving alternative public transport and so reducing the need to use cars. Car parking on the Downs should not be allowed to increase substantially.

In the past conservation and tourism have often been in conflict. By working together in a partnership the two sides can achieve a lot in terms of conservation and developing the local economy. Partnership schemes beginning elsewhere in the country, for instance, in the Lake District and the New Forest, originate projects, educate the tourist industry on how to protect the environment and focus on the need to put something back into the landscape from which they are making money.

Urban-fringe downland poses special difficulties. The continuation of farming in such a zone is problematic, especially in Brighton's downland, being such a popular and accessible countryside to a coastal conurbation of 250,000 people. Over a long period before 1939

150   West Dean House is the focus of the 6,000-acre estate of the Edward James Foundation which, by giving a high priority to conservaton, is a prime example of good Downland management.

Brighton Coorporation acquired approximately 11,000 acres of downland forming a crescent about half a mile wide between Portslade in the west and Saltdean in the south-east, comprising tenanted farms, the villages of Stanmer and Falmer and Stanmer Park. The National Trust has also recently built up its holdings in the area by acquiring—by means of its highly successful South Downs Escarpment Appeal—Wolstonbury Hill, Pangdean and Saddlescombe Farms, the Devil's Dyke and the Fulking Escarpment, together with Black Cap and Frog Firle further afield.[18] The opportunity for further land purchases may well occur. There is thus a unique opportunity for policies which address the needs of the urban population. Here the urban fringe should be a special target for landscape restoration, the designation of country parks, the extension of more public ownership, farmland diversity, the removal of eyesores and the prevention of intrusive development and noise pollution in the interest of improved public access and quiet enjoyment. An imaginative project of this kind, democratically planned, would command national interest, and hopefully attract external funding. It would also be a contribution to the rejuvenation of Brighton and Hove and a way of bringing a potentially beautiful heritage into the next century so that an urban public could regain their old custom of wandering over the Downs. In the changed circumstances of agricultural use a general right to roam would not be appropriate, and many existing footways and bridleways are little used, but there may be special cases where negotiated agreements with landowners might be desirable to extend public access.

In its way, the South Downs is one of the most historical parts of England. The surviving rich heritage of historic monuments, sites and buildings will require careful management if we are to pass these on to future generations. Today, as we search for an identity as a community, they are a potent reminder of our links with the past and with the rest of Europe. In our highly visual age, episodes in prehistory and history are likely to stick in popular memory only when attached to visible physical remains. It has been suggested by Peter Fowler that our lives can only be made richer and our understanding of the contemporary countryside made deeper by a knowledge of the achievement of earlier peoples.[19]

An important consideration with respect to the future protection of the Downs is the potential adverse impact on views from the Downs across the Weald, even if beyond the bounds of the AONB, now that the district of the Low Weald is subject to threats of major development. These views are one of the most valued qualities of the Downs and every effort should be made to preserve them for posterity. A changed attitude on the part of the government is necessary with respect to radio masts and other visual clutter and opportunities should be pursued to put underground stretches of electricity cables and pylons which are especially damaging.

## Providing for the future needs of the Downs

In theory, the designation of the Sussex Downs and the East Hampshire Downs as parts of Areas of Outstanding Natural Beauty should have given them as much protection as being a National Park. In reality, it did not. AONBs are perceived to be of lesser status because they do not have statutory administrative and financial arrangements. Moreover, National Parks are currently provided with 75 per cent of their funding from central government, a much higher percentage from the national exchequer than is available to AONBs, and to the South Downs, in particular, and a sum much larger than currently available to protect and manage them. The enhanced profile of a National Park Authority would focus both on the protection and recreational management of the Downs, the latter aspect not being a function of AONBs. As the Sussex Downs are more visited than any National Park this is a serious issue.

These potential advantages associated with a National Park have inevitably led to a debate over more than 60 years as to the best way of securing the South Downs' permanent future. In the 1980s there was a resurgence of opinion in favour of national park status for the Downs.

**151** Tourism at Ditchling Beacon.

**152** The Hollingbury Industrial Estate was created on former downland in the 1960s when light industry remained an important part of the Brighton economy. It is now reverting to retail development and other uses and a general air of *déjà vu* has prompted the local authorities to plan for greenfield science parks on unspoilt downland nearby.

**153** Traffic in Steyning High Street has probably increased to much the same level as in 1970 before the by-pass was constructed.

Many organisations including the Ramblers' Association, the C.P.R.E., the Sussex Wildlife Trust and some local authorities, including Hove and Worthing Borough Councils, together with individuals, campaigned for the Downs to be given this status. Supporters recalled that the South Downs were the sole unfulfilled candidate for National Park status of all those selected by the Hobhouse Committee in 1947, the Norfolk Broads having become a National Park in all but name in 1988. It was noted that the South Downs were already so, in effect, receiving more visitors than several of the national parks, though as an undeclared National Park it lacked government funding for its management and there were inconsistencies and anomalies in the application and interpretation of planning controls by the various local authorities responsible for the Downs.

In the event, the campaign for national park status failed to win favour with the Countryside Commission and most local authorities, and an alternative scheme was put into effect. These bodies entered into a formal agreement under section 102(1) of the Local Government Act 1972 to establish a joint committee called the Sussex Downs Conservation Board for the purpose of discharging certain functions of the AONB The three parties to the agreement, the Countryside Commission, the County Councils and the District Councils each had twelve members on the Board. The County Councils delegated their function of countryside management and the maintenance of rights of way to the Board and local planning authorities agreed to consult the Board on relevant applications in the AONB outside settlement areas. This was a remarkable achievement on the part of the local authorities concerned. It owes much to the vision of the West Sussex County Council and will be recognised as a milestone in the history of town and country planning.

The Board was set up in April 1992 on a six years' experimental basis, and is the only one of its kind in the country. After a necessarily slow beginning, the SDCB has proved to be a positive initial step in protecting and enhancing the Downs but there is not a long-term agreement on funding. There is moreover, no legal requirement of local planning authorities to consult the Board and it has no veto over local authorities' planning decisions. The East Hampshire Downs are excluded from its remit and several local authorities, e.g. Brighton and Eastbourne have not delegated downland management functions to the Board. Nevertheless the Board's achievements have been considerable. It has created an integrated management service and a first management strategy for the whole of the Sussex Downs AONB and has secured an influential voice in the planning process.

With the coming to an end of the six-year experimental period of the Sussex Downs Conservation Board (subsequently extended to 2001), the Countryside Commission in 1997 decided to seek views on the most appropriate form of administration for the whole of the South Downs.[20] The result of this process was the decision of the Countryside Commission to advise government ministers that the most appropriate long term management of the South Downs is as an AONB (Sussex Downs and East Hampshire managed concurrently) with a statutory Conservation Board having the benefit of the powers and measures to be proposed for AONBs generally.

The South Downs Campaign, comprising the C.P.R.E., the Council for National Parks, the Ramblers' Association, the Sussex Wildlife Trust, Brighton Friends of the Earth, and other groups, have instigated a campaign for a National Park. Sixty per cent of respondents favoured this option. The question as to whether the Downs will have National Park status now rests with the Secretary of State for the Environment.

Brian Redhead has recently remarked that 'future generations will have inventions we cannot even dream of, and if we act in time, they will also have the South Downs we know and love—protected and more beautiful'.

# EPILOGUE

We have found the South Downs not to be the one unchangeable, permanent, thing in the world that some of us would have liked them to be. Readers may well wonder how they survived at all, seeing that they appear to have been done to death so many times in the past. Reading over previous chapters, one cannot fail to note how each generation has mourned the passing of the Downs-before-yesterday. Open the pages at random and people will be found saying that the Downs have gone to the dogs since their childhood and that they are finally and irrevocably doomed. The present generation rails against agribusiness, phosphate fertiliser and pesticides and yearns for the miles of pre-1939 chalk turf, yet farmers in the inter-war years were eaten up with worries of agricultural depression. They looked back to the 'prosperity' and 'stability' of high farming in the mid-to-late 19th century, but it turns out that some thought the downs had gone downhill with the coming of the steam thresher. Coming back to Cobbett, who inveighed against changes since his own childhood, we learn from other sources that the Agricultural Revolution was then creating untold misery for others. Such an idea of past adverse changes in the South Downs can certainly be traced back to Sir Thomas More's *Utopia* (1516), when 'sheep ate up men' and decimated rural communities.

Yet the history of the Downs also reveals their indomitable character and the extraordinary affection and love they have inspired universally over generations. This prompts an unfailing confidence that the present problems, deficiencies and mistakes will be put right. A 20th-century Zeitgeist was, and is, against them, but people are now prepared to do battle with the Zeitgeist. Another period of change hopefully lies ahead for the Downs, oriented towards the health, beauty and permanence of the landscape and a better deal for those living and working in them. For an England becoming steadily more built over and uniformly filled with the ugly debris of the 20th century it is of momentous importance that there should remain a range of hills undesecrated by human hands and adequately protected against the sort of pressures mentioned in this book. Provided we ensure that the motives and purposes we avow for the Downs are not at variance with what we actually do to them (which is the main failing of the 20th century), we shall fulfil what John Ruskin said we should when he wrote over one hundred years ago that the Earth belongs to those who are to come after us, as to us, and that amongst our duties was 'the practising of present economy for the sake of debtors yet unborn'.

The future South Downs of one's dreams is not yet, nor ever wholly will be, but one refuses to believe that it will be never.

# BIBLIOGRAPHY

Abbreviations:    Sussex Archaeological Collections      *SAC*
Sussex Record Society      *SRS*
Agricultural History Review      *Agric.Hist.Rev.*
English Place Name Society Journal      *EPNSJ*

| | |
|---|---|
| Aldsworth, Fred and Harris, R. | 'The Chilgrove Valley Project' in Alec Down (ed.), *Chichester Excavations* 4 (1979), 22-40 |
| | 'The Tower and "Rhenish Helm" spire of St Mary's Church, Sompting', *SAC* 126 (1988), 105-44 |
| Allcroft, A. Hadrian | *Earthwork of England* (Macmillan, 1908) |
| | *Downland Pathways* (London, 1924) |
| | *Waters of Arun* (London, 1930) |
| Allen, Andrew | *A Sussex Dictionary of Medicine* (Newbury, 1995) |
| Anderson, William | *The Face of Glory* (London, 1996) |
| Andrews, Colin | *The Life and Songs of Michael Blann of Upper Beeding* (Worthing, 1979) |
| Angus, Peggy | *Furlongs: Peggy Angus and Friends* (Towner Gallery, Eastbourne, 1987) |
| Ashwell, A.R. | *Life of William Wilberforce* (London, 1880-2) |
| Avebury, Lord | *The Scenery of England* (London, 1902) |
| Bailey, Mark | 'The Rabbit in Medieval East Anglian Economy', *Agric.Hist.Rev.* 36 (1988), 1-20 |
| Baker, A. | 'Lewes Priory and the early group of Wall Paintings in Sussex', *Walpole Society* 31 (1942-3), 1-44 |
| | 'The Wall Paintings in the Church of St John the Baptist, Clayton, Sussex', *SAC* 108 (1970), 58-81 |
| Baker, A.R.H. | 'Some evidence of a reduction in the acreage of cultivated land in Sussex during the early fourteenth century', *SAC* 104 (1966), 1-23 |
| Baldwin, Stanley | *On England* (London, 1925) |
| Barker, Eric | 'Sussex Anglo-Saxon Charters', *SAC* 86 (1947), 42-101; 87 (1949), 112-63; 88 (1950), 51-113 |
| | 'Some Woolavington and Wonworth leases', *SAC* 94 (1956), 43-69 |
| Barr-Hamilton, Alec | *Saxon Sussex* (London, 1953) |
| | 'The excavation of Bargham church site', *SAC* 99 (1961), 38-65 |
| Baxter, John | *Library of Practical Agriculture* (Lewes, 1846) |
| Bayliss-Smith, T.P. and Owens, S.E. (eds.) | *Britain's Changing Environment from the Air* (Cambridge, 1990) |
| Beckett, Arthur | *The Spirit of the Downs* (London, 1909) |
| Beetles, Chris | *S.R. Badmin* (London, 1985) |
| | *The Art of George and Eileen Soper* (London, 1995) |
| | *Landscapes of Charles Knight* (London, 1997) |

| Bell, Martin | 'Excavations at Bishopstone', *SAC* 115 (1977) |
|---|---|
| Bell, Quentin | *Bloomsbury* (London, 1986) |
| Belloc, Hilaire | *Hills and the Sea* (London, 1906) |
| | *Sussex* (illustrations by W. Ball) (London, 1906) |
| | *The Four Men* (London, 1912) |
| | *The County of Sussex* (London, 1936) |
| | *Complete Verse* (London, 1954) |
| Binyon, Helen | *Eric Ravilious* (London, 1983) |
| Birkenhead, Lord | *The Hundred Best Essays* (London, 1929) |
| Blaauw, W.H. | 'Letters to Ralph de Nevill Bishop of Chichester, 1222-1244', *SAC* 3 (1850), 54 |
| Blair, J. (ed.) | *Minsters and Parish Churches: the local church in transition, 950-1200* (OUCA Mono 17: Oxford) |
| Bleach, J. and Coates, R. | 'Three more Walcots', *EPNSJ* 19 (1986-87), 56-63 |
| Bleach, J. | 'Walecote: a British Settlement in an Anglo-Saxon Estate', *Ringmer History* 7 (1986), 35-41 |
| Blencowe, R.W. | 'On Shepherds and their Songs', *SAC* 2 (1849), 247-56 |
| Blunt, Wilfrid Scawen | *Collected Works* (London, 1914) |
| Boardman, John | 'Severe Erosion on agricultural land in East Sussex', October 1987, *Soil Technology*, vol.I (1988), 333-48 |
| | 'Damage to Property by run-off from agricultural land, South Downs, southern England, 1976-93', *Geographical Journal* 161 (1995), 177-91 |
| and Robinson, D.A. | 'Soil Erosion, climatic vagary and agricultural changes on the Downs around Lewes and Brighton', autumn 1982, *Applied Geography* 5 (1985), 243-58 |
| Bogarde, Sir Dirk | *Great Meadow* (London, 1992) |
| Boxall, J.P. | 'The Sussex breed of cattle in the nineteenth century', *Agric.Hist.Rev.* 20 (1972), 17-29 |
| Bowie, G.G.S. | 'New sheep for old: change in sheep farming in Hampshire', *Agric.Hist.Rev.* 35 (1987), 1524 |
| Bowness, Alan | *Ivon Hitchens* (London, 1973) |
| Bradley, Richard | 'Stock raising and the origins of the hill fort on the South Downs', *Antiquaries Journal* (1971), 8-29 |
| Brandon, P.F. | 'The enclosure of the Keymer Commons', *Sussex Notes and Queries*, 15 (1960), 181-6 |
| | 'Arable farming in a Sussex scarpfoot parish during the later middle ages', *SAC* 100 (1962), 60-72 |
| | 'The Common Lands and Wastes of Sussex', unpublished Ph.D. thesis, University of London, 1963 |
| | 'Demesne arable farming in coastal Sussex during the late middle ages', *Agric.Hist.Rev.* 19 (1971a), 13-34 |
| | 'The Origin of Newhaven and the drainage of the Lewes and Laughton Levels', *SAC* 109 (1971b), 94-106 |
| | 'Cereal yields on the Sussex estates of Battle Abbey during the later middle ages', *Economic History Review* 25 (1972), 403-20 |
| | *The Sussex Landscape* (London, 1974) |
| (ed.) | *The South Saxons* (Chichester, 1978) |
| | 'Designed Landscapes in South-East England', *Trans. Institute British Geographers*, Special Number 10 (1979) |
| | 'Philip Webb, the Morris Circle and Sussex', *Sussex History* 2 (1981), 8-14 |
| | *Applesham Farm: a case study of farming and conservation* (CPRE, 1987) |
| and Short, B. | *South East England from 1000 A.D.* (London, 1990) |

Brent, Colin                 'Rural population in Sussex between 1550-1640', part II, *SAC* 116 (1978), 41-56

Brent, J.A.                  'Alciston Manor in the middle ages', *SAC* 106 (1968), 89-102

Briault, E.W.H.              *The Land of Britain: Sussex* (London, 1942)

Brooke, Stopford A.          *Life and Letters of F.W. Robertson* (London, 1865)

Budgen, Revd W.              'Excete and its parish church', *SAC* 58 (1916), 67-70

Bumpus, Judith               *Adrian Berg: a sense of place*, introduction to exhibition catalogue, Barbican, 1993

Burke, John                  *Musical Landscapes* (Exeter, 1983)

Burleigh, G.R.               'An introduction to deserted medieval villages in East Sussex', *SAC* 91 (1973), 45-53

                             'Further notes on deserted and shrunken medieval villages in Sussex', *SAC* 114 (1976), 61-8

Burroughs, John              *Fresh Fields* (Boston, 1904)

Bush, M.B.                   'The Age of Britain's climax grassland', *Nature* 329 (1987), 434-6
  and Frenley, J.R.

Caird, J.                    *English Agriculture in 1851-2* (London, 1852)

Camden, William              *Britannia* (1586)

Camp, Jeffery                *Paint* (London, 1996)

Campbell, L.H.               *The indirect effects of Pesticides on Birds* (Joint Nature Conservation Committee, 1997)
  and Cooke, A.S.

Chatt, J.                    *New Trends in the Chemistry of Nitrogen Fixation* (Lisbon, 1982)

Clifton-Taylor, Alec         *Six More English Towns* (BBC, 1981)

Clough, M.                   'Two Fitzalan Surveys', *SRS* 67 (1969)

Coates, R.                   'Remarks on "pre-British" in England with special reference to *uenta cilla* and *cunaco*', *EPNSJ*
                             16 (1983-84), 1-24

                             'The Name of Lewes: some problems and possibilities', *EPNSJ* 23 (1990-91), 5-15

Coatts, Margot               *A Weaver's Life: Ethel Mairet 1872-1952* (Crafts Council, Bath, 1983)

Cobbett, William             *Political Register* (1821-26)

Cole, Ann                    'The distribution and usage of the place-name elements *botm*, *bytme* and *botn*', *EPNSJ* 20
                             (1988), 39-46

                             'The meaning of the Old English place-name element *ora*', *EPNSJ* 21 (1989), 15-22

                             'The origin, distribution and usage of the place-name element *ora* and its relation to the
                             element *ofer*', *EPNSJ* 22 (1990), 26-41

Cole, G.D.H.                 *Rural Rides of William Cobbett* (London, 1930)
  and Cole, Margaret

Collins, Margaret            'Some evidence of the influence on land use of the distribution of non-calcareous soils on
                             the chalk downs of southern England', MA thesis, University of London, 1982

Colls, Robert                *Englishness: Politics and Culture 1880-1920* (London, 1986)
  and Dodd, Philip

Connolly, C.                 *The Condemned Playground* (London, 1945)

                             'Comment', *Horizon* 16 (1947), 68-9

Constable, Freda             *The England of Eric Ravilious* (London, 1982)

Cook, C.F.                   *The Book of Sussex Verse* (Hove, 1914)

Copper, Bob                  *A Song for Every Season* (London, 1975)

                             *Bob Copper's Sussex* (Seaford, 1997)

Cornwall, J.                 'The Ecclesden Outrage: a fresh interpretation', *SAC* 113 (1975), 7-15

Countryside Commission *The East Hampshire Landscape* (Cheltenham, 1993)

| | |
|---|---|
| Cunliffe, B. | 'Saxon and Medieval settlement pattern in the region of Chalton, Hants', *Medieval Archaeology* 16 (1972), 1-12 |
| | *The Regni* (London, 1973) |
| | 'Chalton, Hants: The evolution of a landscape', *Antiquaries Journal* 53 (1973), 173-90 |
| | 'Saxon Sussex', in P.F. Brandon (ed.), *The South Saxons* (Chichester, 1978) |
| | 'Danebury: an Iron-Age hillfort in Hampshire', *CBA Research Report* 52 (1984) |
| Curran, Stuart | *The Poems of Charlotte Smith* (London, 1993) |
| Curwen, E.C. | *Prehistoric Sussex* (London, 1929) |
| | 'Ancient Cultivation', *Antiquity IV*, no.24 (1932), 389-406 |
| | *The Archaeology of Sussex* (London, 1937) |
| | *The Journal of Gideon Mantell* (London, 1940) |
| Davidson, H. | 'The Hill and the Dragon', *Folklore* 61 (1950), 169-185 |
| Dawson, B. | *Flint Buildings in West Sussex* (West Sussex County Council, 1998) |
| Defoe, Daniel | *A Tour through the whole island of Great Britain, 1738* (reprint 1927) |
| Dodgson, J. McNeal | 'The significance of the distribution of the English Place-Name in ingas and inga in South-East England', *Medieval Archaeology* 10 (1966), 1-29 |
| Down, A. (ed.) | *Chichester Excavations* 4 (1979) |
| Drewett, D. | 'Return to Mount Caburn', *Past and Present*, Lewes, 78 (1996), 4; 80 (1996), 6-7 |
| and Rudling, D. | *A Regional History of South East England to AD1000* (London, 1988) |
| and Gardiner, M. | *An extensive survey of plough damage to known archaeological sites in West and East Sussex* (Institute of Archaeology, London, 1976) |
| Dunvan, Paul | *Ancient and Modern History of Lewes and Brighthelmstone* (Lewes, 1795) |
| Ede, Joy | *The Dyke Estate: An archaeology and land-use report* (The National Trust, Slindon, 1997) |
| Edwards, A.M. | *The Design of Suburbia* (London,1981) |
| English Nature | *Crops and Biodiversity* (London, 1997) |
| Fairbrother, Nan | *New Lives, New Landscapes* (London, 1970) |
| Farjeon, Annabel | *Morning has Broken: a biography of Eleanor Farjeon* (London, 1986) |
| Farrant, S. | 'John Ellman of Glynde in Sussex', *Agric.Hist.Rev.* 26 (1978), 77-8 |
| | 'The management of farm estates in the lower Ouse valley, Sussex, and agricultural change', *Southern History* 1 (1979), 155-77 |
| Figg, W. | 'Manorial Customs of Southease-with-Heighton', *SAC* 3 (1850), 249-52 |
| | 'Tenantry customs: the Drinker Acres', *SAC* 4 (1851), 247-56 |
| Fisher, Clive | *Cyril Connolly: a nostalgic life* (London, 1995) |
| Fisher, E.A. | *The Anglo-Saxon Churches of Sussex* (London, 1970) |
| Ford, Ford Madox | *It was the Nightingale* (London, 1934) |
| Fowler, Peter | *Approaches to Archaeology* (London, 1987) |
| Fox, A.H. Lane | 'An examination into the character and probable origin of "hillforts" of Sussex', *Archaeologia* 42 (1869), 27-52 |
| Fussell, G.E. | 'Four centuries of farming systems in Sussex, 1500-1900', *SAC* 90 (1952) |
| Garde, de la *Comte* | *Brighton: Scénes detachées d'un voyage en Angleterre* (2nd ed., Parish, 1834) |
| Garland, Patrick | *Angels in the Sky* (Chichester, 1995) |
| Gaze, John | *Figures in a Landscape: the history of the National Trust* (London, 1988) |
| Gill, Eric | *Autobiography* (1940) |

Gilpin, William        *Picturesque Beauty* (London, 1792)

                       *Observations on the Coast of Hampshire, Sussex and Kent, 1774* (London, 1804)

Gissing, G.            *Collected Letters*, 4 vols., ed. P. Mattheisen, A. Young and P. Coustillas (Athens, Ohio, 1990-93)

Glasscock, R.E.        'The Distribution of lay wealth in Kent, Surrey and Sussex in the early fourteenth century', *Archaeologia Cantiana* 80 (1965), 61-8

Godfrey, W.            'The parish church of Bishopstone', *SAC* 87 (1948), 164-83

   (ed.)               'The book of John Rowe', *SRS* 34 (1928)

Goldsmith, John        *Hambledon* (Chichester, 1994)

Gosse, Philip          *Go to the Country* (London, 1935)

Graham, P. Anderson    *Reclaiming the Waste* (London, 1916)

Granville, A.B.        *Spas of England, Vol.2 The Midlands and South* (London, 1841)

Greatorex, C.          'Eastbourne's Bronze Age find "of national importance"', *Past and Present*, Lewes, 77 (1995), 5

Green, Bryn            'Towards a more sustainable agriculture: time for a rural land-use strategy', *Biologist* 40, 2 (1993), 81-5

                       *Plenty and Wilderness: creating a new countryside* (ECOS 16[2], 1995)

Greene, Graham         *Brighton Rock* (London, 1938)

Grigson, G.            *The Englishman's Flora* (London, 1958)

Grinsell, L.V.         'Sussex Barrows', *SAC* 75 (1934), 217-75

                       'Supplement No.2', *SAC* 82 (1941), 115-23

                       *The Ancient Burial Mounds of England* (London, 2nd edn, 1953)

Gunther, R.            *Early British Botanists* (London, 1922)

Haggard, Rider         *Rural England*, vol.1 (London, 1902)

Hall, A.D.             *A Pilgrimage of British Farming, 1910-12* (London, 1914)

and Russell, E.J.      *A Report on the Agriculture and Soils of Kent, Surrey and Sussex* (London, 1911)

Hampshire County       *Hampshire's Countryside Heritage* (Winchester, 1984)
   Council

Hare, Augustus         *A Guide to Sussex* (London, 1894)

Harvey, Graham         *The Killing of the Countryside* (London, 1997)

Hawkes, Jacquetta      *A Land* (London, 1951)

Henderson, P.P.        *Letters of William Morris* (London, 1950)

Heron, Patrick         *Ivon Hitchens* (London, 1955)

Hill, D.               'The Origins of Saxon towns in Sussex' in P. Brandon (ed.), *The South Saxons* (Chichester, 1978)

Hodgson, J.M.          *The Soils of the West Sussex Coastal Plain*, Soil Survey of Great Britain (London,1967)

Holden, E.W.           'Excavations at the deserted medieval village of Hangleton', Part 1, *SAC* 119 (1963), 117-48

   and Hudson, T.P.    'The Salt Industry in the Adur Valley', *SAC* 119 (1981), 117-48

Holleyman, G.          'The Celtic Field System in South Britain: A Survey', *Antiquity* 9 (1935)

                       *Herbert Toms* (unpublished, 1994)

Hopkins, G. Thurston   *Sussex Pilgrimages* (London, 1927)

   and R. Thurston     *Literary Originals of Sussex* (Gravesend, 1936)

House of Commons       *Agricultural Committee Second Report*, vol.2 (1997)

Howkins, A.            'The Discovery of Rural England' in R. Colls and P. Dodd (eds.), *Englishness: Politics and Culture, 1880-1920* (London, 1986)

Hudson, W.            'On a series of rolls of the manor of Wiston', *SAC* 53 (1911), 94-118

Hudson, W.H.          *Nature in Downland* (London, 1900)

Hulton, E.            'Can we save the real England', *Picture Post* (21 October 1944), 21-3

Hurdis, James         *The Favourite Village* (Bishopstone, 1800)

Hurst, J.G. and D.G.  'Excavations at a deserted medieval village, Hangleton', part 11, *SAC* 102 (1964), 94-112

Hussey, A.            'On Rottingdean Church', *SAC* 9 (1857), 67-70

Ingrams, Richard      *England: an anthology* (London, 1989)

Jefferies, R.         *Nature near London* (London, 1908 edn)

                      *The Open Air* (London, 1913)

Jennings, Louis J.    *Field Paths and Green Lanes* (London, 1878)

Jeremy, R.C.A.C.      *Chalk Grassland: studies in its conservation and management in South-East England* (Kent Trust for
  and Stott, P.A. (eds.)     Nature Council, Maidstone, 1973)

Jesse, R.H.B.         *A survey of the agriculture of Sussex Royal Agricultural Society of England* (London, 1960)

Joad, C.E.M.          *The Testament of Joad* (London, 1937)

                      'The Face of England', *Horizon*, V, no.29 (May 1942), 335-47

                      *The Untutored Townsman's invasion of the country* (Folly Farm, London, 1947)

Johnson, W.H.         *Crime and Disorder in late Georgian Alfriston* (Eastbourne, 1994)

Jones, D.K.C. (ed.)   *The Shaping of Southern England* (London, 1980)

                      *The Geomorphology of the British Isles: Southeastern and Southern England* (London, 1981)

  and Rose, Francis   'The Downs that are England', *Geographical Magazine* 52 (1979-80), 618-31
  and Hebbert, M.

King, S.H.            'Domesday Sussex' in H.C. Darby and E.M.J. Campbell, *The Domesday Geography of South-East
                        England* (Cambridge, 1971)

Kipling, Rudyard      *Something of Myself* (London, 1937)

                      *The Complete Verse*, ed. M.M. Kaye (1990)

Kirby, D.P.           'The Church in Saxon Sussex', in P.F. Brandon (ed.), *The South Saxons* (Chichester, 1978)

Lamond, E. (ed.)      *Walter of Henley's Husbandry* (London, 1890)

———                   *Land at War*, Ministry of Information (London, 1945)

Lang, Cecil M. (ed.)  *The Swinburne Letters*, vol.5

Lankester, Edwin      *The Correspondence of John Ray* (The Ray Society, London, 1948)

Laurie, Gordon        *All is Safely Gathered In: Granary Storage on the Wiston Estate 1350-1900* (Wiston, 1990)

Leach, Bernard        *Beyond East and West* (London, 1978)

Lee, Hugh A. (ed.)    *A Cézanne in the Hedge* (London, 1992)

Leconfield, Lord      *Petworth Manor in the Seventeenth Century* (Oxford, 1954)

Lewes, Jeremy         *Cyril Connolly: A Life* (London, 1997)

Lousley, J.E.         *Wildflowers of Chalk and Limestone* (London, 1950)

Lower, Mark A.        *Contributions to Literature* (London, 1854)

                      'The churches of Newhaven and Denton', *SAC* 9 (1857), 89-100

                      'Old Speech and Manners', *SAC* 13 (1861), 219-31·

                      *A Compendious History of Sussex* (London, 1870)

Lower, Richard        *Stray Leaves* (Lewes, 1862)

Lowerson, J.L.        *A Short History of Sussex* (Folkestone, 1980)

Lusted, Andrew        *Arthur Duley: the story of a Southdown shepherd* (Lewes, 1988)

| | |
|---|---|
| Lynton, Norbert | *The Sussex Scene* (Hove Museum, 1993) |
| MacCarthy, Fiona | *Eric Gill* (London, 1989) |
| Mais, S.P.B. | *Round about England* (London, 1935) |
| | *Hills of the South* (Southern Railway, 1939) |
| | *England's Pleasaunce* (London, 1945) |
| | *Listen to the Country* (London, n.d.) |
| Mantell, Gideon | *The Fossils of the South Downs* (London, 1822) |
| | *The Geology of the South-East of England* (London, 1833) |
| | *A Day's Ramble in Lewes* (London, 1846) |
| Marler, Regina (ed.) | *Selected Letters of Vanessa Bell* (London, 1983) |
| Marr, Murray | *A Survey of the Chalk Grassland on the Western South Downs 1981-2* (Chichester, 1984) |
| Marsh, Jan | *Back to the Land* (London, 1982) |
| Marshall, William | *The Rural Economy of the Southern Counties*, Vol.2 (London, 1798) |
| | *A Review and Abstract of the County Reports to the Board of Agriculture, Southern and Peninsular Departments* (London, 1817; David and Charles reprint, 1968) |
| Martin, Edward | *Life in a Sussex Windmill* (London, 1921) |
| Martins, Susanna Wade | *An Estate at Work: Holkham estate, its inhabitants in the nineteenth century* (London, 1980) |
| | 'From black face to white face: An aspect of the Agricultural Revolution in Norfolk', *Agric.Hist.Rev.* 41 (1993), 20-30 |
| Mason, R.T. | 'Alciston Court: A manor of Battle Abbey', *SAC* 116 (1978), 159-68 |
| Massingham, H.J. | *Where Man Belongs* (London, 1946), 248 |
| Mee, Arthur | *Sussex: The Garden by the Sea*, The King's England (London, 1938) |
| Mellor, David, Saunders, Gill and Wright, Patrick | *Recording Britain: A Pictorial Survey of Pre-War Britain* (London, 1990) |
| Mercer, Peter and Holland, Douglas | *The Hunns Mere Pit: The Story of Woodingdean and Balsdean* (Lewes, 1993) |
| Merrifield, Mrs. | *A Sketch of the Natural History of Brighton* (Brighton, 1864) |
| Milner-Gulland, R. | 'The Problem of the Early Sussex Frescoes', *Southern History* 7 (1985), 25-54 |
| Ministry of Agriculture | *Botanical Monitoring of Grassland in the South Downs ESA Scheme, 1987-1995* (London, 1996) |
| Monro, Alida | *Collected Poems of Harold Monro* (London, 1933) |
| Moore, G. | *Esther Waters* (London, 1894) |
| | *Ave* (London, 1911) |
| Mortimore, R.N. | *A Guide to the Chalk of Sussex* (Brighton, n.d.) |
| Murchison, R. | *Agricultural Sir John: A biography of Sir John Sinclair* (London, 1962) |
| Murray, M.A. | 'England a field for folk-lore research', *Folklore* (1954), 1-9 |
| Nairn, I. and Pevsner, N. | *The Buildings of England: Sussex* (London, 1965) |
| National Trust | *Saddlescombe Farm Vernacular Building Survey* (Slindon, 1996) |
| Neve, Christopher | *The Unquiet Landscape: Place and Idea in twentieth-century English painting* (London, 1990) |
| Nicholson, Andrew | *William Nicholson: Paintings, Woodcuts and Writings* (London, 1996) |
| Nicolson, Nigel (ed.) | *The Letters of Virginia Woolf* (London, 1975-8) |
| Noyes, Alfred | *Collected Poems* (London, 1950) |
| O'Connor, J. and Shrubb, Michael | *Farming and Birds* (Cambridge, 1986) |
| Parish, W.D. | *A Dictionary of the Sussex Dialect* (Chichester, 1957) |

Park, D.                     'The Lewes Group of Wall Paintings in Sussex', *Anglo-Norman Studies* 6 (Suffolk, 1983), 200-39

Parker, A.C.                 *Coke of Norfolk* (Oxford, 1975)

Partridge, Frances           *Memories* (London, 1981)

                             *Hanging On* (London, 1990)

                             *Other People* (London, 1993)

Patmore, P.                  *Letters in England by Victoire, Count de Soligny* (London, 1823)

Peake, Harold J.E.           *South-Eastern Naturalist and Antiquary* 36 (1931), 62

Peckham, W.D.                *Thirteen Custumals of the Sussex Manors of the Bishops of Chichester*, *SRS* XXXI (Cambridge, 1925)

Pelham, R.A.                 'The Distribution of sheep in Sussex in the early Fourteenth Century', *SAC* 75 (1934), 128-35

Pennington, Janet            'Steyning Town and its Trades 1559-1787', *SAC* 130 (1992), 164-188
  and Sleight, Joyce

Pennington, W.               *The History of British Vegetation* (London, 1969)

Pentecost, Evelyn            *A Shepherd's Daughter* (Petworth, 1987)

Piozzi, Mrs.                 *Anecdotes of the late Samuel Johnson LL.D.*, ed. Robina Napner (London, 1884)

Pitts, Michael               *Fairweather Eden* (London, 1997)
  and Marr, Robert

Porter, Valerie              *The Southdown Sheep* (Singleton, 1991)

Potts, G.R.                  *The Partridge* (London, 1986)

Powys, J.C.                  *Autobiography* (London, 1967)

Pragnell, V.P.               *The Story of the Sanctuary* (Steyning, 1928)

Pruden, Winefride            'The Guild of St Dominic and St Joseph' (Ditchling, unpublished, 1994)

Pückler-Muskau, *Prince*     *Tour in Germany, Holland and England, 1826-28* (London, 1832)

Pull, J.                     *The Flint Mines of Blackpatch* (London, 1932)

Rackham, Oliver              *The History of the Countryside* (London, 1986)

Ray, John                    *The Wisdom of God manifested in works of Creation* (Cambridge, 1701 ed.)

Reece, M.M.                  *Goodwood's Oak* (London, 1987)

Redwood, B.C.                *Custumals of Sussex Manors of the Archbishop of Canterbury*, SRS 57 (1958)
  and Wilson, A.E.

Rees, Simon                  *The Charlton Hunt* (Chichester, 1998)

Relhan, A.                   *A short history of Brighthelmstone* (London, 1829)

Reynolds, Peter              *Iron-Age Farm* (London, 1979)

Roberts, Morley              *W.H. Hudson: A Portrait* (London, 1924)

Robinson, Maude              *A South Down Farm in the Sixties* (London, 1938)

Robinson, J.M.               *The Dukes of Norfolk: A Quincentennial History* (London, 1982)

Rose, Francis                *Habitat and Vegetation of Sussex* (Booth Museum, Brighton, 1995)

                             *The Flora of Hampshire* (Colchester, 1997)

Ross, Alan                   'A Human Landscape' in *Poems 1942-67* (1976), 156

Rouse, Clive                 'Wall Paintings in Coombes Church', *Sussex Notes and Queries* XII (1948), 12-13

Royal Society for the        *Review of the South Downs Environmentally Sensitive Area Scheme* (London, 1996)
  Protection of Birds

Ryman, Ernest                *The Devil's Dyke: A Guide* (Brighton, 1994)

Salisbury, Sir E.J.          *Downs and Dunes* (London, 1952)

                             *The South-Eastern Naturalist and Antiquary* 38 (1933), 9

Salzman, L.F.    'The Property of the Earl of Arundel', *SAC* 91 (1953), 132-52

Sanderson, N.A. and Rose, F.    *Potential Special Areas of Conservation in the Western World* (Hampshire Wildlife Trust, 1996)

Selincourt, Hugh de    *The Cricket Match* (London, 1924)

Sharp, Thomas    *Town and Countryside* (London, 1932)

Sheail, John    'The distribution of taxation: Population and Wealth in England during the sixteenth century', *Trans. Inst. British Geographers* 55 (1972), 111-26

*Nature in Trust* (London, 1976)

'The South Downs and Brighton's water supplies: an inter-war study of resource management', *Southern History* 14 (1992), 93-102

Sheffield, *Lord*    *Remarks on the Deficiency of Grain*, Part 1 (London, 1801)

Shoard, M.    *The Theft of the Countryside* (London, 1980)

Short, Brian    'South-East England: Kent, Surrey and Sussex' in Joan Thirsk (ed.), *The Agrarian History of England and Wales*, vol.V(1), 1640-1750 (Cambridge, 1984)

Shrubshall, Dennis and Coustillas, Pierre    *Landscape and Literati: Unpublished Letters of W. Hudson and George Gissing* (London, 1985)

Sleight, Joyce    *Yeoman Farmers and Gentlemen: People of Wiston, West Sussex, 1612-1732* (Wiston, 1993)

Smith, Bernard and Haas, Peter    *Writers in Sussex* (Bristol, 1985)

Smith, C.J.    *The Ecology of the English Chalk* (London, 1980)

Smith, Michael    *Rudyard Kipling: The Rottingdean Years* (Rottingdean, 1989)

Somerville, W.    'Some notes on the Society's experiment at Jevington and on the improvement of poor pasture near Shoreham (Applesham)', *Journal of the Bath and West and Southern Counties*, 5th series (1911), 90-8

Spargo, Demelza    *This Land is our Land: Aspects of Agriculture in English Art* (Royal Agricultural Society of England, 1988)

Sparks, B.W.    *Geomorphology* (London, 1986)

Spink/Nevill Keating    *Douglas Stannus Gray, 1890-1959* (London, 1986)

Stang, J. and Cochan, K.    *The Correspondence of Ford Madox Ford and Stella Bowen* (Indiana U.P., 1993)

Stapledon, Sir George and Davies, W.    *Ley Farming* (London, 1946)

Stephens, Sir Leslie    'Stray Thoughts on Landscape', *Cornhill Magazine* (1878), 76-7

Stephens, Nicholas (ed.)    *Natural Landscapes of Britain from the Air* (Cambridge, 1990)

Strong, Sir Roy    *Arcadia* (London, 1996)

Tansley, Sir Arthur    *The British Isles and their Vegetation* (Cambridge, 1949)

and Adamson, R.S.    'Studies of the vegetation of the English chalk', III: 'The chalk grasslands of the Hampshire-Sussex border', *Journal of Ecology* 13 (1925), 177-233; IV: 'A preliminary survey of the chalk grassland of the Sussex Downs', *Journal of Ecology* 14 (1926), 1-32

Taylor, Christopher    *Village and Farmstead* (London, 1983)

Taylor, H.M. and J.    *Anglo-Saxon Architecture* (Cambridge, 1965)

Taylor, James    *The Sussex Garland* (Newick, 1851)

Thomas, A.S.    'Chalk, Heath and Man', *Agri.Hist.Rev.* 8 (1960-1), 38-56

Thomas, Helen and Myfanwy    *Under Storm's Wing* (Manchester, 1988)

Thomas, R. George    *The Collected Poems of Edward Thomas* (Oxford, 1978)

Titow, J.Z.    *Winchester Yields: A Study in Medieval Agricultural Productivity* (Cambridge, 1972)

Tittensor, A.M. and Ruth, M.   'The Rabbit Warren at West Dean near Chichester', *SAC* 123 (1985), 151-181

'Tramp', The   *The South Downs*, London, Brighton and South Coast Railway (London, 1914)

Turner, E.   'On the military earthworks of the Sussex Downs', *SAC* 3 (1850), 173-84

University of Sussex   *Sussex: Environment, Landscape and Society* (London, 1983)

Unwin Cobden, Mrs.   *The Hungry Forties* (London, 1904; Irish University Press, 1971 reprint)

Vanderzee, G.   *Nonarum Inquisitiones in Curia Scaccari* (Record Commission, 1807)

Walpole, Horace   *The History of the Modern Taste in Gardening*, ed. J. Dixon Hunt (Ursus Press, New York, 1995)

Watt, A.S.   'Yew Communities of the South Downs', *Journ. Ecology* 14 (1926), 282-316

Waugh, Evelyn   *Labels* (London, 1930)

Waugh, Mary   *Smuggling in Kent and Sussex, 1700-1840* (Newbury, 1985)

Weight, R.V.   *Carol Weight: A Haunted Imagination* (Newton Abbot, 1994)

Welch, M.G.   'Late Romans and Saxons in Sussex', *Britannia* 2 (1971), 232-37

  *English Heritage Book of Saxon England* (London, 1992)

Wellings, S.R. and Bell, J.P.   'Physical controls of water movement in the unsaturated zone', *Q.J.Eng..Geology* (1982), 15, 235-41

Wells, H.G.   *Tono-Bungay* (1909, reprint 1964)

  *The Research Magnificent* (1915)

  *Experiment in Autobiography* 1 (1924)

  *The Wheels of Chance*, ed. B. Bergonzi (Everyman edition, 1984), v-xi

Wells, R.   'Popular protest and social crime: the evidence of criminal gangs in rural southern England' in Barry Stapleton (ed.), *Conflict and Community in Southern England* (1992), 139-49

West Sussex County Council   *D-Day West Sussex* (Chichester, 1994)

White, Gilbert   *The Natural History and Antiquities of Selborne* (1836 edition, London)

Wilcox, T. (ed.)   *Eric Gill and the Guild of St Joseph and St Dominic* (Hove Museum, 1991)

Wilkinson, Walter   *A Sussex Peep-Show* (London, 1933)

Williamson, J.   *The Great Yew Forest* (London, 1978)

Williamson, Tom and Bellamy, Liz   *Property and Landscape* (London, 1987)

Wills, Barclay   *Shepherds of Sussex* (London, 1938)

Wood, Frederick   *Sport and Nature in the Sussex Downs* (London, 1928)

Woolf, L.   *Autobiography Vol.4 Downhill all the Way* (London, 1967)

Woolf, V.   *The Death of the Moth* (1947)

  *Diaries*, ed. Anne Olivier Bell, 5 vols. (London, 1977-84)

Yates, E.M.   *A History of the Landscape in the parishes of South Harting and Rogate* (Chichester, 1972)

Young, Arthur   *Annals of Agriculture* (London)

  *The Agriculture of Sussex* (1794)

  *A General View of the Agriculture of the County of Norfolk* (London, 1804)

Young, Rev. Arthur   *A General View of the Agriculture of the County of Sussex* (London, 1813)

# CHAPTER NOTES

Manuscript sources are given in full. Articles and books are given by author and date, by which they can be located in the Bibliography.

Manuscript abbreviations:

| | |
|---|---|
| ESRO | East Sussex Record Office |
| PRO | Public Record Office |
| WSRO | West Sussex Record Office |
| SDCB | Sussex Downs Conservation Board |

Other abbreviations:

| | |
|---|---|
| BPP | British Parliamentary Papers |
| CPRE | Council for the Protection of Rural England |
| Downsmen | Society of Sussex Downsmen |

## Introduction, *pp.xv-xvi*

1 Mee (1938), 1
2 Kipling (1990), 676

## 1 The Character of the Downs, *pp.1-19*

1 White (1836 ed.), 255
2 Young, *Annals* 3 (1785), 133; Marshall (1798), 2, 294, 359
3 Lane Fox (1869), 27
4 Hudson (1900), 19
5 Anderson (1996), 28
6 Clifton-Taylor (1981), 103
7 Hudson (1900), 21
8 Wells (1915), 141
9 Ashwell (1880-82), 1, 239
10 White (1836 ed.), 255
11 Hudson (1900), 22
12 Ross (1976), 156
13 Lankester (1948)
14 Kipling (1990), 174-8
15 Wells (1909), 25
16 Tansley (1949)
17 Williamson (1978)
18 Holden and Hudson (1981), 119-48
19 Joad (1937), 279
20 Burke (1983), 67-70
21 Heron (1955), 1-3
22 Ford (1934), 93-7

23 Robinson (1982), v
24 Gunther (1922)
25 Henderson (1950), 115
26 Brandon (1981), 8-14
27 *Country Life* 97 (1945), 252

## 2 The Chalk Takes Care of All, *pp.20-31*

1 Hawkes (1951), 18
2 Smith (1980)
3 Mortimore (n.d.)
4 Jones (1981)
5 Sparks (1986), 22, 28, 70-1, 189-90, 211
6 Bayliss-Smith and Owens (1990), 94-5; Stephens (1990), 43
7 Cole and Cole (1930), 2, 478
8 Belloc (1911), 189-90
9 Cole and Cole (1930), 2, 454
10 Wellings and Bell (1982), 235-41
11 Young (1804), 21-2
12 Hawkes (1951), 134, 229
13 Clifton-Taylor (1981), 104
14 BPP Agriculture, 10 (1867-8), 95

## 3 Early Man, *pp32-46*

1 Pitts and Roberts (1997)
2 Lane Fox (1869), 28; Cf, Turner (1850), 173-4
3 E. Cecil Curwen (1929, 1937)
4 Holleyman (unpublished, 1994)

5   Grinsell (1953), 186-9
6   Reynolds (1979)
7   Curwen (1929), 14-21
8   Pull (1932)
9   Drewett (1988), 96-116
10  Grinsell (1934, 1941); *Suss.Arch.Coll.* 7 (1854), 50-3
11  Bradley (1971)
12  Cunliffe (1973), 126-39
13  Cunliffe (1973), 173-90
14  Aldsworth in Down (1979)
15  Curwen (1932), 6, 38-46
16  Holleyman (1935), 443-55
17  Reynolds (1979)
18  *The Times*, 21 September 1996, *Weekend*, 3

## 4 The Saxon South Downs, *pp.47-56*

1   Taylor (1983), 109-24
2   Welch (1971), 232-6
3   Bell (1977), 193-241
4   Cunliffe (1978), 223
5   Cunliffe (1972), 1-12; (1993), 173-90
6   Brandon (1978), 10
7   Welch (1992), 42
8   Barker (1947), 65-9
9   Dodgson (1966), 1-29
10  Coates (1983-84), *16*, 1-24
11  *Ibid.*
12  Coates (1990-91), *23*, 5-15
13  Bleach and Coates (1986-87), *19*, 56-63
14  Cole (1989), 21, 15-22
15  Cole (1988), 20, 39-41, 45-55
16  Cole (1990), 26-41
17  Brandon (1978), 6
18  Taylor (1983), 109-24
19  King in Darby and Campbell (1971), 463-72
20  Hill (1978), 185-6

## 5 Farming Communities in the Middle Ages (1100-1500), *pp.58-78*

1   Brandon (1971b)
2   Birkenhead (1929), 1-3
3   Peckham (1925); Clough (1969)
4   Brandon (1963), 263
5   *Ibid.*, 265
6   Williamson and Bellamy (1987), 22-5
7   Barker (1947), 65-9
8   The Sussex Domesday (Alecto Historical Editions, London, 1988), f.26
9   Blaauw (1850), 35-76
10  Vanderzee (1807)
11  Salzman (1953), 32-52
12  Brandon (1972)
13  White (1836 ed.), 255
14  *Ibid.*
15  Brandon (1960)

16  *Ibid.*
17  *Ibid.*
18  Brandon and Short (1990), 70-4
19  PRO C 135/162/11
20  Brandon (1971a); ESRO G/451 and *passim*; PRO SC6/1026/19 and *passim*
21  Brandon (1971a)
22  *Ibid.*
23  Pelham (1934), 129-35
24  Brandon (1972)
25  *Ibid.*
26  ESRO/G/I/5
27  Lamond (ed.) (1890), 67, 71
28  Brandon (1972)
29  Camden (1586), 154
30  Baker (1966), 1-6
31  Allcroft (1924 ed.), 60
32  Brandon (1974), 162-4
33  *Ibid.*
34  *Ibid.*
35  *Ibid.*
36  Burleigh (1973), 45-83; (1976), 61-8; Brandon (1974), 162-4
37  Brandon (1974), 162-4
38  *Ibid.*
39  *Ibid.*
40  Budgen (1916), 138-70
41  *Ibid.*
42  Holden (1963), 54-181; Hurst and Hurst (1964), 94-142
43  Brandon (1962), 60-72
44  Brandon, *ibid.*; Brent (1968), 89-102
45  Brandon (1962), 60-72
46  Mason (1978), 159-62

## 6 The Saxon and Early Medieval Downland Church, *pp.79-89*

1   Nairn and Pevsner (1965), 23
2   Taylor and Taylor (1965), 2, 730
3   Fisher (1970), 227-34
4   Kirby in Brandon (1978), 170
5   Barr-Hamilton (1961), 38-65
6   Taylor and Taylor (1965), 2, 537
7   The present spire dates from the 14th century. Aldsworth (1988), 105-44
8   Nairn and Pevsner (1965), 111
9   Camden (1586)
10  Taylor and Taylor (1965), I, 71; Godfrey (1948), 164-83
11  Brandon (1974), 126-7
12  Lower (1857), 92-3
13  Taylor and Taylor (1965), 2, 544
14  Davidson (1950), 175
15  Hussey (1857), 69
16  Nairn and Pevsner (1965), 577
17  Nairn and Pevsner (1965), 270

18  *The Spectator*, 3 September 1994, 32
19  Brandon (1974), 211
20  Baker (1942-3), 1-4; (1970), 58-81
21  Rouse (1948), 12-13
22  Baker (1942-3), 13
23  Milner-Gulland (1985), 25-54
24  *The Daily Telegraph*, 8 September 1990, *Weekend*, 1

## 7 Sowing the Seeds of Change: the 16th and 17th Centuries, *pp.90-101*

1   Godfrey (1928)
2   *Ibid.*, 40
3   *Ibid.*, 6
4   *Ibid.*, 235-9
5   Fussell (1952), 62-4
6   Godfrey (1928)
7   Figg (1851), 307
8   Hudson (1911), 177-8
9   *Ibid.*, 177
10  ESRO Preston WS/DJ/BI/F69
11  Barker (1956), 53 *et seq.*
12  Brandon (1963), 308-11
13  ESRO/SAV/CP 193
14  Brandon (1971b)
15  *Ibid.*
16  Sussex Record Society 27 (1921), 41-2
17  WSRO Add.Ms. 524
18  Brandon (1963), 289
19  Godfrey (1928), 69
20  Kent County Record Office, Sackville Ms.14
21  Brandon (1963), 203-5
22  ESRO Shiffner Ms. 2028
23  ESRO SAT DN 185; SAT Woolgar Ms ii, 51
24  ESRO SAT DN 185; Shiffner Ms. 2028
25  WSRO SAT B 604; PRO SC12/15/76; SC12/3/57
26  WSRO Acc 751/9; PRO SC12/25/76
27  Marshall (1798), 2, 203-6
28  WSRO Add.Ms. 524; Acc 939 f.19 *et seq.*

## 8 The 'New Farming' (*c.*1780-1880), *pp.102-115*

1   Sheffield (1801), Part 3
2   Cobbett (1821), 39, 274-80, 312, 361-415, 415-16, 468-70, 491-4, 505-66; (1826), 40-1, 129-50, 154-87
3   *Ibid.* (1826), 39, 275-312
4   Cole and Cole (1930), 1, 65-6
5   Farrant (1978), 261-8
6   Marshall (1798), 2, 92-164; *see also* Arthur Young (1794), 616
7   Baxter (1846), 2, i-lxiv; Farrant (1978), 77-8
8   White (1836 ed.), 256
9   Marshall (1798), 2, 345, 370-1
10  Murchison (1962), 178-9
11  Spargo (1988), 60
12  Young (1789), 98; A. Young (1794), 511
13  Parker (1975); Wade Martins (1980); Porter (1991)
14  *The Times*, 11 July 1861, 7ff.
15  Marshall (1798), 2, 346
16  Marshall (1817), 399
17  *Ibid.*, 400
18  *Ibid.*, 350
19  *Ibid.*, 94
20  *Ibid.*, 400
21  Wade Martins (1993), 20-30
22  Marshall (1798), 351
23  Boxall (1972), 17-29
24  Revd. A. Young (1813), 301-2
25  Marshall (1817), 91
26  *Ibid.*, 224-5
27  *Ibid.*, 347
28  Board of Agriculture, Prize Essay (1801)
29  Hudson (1900), 36
30  Revd. A. Young (1794), 22; *see also* Marshall (1798), 367
31  Hodgson (1967)
32  Somerville (1911); Jesse (1960), 129
33  Graham (1916), 63-73
34  Young (1797), 8 June
35  *Ibid.*, 445
36  Brandon and Short (1990), 251 and *passim*
37  Jefferies (1908 ed.), 199-202
38  Revd. A. Young (1813), 55; (1794), 375-83
39  Martin (1921), 24-30; *The Independent*, 8 November 1997, p.11

## 9 Traditional Farm Buildings and Rural Life (*c.*1780-*c.*1880), *pp.116-134*

1   Young (1792), 152-3
2   Robinson (1938), 16-19
3   Census 1861
4   Andrews (1979)
5   BBP *Agriculture* 10 (1867-8), 89
6   Arthur Young, *Annals*, 22, 141
7   BPP *Agriculture* 6 (1843), 193
8   BPP *Poor Law* 8 (1834), 477
9   BPP *Poor Law* 2 (1820-8), 15, 464, 468, 475
10  BPP *Poor Law* 1 (1820-8), 19-23
11  BPP *Poor Law* 8 (1834), 413; *Agriculture* 6 (1843), 193; 10, 77
12  *The Times*, 25 November 1830; *The Sussex Advertiser*, Nov-Dec 1830; ESRO LEW/CI/3, pp.220-2
13  Wells (1992)
14  Waugh (1985)
15  Cobden Unwin (1904)
16  *Ibid.*, 17-18
17  *Ibid.*, 21-3
18  *Ibid.*, 24-7
19  *Ibid.*, 31-6
20  *Ibid.*, 36-41

21 *Ibid.*, 48-50
22 Lower (1854), 168
23 *Ibid.*, 167
24 *Ibid.*, 164-5
25 *Ibid.*, 168
26 Hurdis (1800)
27 Blencowe (1849), 247-56
28 *The Times*, 28 February 1964, 14ff.
29 ESRO PAR/464/7/5
30 Lower (1861), 162
31 *Ibid.*, 230
32 Parish (1957 ed.)

## 10 Nature, Man and Beast, *pp.135-145*

1 Ray, John (1701), 213; Lankester (1948), 14
2 Peake (1931), 62
3 Salisbury (1933), 9; (1952), 21
4 Tansley (1925), 177-223; (1926), 1-32; (1949), I, 164-5
5 Rose (1997), 618-37
6 Bell (1977), 193-273; *see also* Evans and Dimbleby (1976), 42, 150-9
7 Rose (1997), 618-37
8 *Ibid.*, 628
9 Cunliffe (1984), 5
10 Collins (1982)
11 Rose (1995), 5-6
12 Hampshire CC, *Chalk Grasslands* (1983)
13 Lousley (1950), 67-77
14 CPRE archives, Reading University
15 Rose (1995), 6; Sanderson and Rose (1996), 21
16 Thomas (1960), 57-65
17 Allen (1995)
18 Grigson (1958)
19 Tansley and Adamson (1925, 1926)
20 Bailey (1988), 1-20
21 Tittensor (1985), 153-5
22 Moore (1911), 307-11
23 Tansley (1949), 376-80; Williamson (1978)

## 11 The Making of an Icon, *pp.146-156*

1 ESRO Glynde MS 1520
2 Ray (1701 ed.), 224
3 Defoe (1927 ed.), 129, 132
4 Taylor (1851), 60-83; Cook (1914), 39-44
5 White (1836 ed.), 255
6 Blunt (1914)
7 Robinson (1938), 1
8 Cook (1914), 39-41
9 Cole and Cole (1930), I, 356-7
10 *Ibid.*, I, 302
11 *Ibid.*, III, 702-3
12 *Ibid.*, II, 514-15
13 *Ibid.*, I, 163-9
14 *Ibid.*, I, 96, 125
15 *Ibid.*, I, 62-5, 66-7, 96, 125

16 Gilpin (1792)
17 Walpole (1995 ed.), 57
18 Cole and Cole (1930), I, 40; *see also* I, 125
19 Piozzi (1884), 54, 106
20 Pückler-Muckau (1826-8), 318-24
21 Granville (1841), 580-1
22 Anon (1822), 67-8
23 Patmore (1823), I, 17-18
24 de la Garde (1834), 393
25 Merrifield (1864), 21
26 Lower (1854), 146-7. His love of the Downs was matched by Gideon Mantell's. *See A Day's Ramble in Lewes* (1846)
27 Brooke (1865), 89-90
28 Hare (1894), 134-5
29 *The Speaker*, April 1898
30 *Cornhill Magazine* (1878), 76-7
31 Shrubshall and Coustillas (1985), 87
32 Thomas (1978), 50
33 *Ibid.*
34 Moore (1911), 307-11
35 Hudson (1900), 32
36 Allcroft (1908), 625
37 Noyes (1950), 372
38 Copper (1975), 97-8
39 Robinson (1938), 2
40 Powys (1967), 208-9
41 Massingham (1946), 243-50
42 Burroughs (1904 ed.), 30-1
43 Avebury (1902), 424-5

## 12 The Downs that were England (1900-1939), *pp.157-166*

1 *Time and Tide* (1953), 42
2 Symbolised by a miniature masterpiece (Selincourt, 1924)
3 Miss Beryl Gill, personal communication
4 BPP, *Agriculture* 10 (1867-8), 89
5 Haggard (1902), 1, 104-14
6 Farrant (1979), 155-70
7 Massingham (1946), 146
8 Gill (1940), 75-6
9 V. Woolf (1947), 12
10 Copper (1975 ed.), 75-6
11 Bogarde (1992)
12 Lower (1854), 148
13 Hopkins (1927), 18-19
14 Beckett (1909), 3
15 Gissing, *Thyrza* (1892 ed.), 481-4, 487-9; Gissing (1990-93), 4, 83, 195
16 Jefferies (1908 ed.), 211
17 *The Speaker* (April 1898)
18 Mais (n.d.), 221-7; Gosse (1935), 113-15
19 Murray (1954), 3
20 *The Sunday Telegraph*, 25 February 1966
21 Eric Holden, personal communication

22  Sandgate Newsletter (Storrington), 1987-1994; Ham (1982)
23  Baldwin (1925), 6-9
24  *Emma* (1816), 191-2
25  Avebury (1902), 424-5
26  *The Longest Journey* (1924 ed.), 146
27  This was the idea of the Downs conveyed at the end of the Second World War. *Picture Post*, 21 October 1944, 21-3
28  Connolly (1945), 207
29  *Ibid.*, 201-2
30  Evelyn Waugh (1930), 55-6. I am indebted to Geoffrey Mead for the last reference. Joad (1937), 17-18, 25-6; (1947), 34-5, 52, 157-8, 208-11
31  Joad (1937), 174-5
32  Allcroft (1908), 626
33  *The South Eastern Naturalist* (1920), lvi-lvii
34  Mais (1935), 79-80

## 13  The Call to Arms, *pp.167-180*

1   Gaze (1988), 35-6
2   ESRO GIL3/161/2
3   ESRO GIL3/162/9-14
4   ESRO GIL3/171,174/1-4
5   ESRO GIL3/183/1-2
6   Mercer in Holland (1993), 138-220
7   ESRO C/C6/79; Sales Particulars, 1903, 1905
8   Sharp (132), 158-9
9   Nairn and Pevsner (1965), 578
10  Greene (1938), 107-13
11  Woolf (1967), 146-8
12  Edwards (1981), 123-4; *see also* Brighton, Hove and District Regional Planning Scheme (1932), 19-20; *Picture Post*, 21 October 1944, 21-23; ESRO C/C11/63/26
13  ESRO AMS/5798/1-13
14  Woolf (1977-84), IV, 85, 124 *et seq.*; ESRO C6/86
15  Downsmen Annual Report, 1926
16  *The Times*, 31 May 1928, 19a; 30 October 1929, 11d; 27 November 1933, 15c, 15e; 12 December 1933, 10a, b, 15c
17  Brighton Corporation, Jubilee issue; *Sussex Daily News* 11, 31 July 1936; *Country Life*, 11 July 1936
18  ESRO C/C2/56, 1-5; 57; C/C2/47; C/C2/96; *The Times*, 27 November 1933, 15c, 15e; 10 January 1934, 5e; ESRO C/C256, 1-5; C/C2/15;C/C2/9; *The Times*, 27 November 1933, 15c; ESRO C/C2/56, 1-5; ESRO C/C2/47,58; Brighton, Hove and District Regional Planning Scheme (1932)
19  *The Spectator*, 13 July 1934; *Country Life*, 20 January 1934; Downsmen Annual Reports, 1928-34; *The Times*, 27 November 1933, 15e, 15c; 2 December, 15c; 10 January 1934, 6a (Brighton's case); 4 December 1933, 16a (racing driver Lord Howe's support for the race track); *Punch* 186 (1934), 543; *see also* 521.
20  ESRO C/C2/56. For a summary of the dispute

over Brighton's attitudes see Parliamentary Debates, House of Lords, 96 (1934-5) and Brighton's refutation in the *Sussex Daily News*, 31 July 1936.
21  WSRO CS/PL/1970/28,29; *The Morning Post*, 3 June 1936; *The Times*, 3 December 1935
22  For the new strategy of the East Sussex County Council, *The Times*, 12 February 1936, 6e
23  *The Times*, 27 April 1938, 12e reported the success of negotiations with landowners covering 27,000 acres of downland; *The Times* similarly reported protection for a further 11,000 acres in Hailsham Rural District (25 February 1938, 164).
24  *The Times*, 12 February 1936, 6e; 25 February 1938, 16ff.; 27 April 1938, 12e; ESRO C6/79,C6/5,C69/152
25  CPRE Archives, Reading University, 1938
26  *The Times*, 2 November 1939, 2f; Mellor (1990), 11-13. A similar scheme was revived in 1964 but it was not approved by local planners, *Evening Argus*, 25 April 1964
27  *The Times*, 13 April 1938, 10d; WSRO HLG4/60; *The Herald*, 12 and 19 January 1938; *Worthing Herald*, 16 August 1938

## 14  After Eden, *pp.181-194*

1   ESRO C/C69/164
2   *Ibid.*
3   *West Sussex at War* (1994); *The Land at War* (HMSO, 1945); Joad (1942), 127
4   ESRO C/C69/164
5   ESRO C69/198; Downsmen Annual Reports, 1946, 1947
6   *The Times*, 14 August 1947, 6b
7   *The Times*, 14 November 1945, 7a
8   Mr. Granshaw, personal communication
9   *The Times*, 16 February 1946, 4g; ESRO C/69/198; C/C11/63/26
10  *Horizon* (1942), 167; *The Times*, 16 February 1949, 5ff.; 5 December 1950, 7e; 14 December 1950, 7c; 18 August 1952, 2e; 8 August 1955, 8d
11  Barclay Wills (1938), 1
12  *The Times*, 16 February 1946, 4g; 10 February 1950, 8b; 9 May 1950, 9b
13  Report of the National Parks Committee, Cmnd.3851 (1931), Appendix 2
14  ESRO C/C69/198
15  *The Times*, 14 August 1954, 5ff.; *see also*, *ibid.*, 3 August, 3d
16  ESRO C/C69/198; *The Times*, 10 August 1956, 7d
17  ESRO C/C69/198
18  *Ibid.*; ESRO C/C2/151/1-2
19  Downsmen Annual Report, 1949; ESRO C11/63/6
20  Downsmen Annual Reports, 1948, 1949, 1950
21  CPRE archives, Reading University; *The Times*, 10 May 1956, 7d; ESRO C/C69/198

22 *The Sussex Weekly Herald*, 4 April 1953
23 Parliamentary Debate, House of Lords, 192 (1954-5), 147-52. *See also, The Times*, 17 August 1956, 7e
24 *Ibid.*
25 *Ibid.; The Times*, 2 May 1955, 5f; 27 November 1957, 4a; 13 December 1958, 7f; 15 December 1958, 9f
26 *Country Life*, 19 November 1959; *see also, The Times*, 17 August 1957, 7ff.
27 *The Times*, 6 September 1948, 5e; ESRO C/C11/63/50
28 National Parks Commission, Annual Report 1958, 145; PRO Kew COU2/2 (1956-62); COU2/154; COU1/288
29 Downsmen Annual Report, 1967; *The Times*, 15 April 1966, 4d; WSRO CS/PL/1970/1103
30 *The Times*, 3 March 1959, 6c
31 WSRO CS/PL/1970/1103; *The Times*, 15 April 1966; Downsmen Annual Report, 1967
32 *Architectural Review* 84 (1964), 126; Downsmen Annual Reports, 1964-8; *The Times*, 22 July 1964, 6a
33 *The Times*, 13 November 1966, 4d
34 *The Times*, 14 April 1963, 6f
35 Massingham (1946), 250

## 15 Places and Ideas: The Downs in Literature and Painting, *pp.195-204*

1 Monro (1933), 125
2 Hudson (1900), 7
3 Taylor (1851)
4 Hurdis, (1800)
5 Curran (1993)
6 Blunt (1914)
7 *Apollo* (1947), 45, 162
8 McCarthy (1989), 128-42
9 Pruden (1994)
10 Wilcox, 50-84
11 Leach (1978), 30
12 Mellor (1990), 9-13
13 Diana de Vere Cole, personal communication
14 Kipling (1937), 136
15 Smith (1989), 5
16 Copper (ed.) (1975), 12-13; *Journal Folk Song Society* (1899-1904), 11, 19-25
17 Nicholson (1996)
18 Bell (1978), II, 62-3, 127, 205; (1980), III, 60;

(1982), IV, 349
19 Bell (1968); *Charleston Newsletter*, nos.1-24 (1972-84); Lee (1992)
20 Partridge (1990), 173-4; (1993), 89-91
21 Angus (1987)
22 Constable (1982); Binyon (1983)
23 Lower (1854), 192
24 Garland (1995), (1995), 13
25 Bowness (1973)
26 Beetles (1985)
27 Camp (1996), 87, 116-17, 167-9 *et seq.*
28 Spink/Nevill Keating (1986)
29 Weight (1994)

## 16 The Austere Present, *pp.205-218*

1 *Environmental Capacity in West Sussex*, West Sussex County Council, Chichester (1996), 112-20, 148-50
2 Downsmen Annual Reports, 1986, 1987
3 Downsmen Annual Report, 1991
4 CPRE archives, Wetland File, University of Reading
5 Downsmen Annual Reports, 1980, 1981
6 *Environmental Capacity in West Sussex*, 70-80
7 Chatt (1982); Campbell and Cooke (1997); House of Commons, Agricultural Committee, second report, 1997; *Growing Greener: sustainable agriculture in the UK*, CPRE (1996)
8 Potts (1986), 74-93
9 Harvey (1996), 4, 28
10 *The Times*, 14 August 1956, 5ff.
11 The Game Conservancy Trust, 1994 Review, issue 2676-875; Potts (1996); Aebischer and Potts (1997)
12 Potts (1996)
13 Boardman and Robinson (1982); Boardman (1988), 333-48; Boardman (1995), 177-91
14 SDCB, *A Management Strategy for the Sussex Downs*, AONB (1995); *Landscape Design Guidelines* (1997); Ditchling Beacon Project (forthcoming)
15 SDCB, Anniversary Conference (1997)
16 *Applesham Farm*, Stoneleigh (1997)
17 SDCB, Anniversary conference (1997), 11
18 The National Trust, *The Devil's Dyke Estate* (1997)
19 Fowler (1977), 189-92
20 Parliamentary Debates, House of Lords, 22 July 1997, 1408-32

# INDEX

*compiled by Ann Winser*

Note: Small Roman figures refer to the preliminary pages; large Roman figures refer to colour plates; figures in **bold** type are the page numbers of illustrations in the text